THE NATURAL LAW READER

Edited by
Brendan F. Brown

Professor of Law
Loyola University of the South
New Orleans, Louisiana

DOCKET SERIES
Volume 13

Oceana Publications
New York City

1960

*This Book is affectionately dedicated to my
Mother and the memory of my Father*

© Copyright, 1960, by Oceana Publications, Inc.
All rights reserved

Library of Congress Catalog Card Number: 59-8601
Printed in the U. S. A.

TABLE OF CONTENTS

PREFACE V

ACKNOWLEDGMENTS VII

INTRODUCTION IX

PART I—THE REVIVAL OF NATURAL
LAW JURISPRUDENCE 1

  A. The Doctrine of Natural Law
     in Jurisprudence 1
  B. Causes of the Decline of
     Natural Law Thinking 3
  C. Causes of the Revival 19
     1. In General 19
     2. United States 24
     3. Latin America 30
     4. France 32
     5. Germany 33
     6. Italy 39

PART II—SCHOLASTIC NATURAL LAW
JURISPRUDENCE 47

  A. Plato, Aristotle, and Cicero 47
  B. The School Men 61
     1. In General 61
     2. In Particular
        St. Thomas Aquinas 68

C.	Continuation of Scholastic Thinking After the Reformation by Non-Catholics	99
D.	Impact of Scholastic Natural Law Jurisprudence on Positive Law	108
	1. Public Law	109
	A. International Law	109
	B. National Law	110
	2. Private Law	128
	a. The Family	128
	b. Contracts, Torts, Property, Criminal Law and Procedure, Corporations, Law Merchant and Equity	134
E.	The Dynamism of Scholastic Natural Law	153

PART III—NON-SCHOLASTIC NATURAL LAW JURISPRUDENCE 172

A.	Neo-Kantian Absolutism, Transcendental Idealism	172
B.	Ethical Rationalism, Relative Idealism	180
C.	Sociological Rationalism, Quasi-Idealism	194
	1. In General	194
	2. In Particular	197

INDEX 227

PREFACE

The inclusion of The Natural Law Reader in the well known Docket series is timely and imperative. The philosophy of natural law, as such, has not been formally projected by any of the other Readers in this Series. Indeed, conflicting and competing legal philosophies have already been illustrated, notably in the Holmes and Brandeis Readers. But the modern resurgence of natural law thinking has been so great as to propel it to a commanding position in the contemporary development of the legal order. Natural law jurisprudence, which is based on a moral attitude toward law, is slowly but surely winning its final battle with the force concept of law contained in positivism which makes the essence of law depend on the will of the political sovereign.

The revival of natural law thinking has proceeded in two general directions, namely, the scholastic and non-scholastic. First, it has moved in the direction of the perennial philosophy of the scholastics, symbolized by the person of the angelic doctor, St. Thomas Aquinas. This philosophy has for its core the ideal of an objective natural law in the sense of a regulatory norm for human conduct, promulgated by a personal divine Law-giver, knowable by reason alone as distinguished from revelation. This norm is as immutable as the essence of human nature and the will and reason of this Law-giver in regard to the most general principles of doing good and avoiding evil, and of recognizing in action the supreme worth of human personality, by respecting life, property, liberty and the pursuit of happiness. But the moral principles governing human behavior which from time to time flow from the application of those general principles to ever changing sociological facts are variable.

Secondly, the revival of natural law jurisprudence has also moved in a non-scholastic direction. All non-

v

scholastic natural law jurists omit the factor of the rationally knowable divine Law-giver. Who has promulgated the natural law in the reason and conscience of every human being. Some deviate no further than this from the scholastic doctrine. Accordingly, they believe, like the scholastics, in the existence of an immutable, objective, transcendental ideal of conduct to which man should conform his conduct. Immanuel Kant is for this subdivision of natural law jurisprudence what St. Thomas is for the scholastic.

Other natural law jurists deviate still further from the scholastic doctrine by accepting the existence of only relative ideals for human conduct. But these ideals do exist *a priori* in an objective order, and do not arise solely from facts. The "ought" stands in juxtaposition with the "is". In ultimate analysis, these ideals are rational.

Finally, certain natural law jurists reduce that law to the level of a quasi-ideal. This ideal is derived from a sociological rationalism by these jurists. Their position represents the maximum deviation from the scholastic concept of the natural law.

This book is intended for both professional and popular purposes. It makes available in compact form highly original source materials which coordinate the several facets of natural law thinking. It is hoped that these materials will prove convenient for the use of law makers, whether participating in the judicial, legislative, or administrative process. These materials are also offered for the convenience of legal scholars, political and social scientists, and philosophers in general.

Beyond strictly professional purposes, it is earnestly hoped that this book will meet with an enthusiastic popular response. Its message is relevant to readers, not only as professional experts in the field of law, but also as human beings. It relates to the most fundamental values of every day living. It is pertinent to the choice of the best future legal and political order, and the kind of civilization which will be most conducive to man's happiness.

The only change in the original materials is that the footnotes have been renumbered and collected at the end of each section.

The editor expresses his appreciation to Mr. Patrick A. Mitchell, Jr., Librarian and Instructor in Law at Loyola University of the South, and to Miss Audrey Ayo for her assistance in the preparation of the manuscript.

ACKNOWLEDGMENTS

The editor expresses his gratitude and appreciation to the following authors, publishers and periodicals for granting permission to reprint excerpts from their books and articles, originally copyrighted by them:

Dr. Mortimer Adler and the University of Notre Dame for "The Doctrine of Natural Law Philosophy";
Ben W. Palmer, Esq., and The American Bar Association Journal for "Defense Against Leviathan";
Professor W. Friedmann and Stevens and Sons, Ltd., for Legal Theory;
Professor Roscoe Pound and the Boston University Press for "Introduction, General Principles of Law by Giorgio Del Vecchio";
Professor Joseph P. Witherspoon and the Texas Law Review for Philosophy and the Law";
The American Catholic Philosophical Association for "The Movement for a Neo-Scholastic Philosophy of Law in America" by Dean Miriam Theresa Rooney;
Professor Josef L. Kunz and The American Journal of Comparative Law for "Contemporary Latin-American Philosophy of Law";
Dr. Freiherr von der Heydte and the Natural Law Forum for "Natural Law Tendencies in Contemporary German Jurisprudence";
Dr. Guido Fasso and the Natural Law Forum for "Natural Law in Italy in the Past Ten Years";
The Clarendon Press, Oxford, England, for The Dialogues by Plato;
The Oxford University Press, Inc., Random House, and The Clarendon Press, Oxford, England, for The Politics, Rhetoric, and Ethica Nicomachea by Aristotle.
Bohn's Classical Library for On the Commonwealth and On the Laws by Cicero;
Dr. Heinrich A. Rommen and the B. Herder Book Company for The Natural Law;
Benziger Brothers, Inc., for Summa Theologica by St. Thomas Aquinas;
Dr. John C. H. Wu and Sheed and Ward for Fountain of Justice;
William Muchall for Doctor and Student by Christopher Saint Germain;
Georgetown Law Journal for De Legibus ac De Legislatore by Francisco Suarez;
Rev. Thomas E. Davitt, S. J., and the Southern Methodist University Press for "St. Thomas Aquinas and the Natural Law" in Origins of the Natural Law Tradition;
Callaghan and Company for Commentaries on the Laws of England by Sir William Blackstone;
Professor Edward S. Corwin and the Harvard Law Review Association for "The 'Higher Law' Background of American Constitutional Law";

Professor Edward S. Corwin and the University of Notre Dame for "The Natural Law and Constitutional Law";

Dean Harold G. Reuschlein and the Bobbs-Merrill Co., Inc., for **Jurisprudence—Its American Prophets**;

Viscount Kilmuir, The Lord High Chancellor of Great Britain, and **The American Bar Association Journal** for "Address of the Opening Ceremony in Westminster Hall of the London Meeting of the American Bar Association in 1957";

Rev. Wm. J. Kenealy, S. J., and the **Loyola Law Review** of New Orleans for "The Majesty of the Law";

Charles S. Rhyne, Esq., and **The American Bar Association Journal** for "The Magna Carta Memorial Ceremonies: Runnymede';

Lord Evershed, Master of the Rolls, and **The American Bar Association Journal** for "The Magna Carta Memorial Ceremonies: Runnymede";

Rev. Francis E. Lucey, S. J., and the Tennessee Law Review for "Liability without Fault and the Natural Law";

Dean A. E. Papale and the **Northwestern University Law Review** for "Judicial Enforcement of Desegregation: Its Problems and Limitations";

Professor Giorgio Del Vecchio and the Catholic University of America Press for **Philosophy of Law;**

The Free Press at Glencoe, Illinois, for **Reason and Nature** by Morris R. Cohen;

Columbia Law Review for "Justice Holmes and the Nature of Law" by Morris R. Cohen;

The Julius Rosenthal Foundation of Northwestern University and the Boston Law Book Company for "My Philosophy of Law" by John Dickinson;

Professor Joseph P. Witherspoon and the **Natural Law Forum** for "Book Review, The Moral Decision by Edmond Cahn";

Professor Thomas A. Cowan and the **Columbia Law Review** for "A Report on the Status of Philosophy of Law in the United States";

Professor Lon L. Fuller and the Foundation Press for **The Law in Quest of Itself;**

Professor Lon L. Fuller and the Association of American Law Schools for "American Legal Philosophy at Mid-Century";

Professor Joseph P. Witherspoon and the **Natural Law Forum** for "The Relation of Philosophy to Jurisprudence";

Simon and Schuster for **Fate and Freedom** by Jerome Frank;

Professor Jerome Hall and the Southern Methodist University Press for "The Progress of American Jurisprudence" in **The Administration of Justice in Retrospect;**

Professor Jerome Hall and the Bobbs-Merrill Co., Inc. for "Living Law of Democratic Society";

To the publishers mentioned below for the following articles written by Brendan Francis Brown:

Notre Dame Lawyer for "Natural Law and the Law-Making Function in American Jurisprudence";

The Catholic Lawyer for "The Influence of St. Thomas Aquinas on Jurisprudence";

Georgetown Law Journal for "Book Review, Philosophy of Law in Historical Perspective by Carl Joachim Friedrich";

Fordham Law Review for "The Natural Law, the Marriage Bond, and Divorce";

The Catholic University of America Law Review for "The Natural Law Basis of Juridical Institutions in the Anglo-American Legal System";

Ohio State Law Journal for "A Scholastic Critique of Case Law";
Tulane Law Review for "Natural Law: Dynamic Basis of Law and Morals in the Twentieth Century";

The Catholic University of America Press for "Introduction, **Philosophy of Law** by Giorgio Del Vecchio".

Specific acknowledgement is made where the passage appears in this Reader.

BRENDAN F BROWN

INTRODUCTION

The doctrine of natural law has existed continuously for almost twenty five hundred years in various forms. During this period, it has been used as a criterion for the evaluation of human positive law, and as an ideal by which legal systems should be guided. It is true that, in the Greek world of Plato and Aristotle, the influence of natural law thinking was principally confined to the speculative or philosophical areas. But in the hands of the practical Roman jurists, such thinking became the foundation of a system of Roman law adequate for the government of the Roman Empire. These jurists adopted the Stoic concept of natural law to their political and juridical needs. Again, in the latter part of the fourteenth century, the philosophy of natural law became the basis of the administration of justice in the Court of Chancery. The Chancellors followed the scholastic natural law, in essence akin to the Stoic idea. Recourse to natural law transformed the English legal system into an instrument for the governance of the British Empire.

But throughout its long history, natural law philosophy has had to compete with the doctrine of positivism. This doctrine proclaims that the authority of the state is supreme in every sense. In the primitive period of law, positivism took the form of codes for the regulation of ancient societies. Positivism was represented by the *Jus Civile* of the Roman law, and by the analytical activities of the Glossators, beginning in the twelfth century at Bologna. Positivism became an elaborated and explicated doctrine in the Leviathan authored by Thomas Hobbes in the latter part of the seventeenth century in England. It received further elaboration and formulation by John Austin in 1832, in his work, "The Province of Jurisprudence Determined."

In the historic struggle, the fate of natural law doctrine has been variable. Thus it has competed successfully with the imperative or positivistic concept of law in the United States. Its triumph is manifest from the emergence and survival of the doctrine of judicial supremacy which subjects positive law to the inhibition of a moral order, constitutionally implemented. But it was not so successful in England where the imperative theory of law, political in nature, overcame the juristic tradition in the sixteenth century and thereafter. Prior to that time, natural law thinking was dominant in England, where the Bractonian maxim that the sovereign must rule under God and the law, (i.e.) the objective natural law, was generally accepted.

The natural law tradition reached a high degree of prestige in the eighteenth century, but later declined until the end of the second world war. Positivism as a way of life in the totalitarian countries bore fruit in the frightful debacle of that conflict. The causes of the rise, decline, and contemporary revival of natural law doctrine will be presented in this Reader.

PART I

THE REVIVAL OF NATURAL LAW JURISPRUDENCE

A. *The Doctrine of Natural Law in Jurisprudence*

Jurists and legal scholars may be divided into naturalists and positivists. The former believe that there is some norm which limits the authority of the political order to make law, whether executively, legislatively or judicially. The latter confer upon the political order the totality of authority so that the essence of law is not justice, based on reason, but the will of the sovereign, either as such, or as the interpreter of the postulated extra-political criterion.

Mortimer Adler, The Doctrine of Natural Law Philosophy,[1] University of Notre Dame Natural Law Institute Proceedings pp. 67-68 (1949); reprinted by permission of the author and the University of Notre Dame.

Let me begin, then, by stating what all these minds hold in common concerning natural law. Let me try thus to state the issue between them as naturalists and the positivists on the other side. I shall call a "naturalist" in law the man who thinks there is something other and more than positive law, a "positivist" the man who thinks that there is only positive law and that there are no rational grounds for the criticism of positive law.

What do all those whom I call "naturalists" agree on? What do they affirm? I must point out at once that they do not all use the words "natural law"; nor do they all have the same concept of natural law. But this they do hold in common: *the laws made by a state or government are not the only directions of conduct which apply to men living in society.*

They affirm that, in addition to such rules as each individual may make for himself, and in addition to the rules of conduct the state may lay down, there are rules or principles of conduct which are of even greater universality—applying to *all* men, not merely to *one* man, and not merely even to *one* society at a given time and place.

They affirm, furthermore, that there are rules of human conduct which no man has invented—*which are not positive in the sense of being posited!* (Subsequently, I shall try to show that the real meaning of positivism involves, as St. Thomas points out, the notion of the arbitrary, an institution of the will as opposed to something natural, discovered by the intellect.)

They agree that man's reason is endowed with the capacity of perceiving these universal laws or principles of conduct, and that, if they are recognized as being laws of reason or rational principles, these laws need no other foundation or authority than the recognition of their truth.

They agree in affirming that these principles are somehow the source of all the more particular rules of conduct, even those which individuals make for themselves or those which governments make in political societies and seek to maintain by force; and they agree that these principles constitute the standard by which all other rules are to be judged good or bad, right or wrong, just or unjust, and in terms of which constitutions and governments are similarly to be judged.

B. Causes of the Decline of Natural Law Thinking

After the eighteenth century, natural law thinking declined because the Stoic-Thomistic doctrine of a duty-imposing, objective natural law was superseded in many quarters by erroneous notions of natural law. Deviations from this doctrine began after the sixteenth century. These deviations mistakenly identified natural law with the positive law itself, or with an order of morality based solely on a unilateral subjectivism, or with an arbitrary social compact, or with the abstract rights of man, or with a particular socio-economic order. These deviations became easy targets for non-philosophical jurists.

The Stoic-Thomistic doctrine continued to be taught in institutions of learning under Catholic auspices, but it was largely ignored by many jurists who erroneously believed that it was only the handmaid of Catholic theology. This doctrine no longer had the prestige and acceptance which it had previously enjoyed. The time was ripe, therefore, for a general decline of natural law thinking not only in the United States but everywhere.

Ben W. Palmer, *Defense Against Leviathan*, 32 *American Bar Association Journal* pp. 329-332, 360 (1946); reprinted by permission of the author and the American Bar Association Journal.

THE CAUSES OF EROSION OF NATURAL LAW

Natural law, however, had largely succumbed to a process of erosion by the earlier part of the present century. The causes of that erosion which is now manifest may be enumerated as follows:

1. *The rise of nationalism.* At first absolutist kings and then nations threw off the restraints of the higher law. The development of the doctrine of sovereignty

by Bodin and his successors, of Erastianism, of Macchiavellian real-politik, destroyed an organic concept of Christendom and made the phrase "family of nations" an anachronistic misnomer concealing disparateness. If externally in relation to other powers the State were subject to no higher law, how was it to be limited in its treatment of the individual or minority groups? Internally dogmas of the divine right of kings and of passive obedience resulted in a carry-over of absolutism from monarchies to the modern state with the philosophies of Kant, Hegel, Fichte, Treitschke and Von Ihring. The state crushed out all opposition, allowed no competition in the field of law, based its own law on force and command rather than on any justification by or appeal to reason or the moral sense of obligation. It became the Leviathan of Hobbes. It became in a less materialistic and semi-mystic emotionalism deity personified or actualized so that resistance or dissent was not merely treason; it was sacrilege to be abhorred.

2. *The rise of capitalism.* With the industrial revolution came an accelerated pursuit of wealth. That pursuit was justified by the flattering unction that wealth was a sign of God's grace, a reward of the prudential virtues, visible sign that the possessor was one of the elect. It was encouraged by opportunity and competitive display of luxury, by the ambition of the rising bourgeoisie first for equality with hereditary aristocracy and then for manifest supremacy over them and county land-owners. It engrossed the attention of more and more of the population with the triumph of the bourgeoisie and the bourgeois mind. It loomed larger and larger in the field of emotion and of thought with the development of cities, of the proletariate, of a class struggle. It was intensified exteriorally with the ruthless competition of finance capital and imperialist States for control of the so-called backward nations and their natural resources and for world markets. And in America this pursuit of wealth tended to monopolize attention because of the

spectacular development or exploitation—some have called it the raping—of the natural resources of a virgin continent.

All these factors contributed to a pronounced secularization of life, a worship of power, a trend towards materialism notwithstanding oases of culture among a leisured minority.

3. *Relativism.* Philosophically belief in absolutes, universals, objective standards, a universal idea of being, was replaced by a view of the world as a chaos of phenomena and by subjectivism. With no recognized authority one man's opinion was as good as another's; what he thought was as likely to be true as what you thought. From this was easy transition to despair at the possibility of finding ultimate truth, doubt and then denial of the existence of truth, acceptance of the proposition that what is true for him is truth, and what is true for you is equally true. *Facilis descensus* came scepticism, agnosticism, atheism unavowed or naked and unashamed.

4. *The anti-intellectualism of Rousseau and the Romanticists.* The great attack upon reason by Rousseau, the arch sentimentalist, who exalted the savage, the peasant and the impulses of the child, was epitomized in his phrase, "The man who reflects is a depraved animal." The obfuscation of reason was exemplified by his sophistry: "I was if not virtuous, at least intoxicated with virtue." The dethronement of reason was accomplished by a denial of standards, both classic and Christian, while concealing the denial by lip-service use of such words as "conscience" and "virtue". The worship of instinct, impulse and vertiginous intoxicating emotion launched by Rousseau was carried on to the further discrediting and submergence of reason by Schopenhauer, Nietsche, Bergson. These, like Aristophanes, cried out "Whirl is King." And Rousseau's praise of ignorance and his contempt for reason and for restraint had correlation with the frontier spirit in America. For that spirit also,

notwithstanding its virile contribution to American life, in its lawlessness, its equalitarian distrust of the professional and contempt for the specialist, its theory that one man is as good as another and that his instinct, especially if in multitude glorified as the voice of God is better than other men's thought, certainly did not glorify reason. And by facile transition from the doctrine that the majority has the right to rule to the dogma that the majority is always right there was easy foundation for a belief that law is command and that might, not physical perhaps, but might at the polls, is right.

5. *Certain adverse tendencies of modern science.* The visible dramatic achievements of the physical sciences and the impact of Darwin's evolutionary hypothesis upon every field of thought profoundly affected the social sciences and through them jurisprudence and the philosophy of law. The triumphs of the physical sciences were manifestly due to emphasis upon the inductive method and a high degree of specialization. The "scientific" age heralded by Comte had arrived to liberate mankind and, removing traditional shackles, carry it to hitherto undreamed-of heights of intellectual achievement. Indeed in the judgment of many enthusiastic heralds of the new age science would take the place not only of theology but of philosophy. And under the leadership of Herbert Spencer the application of the technique of evolutionary biological study to social life would, it was believed, result in similar striking progress in the social sciences.

Leaders in the social sciences therefore set themselves to the greater use of induction and to specialization. Inspired by hope and aided by a fresh approach, undoubtedly the social sciences made marked progress. But there were certain developments in all the sciences that by indirection contributed to the further erosion of the natural law.

The sciences often overemphasized analysis and the mere accumulation of facts at the expense of synthesis, the search for the significant and for principles. Much of it became merely descriptive: Ph.D. theses piled discrete fact on detailed analysis beyond the capacity of comprehension by the most encyclopedic mind. And certainly any possibility of illuminating synthesis for the guidance of mankind was often buried like Pompeii beneath a rain of volcanic ash and lava. There was a general scorn of the *a priori*: deduction was not supposed to be respectable and historians, lost in the minutiae of scholarship, denied the possibility or value of any philosophy of history.

And nineteenth-century science became increasingly materialistic. It often denied the existence of anything that could not be apprehended by the senses or broken down by analysis or reduced to formulae or weighed, counted or measured. Materialistic evolution paved the way for acceptance of the belief that man does not differ in essence from the monkey or the rat. No wonder that Mr. Justice Holmes said that he could see no essential difference between man and a grain of sand or an ape.

Overemphasis on analysis and excessive materialism cooperated with overspecialization. Scientists with eyes glued to microscopes or studying the behavior of rats in ingeniously contrived mazes failed to see the whole man. As a result anthropologists reduced religion to a hangover from savage superstitions. Biochemists made man an aggregate of chemical elements. Physicists said he was merely a complex of electrons and protons. Behavioristic psychologists reduced him to a reflex mechanism, a predominantly subconscious or unconscious organism controlled mainly or entirely by alimentary forces, visceral reactions. Other psychologists took the psyche out of psychology. Economists made man the economic man all of whose motives were profit to himself. Political scientists viewed him only as a voter or maker and administrator of positive law in a moral vacuum. Social planners with their blueprints of an ideal society looked upon men merely as guinea pigs upon which their theories could be tested by successive inoculations of state or federal law. Communists supported the doctrine that all human motives are material, that no one is ever unselfish, that ideas and ideals have no place in human life, that man has no free will, that he is merely the helpless victim of his economic environment.

Social sciences suffered also from a blind copying of the methods of the physical sciences in that they tended to exclude consideration of what ought to be from their studies and concentrated too much on what is. This resulted in an exclusion of the ethical elements in social studies and in the field of law and reduced everything to mere description. By subtle psychological process it also tended to an acceptance of the confusion, stimulated by belief in evolutionary progress, that whatever is is right. Here too was fertile soil for philosophies justifying any existent force in the field of law and political life even though totalitarian.

And Irving Babbitt thought that he saw a curious and unsuspected relationship between coldly objective science and the emotional anti-intellectualism of Rousseau: "The prime virtue of science is to be unemotional and at the same time keenly analytical. Now protracted and unemotional analysis finally creates a desire, as Renan says, for the opposite pole, 'the kisses of the naive being,' and in general for a frank surrender to the emotions. Science thus actually prepared clients for the Rousseauist. The man of science is also flattered by the Rousseauistic notion that conscience and virtue are themselves only forms of emotion."

Finally, as to science, the adoption of successive tentative hypotheses however justifiable as instruments of progress tended to destroy belief in the existence of permanent laws and therefore in absolutes or objective unchanging standards.

6. *Cooperation of laissez faire with evolutionary theories.* Theories of the struggle for existence as a means of producing the survival of the socially fittest

fitted in admirably with laissez faire theories of the Manchester school of economics. Herbert Spencer, Adam Smith and Ricardo were brought into the political and juridical forum as authoritative and "scientific" champions of those who wished to preserve the economic status quo. The idea of Progress dominated the age and it was urged that any interference by law with the struggle of the market place or the relations of master and servant would be an attempted interference with what amounted to the divine plan of the ages. It would be futile. And to the extent that evolution was an impersonal god even to the materialist it would amount to sacrilege. This fitted in with a perversion of natural law later to be discussed.

7. *Utilitarianism.* Bentham, follower of Hobbes, had nothing but contempt for bills of right and attempts to limit sovereign power. Natural law he regarded as without meaning and misleading. Mill's philosophy, notwithstanding his classic plea for liberty, on analysis left to the individual only that sphere of activity which those in control of the state on principles of utility would deem it advisable to leave to him at any given time. True there was an initial presumption as to the utility of as large as possible a sphere, especially in the light of dominant laissez faire, but in last analysis the State would give the command to every man. So it was that utilitarianism could defend totalitarianism as it did in our day when the alleged pre-war efficiency of Germany and Italy was the admiration of too many American men of business. Admitting the tremendous social gains from utilitarianism, the fact remains that for the social utilitarians the immediate end of law was to secure interests. Law became therefore the sovereign's command and not embodiment of reason.

8. *Austinian jurisprudence.* John Austin, accepting Bentham's ideas, carried them out specifically in the field of law. Accepting Kant's rejection of the identification of law and morals, Austin and his followers accomplished a divorce of law from morals and prided

themselves on their accomplishment. They reiterated tirelessly the thesis that law has nothing to do with ethics or with anything outside itself. There was to be no challenge to the commands of the sovereign state.

9. *Denial of the rationality of human conduct and of man's free will.* The overthrow of man from his hitherto high estate was the result of many inconsistent but cooperative forces. Economic determinism strengthened by accelerated infiltration of Marx, Engels, Trotzky and Lenin was aided in the assault on free will by historical materialism. Man, and therefore his institutions and his laws were the result of irresistible forces of geography, race, systems of production, the class struggle. Behavioristic psychology assimilating men to rats joined forces with Freudians who emphasized wish as controlling the conduct of men or disguised, unrecognized forces of sex. The novelty to men of theories of rationalization coincided with the disillusionment and cynicism that followed World War I in a debunking era. These led men to believe that reasons given by any man for his conduct, judge or statesman, were not his real reasons: they were inevitably less noble. This gave point to anarchistic and communistic attacks on the State as merely an engine of exploitation. If, as Proudhon said, property is theft, what of the law that made property possible? And what of the law evidenced during strikes by policemen as the instruments of the exploiting State? Was it strange that many men reverted to the view of Thrasymachus that "justice" is in reality merely "the interest of the ruler and stronger." And, suspicious of rationalization, was it strange that Mr. Justice Holmes should write: "The jurists who believe in natural law seem to me to be in that naive state of mind that accepts what is familiar and accepted by them and their neighbors as something that must be accepted by all men everywhere."

10. *Pragmatism.* Positivism, asserting that knowledge is essentially relative and subjective, character-

istic of the second half of the nineteenth century, found its American variant in pragmatism. Akin to utilitarianism in emphasizing the primacy of will and the practical, truth became nothing else but usefulness as determined by social experience. It is that which works in relation to a purpose. Any efficient conduct is good conduct. Pragmatism does not concern itself with any overall attempt to set up philosophical goals, to answer ultimate questions or set up standards other than utility. It is counterfeit philosophy answering none of the great philosophical questions as to ultimates arising out of man's perennial effort to interpret the universe. It offers its adherents an avoidance of those questions and invites them to live from day to day in successive mansions of skepticism or eclecticism. Its greatest influence has come through the thousands of educators in America who are disciples of its greatest champion John Dewey. And he with his theory of freedom and dislike of discipline and of standards is also in the direct tradition of Rousseau. In that respect his teaching joins forces with utilitarianism and the worship of efficiency in so satisfying men with short term goals and an illusion of philosophy that they have little concern for the vital question of ultimate destinations. And they are therefore often blind to the drift of society, such as a drift towards totalitarianism.

11. *The case system of teaching law.* Begun at Harvard in 1870, the year Mr. Justice Cardozo was born and Mr. Justice Holmes entered that school as teacher, it dominates American legal education. No one of any intelligence would deny the generally beneficial effect of the case system upon American law and upon the competency of the bar. But, like other beneficial developments referred to, its results are now seen to be in some respects harmful. Certainly the case system suffered from that overemphasis on analysis and of the "is" at the expense of the "ought" and the lack of synthesis and overspecialization that affected the inductive science to which it was akin. It

tended to be merely descriptive. It neglected the deeper problems of the law. It ignored philosophy. Dominated by Austinian concepts it isolated law from the social sciences and from morals. It gave lawyers a false conception of the law as a whole by concentrating their attention on litigated cases as the only law in action while disregarding the atmospheric pressure of law on the nonlitigious and the general trends of the law. It tended to make lawyers too exclusively client-caretakers at the expense of their opportunity and duty as leaders of society. Too many American lawyers, therefore, untrained in philosophy, drifted into pragmaticism and joined the worship of efficiency. Infused with the idea of Progress they accepted belief as Pound says, that "whatever is done in the course of judicial decision is law because it is done, not done because it is law." And those who hoped that a sound philosophy of law would result from the mere accumulation of legal "facts" were doomed to disappointment. Moreover, the efficiently developed system of reporting every case and the amazingly ingenious system devised to help the practitioner find an "all fours" case in some respects only contributed to a lack of synthesis and of search for guiding principles.

12. *The spate of legislative law.* The latter part of the nineteenth century and first half of the twentieth witnessed an accelerating deluge of statutory law. The rain of law was due to many causes including the abandonment of laissez faire, the humanitarian movement of the last century, the growing power of women and of organized labor, a decline of individualism and above all the needs of an increasingly urban society. The flood of law produced a marked change in American attitude towards law. In an earlier day there was a greater tendency to regard law as the embodiment of reason because law was primarily the law of decided cases. In these a structure of principle had been laboriously erected by generations of lawyers and judges who laid its walls brick by brick with

anxious thought for the symmetry of reason. But these great masses of statute law were often hastily drawn, inconsistent with each other, made coherent and appealing to reason by no informing principle. Most of all they were all too often obviously mere command. And viewed realistically, perhaps somewhat cynically, they were often regarded as or known to be merely expressions of the will of special interest groups who had secured legislation by the sovereign state ostensibly in the public interest but actually for purely private or selfish purposes. Furthermore legislative law because of its bulk and the publicity given to its enactment was viewed by many as the "law". And so law as a whole was regarded as having no relation to reason or morals. The people forgot natural law.

13. *The discrediting of true natural law by a pseudo-natural law of the late nineteenth century.* The natural law of scholasticism and the founding fathers, like the Roman natural law, was creative. It was not divorced from psychology or other learning. But the tremendous material advancement of the United States that followed the Civil War, opening of the west, transcontinental railroads, phenomenal growth of manufactures, augmented the pioneer trend towards ruthless individualism. As a defence to Granger and liberal legislation, the due process clause of the Fourteenth Amendment was erected into a principle of substantive law against any legislation deemed by the courts to be "arbitrary" and as bulwark of the status quo. This interpretation of the due process clause, more sweeping in effect than a series of constitutional amendments, wrote into the constitution Spencerian laissez faire. "Liberty of contract" found apotheosis in Mr. Justice Field's words in 1885: "The patrimony of the poor man lies in the strength and dexterity of his own hand and to hinder his employing his strength and dexterity in what manner he thinks proper, without injury to his neighbor, is a plain violation of this sacred property." The movement to invalidate statutes under the due process clause ac-

celerated so that between 1920 and 1927 more acts in the field of social and economic legislation were so invalidated than during the preceding fifty-two years. The argument that the clause was being used in the interest of a socially and economically dominant class and as a barrier to humanitarian legislation met increasing acceptance. With that acceptance came a detestation of what was regarded as true natural law. This completed the philosophical erosion of natural law concepts by adding an emotional drive of indignation at what was regarded as the only natural law.

REVIVAL OF TRUE NATURAL LAW
THE DEFENSE AGAINST LEVIATHAN

Totalitarianism triumphed in Europe because it met the opposition of no coherent integrated philosophy of affirmation and of power. It plunged the world into war. Freedom loving peoples awoke from their slumbers. They knew that this was no ordinary war; no war over national boundaries, international markets, oil wells or rubber plantations, or even for the freedom of the seas. It was a battle for the soul of man, the dignity of man, regardless of race or color or economic status or geographical location. Winning that war they are now engaged in the great task of preserving the liberties of men within national boundaries and building a world order in the interest of peace. They will not succeed in that twofold task if they relapse into scepticism, cynicism, indifferentism. They will only succeed if they return to those principles of a true natural law that have again and again triumphed over the divine right of kings and the absolutist state and which will give to the nations of the world that sense of moral unity which is the only foundation for lasting peace.

Brendan F. Brown, Natural Law and the Law-Making Function in American Jurisprudence, 15

Notre Dame Lawyer pp. 12-17 (1939-1940); reprinted by permission of the Notre Dame Lawyer.

Four erroneous deviations from this original notion of natural law may be observed in the history of American law.

In the first place, certain judges and legislators in the formative period of Amercian law at times identified natural law with positive law, i. e., the moral order with the legal. Bills of Rights and constitutional amendments were treated simply as declarations of natural liberty which was identical with common law liberty. Constitutions declared common law principles which were at the same time natural law generalizations. This fallacy had been fostered by Coke and was so deeply imbedded in American politics and jurisprudence that when the American colonists decided in 1776 to throw off the political yoke of England, they approved a Declaration of Independence which asserted a *congeries* of inalienable natural rights which were equivalent to their common law rights which they had set forth in the Continental Congress two years earlier.

What was the result of this confusion of law and morals? The law-makers often idealized the established legal precepts which were regarded as fundamental, immutable and eternal. These rules were not capable of progression toward an extrinsic ethical goal. Many legislators tended to believe that the legislative process was primarily a matter of sustaining a specific legal order rather than of endeavoring to make that order conform, as far as practically possible, to an outside moral ideal. In some nineteenth century decisions, it was held that the judicial process must prevent the alteration of the common law categories of contractual ability by legislation.[1] The theory was that since the common law was the same as natural law and since this latter existed prior to the State and hence was superior to the will of the State, the legislature must not fundamentally change the Common law.[2]

But obviously the concept of a positive law which was identical with natural law was incompatible with the homogeneity of the Thomistic-Aristotelian category. The ultimate notion of *jus naturale* was the denial of an ideal system of human positive law, springing from reason and existing eternal, immutable, and equally applicable to all times and places. The *raison d'etre* of Greek natural law thinking was the subjection of the legal order. But this necessarily implied the existence of these two orders as distinct entities.

Secondly, the natural law was sometimes viewed as a specification of moral rights, which supported legal rights without any corresponding legal duties. Since the natural law, under this interpretation, did not prescribe duties, these moral rights were absolute.[3] The same was true of legal rights. The sole purpose of the positive law, therefore, was to protect and maintain the rights of individuals against other individuals and the state. This juristic theory of rights, whether regarded as moral qualities, inherent in human beings and deducible from the abstract, isolated, individual man, after the doctrine of Grotius, or based upon a social contract, such as that postulated by Rousseau, was individualistic. Whether the basis of these moral qualities was voluntaristic, or non-voluntaristic, they must be given effect by the common law regardless of social consequences. One school of American natural law jurists followed the Coke dogma which identified natural law with the common law, and the other, the doctrine of the French-Dutch publicists, but each was concerned with rights rather than duties.

As a consequence of this second false interpretation of natural law, judges began to speak of the absolute rights of property, freedom of contract,[4] exemption from taxation, and the like. Natural law thus became a weapon against social progress and legal reform. Beneficial labor legislation was invalidated in the name of natural law. Social facts were ignored in the judicial process. Is it surprising that this "led a number of writers who are primarily interested in social reform and in constitutional law to adopt (an) . . . unfriendly attitude toward natural law"[5] in general?

But here again, there was a radical deviation from the content of the *jus naturale* which was evidently not only for the benefit of the individual but also of society, because its original Greek rationale perceived a law which was essentially for the purpose of holding together and aiding cosmos. This in turn was beneficial to the individual units which went into the construction of cosmos. But the secret of the law which made possible cosmos was referable to an equilibrium between the whole and its parts and between the constitutive parts. By analogy, in the field of human society (the human cosmos), such a theory must demand a balancing of rights and duties, the conceptual and the actual, unity and plurality, and stability and motion.

Thirdly, some American jurists and judges were of the opinion that the basis of natural law was subjective rather than objective. From this point of view, natural law was what the individual judge thought it was. It was the reflection of his own personal wishes, sense of justice or intuitive feeling. It was determinable by introspection alone. There was no authority in the form of history, custom, sociology, economics, or the rational sciences to which this intuitive determination of the content of the natural law was subject.

This theory of natural law which refused to recognize any authoritative objective basis could be and frequently was a tool of social injustice. It might be arbitrarily employed by a judge either to uphold a specific precept of law or to overrule it. It afforded judges an opportunity of injecting their own personal sociological and economic predilections into the judicial function. It enabled them to exploit the law for the protection of class interests. It gave the critics of natural law jurisprudence occasion to say that such law was but an empty symbol, a trap for the unwary and a subterfuge for unscrupulous manipulators of the law.

How did such a notion of natural law compare with the classical model of the *jus naturale?* The Greek metaphysical substructure of the *jus naturale* was referable to the observational data of matter, mechanics, and motion fixed in a set pattern. There was general agreement as to the fundamental contour of this objective physical mold. Denial of this pattern did not affect the fact of its existence. The moral order analogously existed as a metaphysical fact despite denial by human intelligences. Besides existence, therefore, this order had definite and specific form, independently of the will of any human individual. Its shape was not ascertainable by abstract reasoning. The rational process must be preceded by an inquiry into the fact-content of sense-perceptions.

According to classical conceptions, no judge could ignore extrinsic *subsidia* in his endeavor to know the meaning of natural law or to apply it in concrete adjudications. Judges might vary to some extent in their conception of this norm, just as physical scientists differed as to the measurements of matter, but the justice of juridical decisions depended upon adherence to this outer authority, however much the individual judge sought to interpose his own mind. Of course a judge would not be morally culpable, if he in good faith followed a misinformed conscience.

Fourthly, there were American jurists who did not derive from their natural law jurisprudence a comprehension of the teleological character of law. Means and end were telescoped by those who merged the legal and moral orders. Positive law had no function to perform except to maintain itself. Justice was to be measured in terms of the maintenance of the existing legal regime rather than by its conformity to an ideal moral order. Some courts reasoned *in vacuo*. Judicial premises were sometimes a little more than meaningless clichés which led to conclusions out of joint with life and experience.

But the regrettable evils which followed in the wake of this deficient legal doctrine are well known since their exposure by the sociological and realist schools of jurisprudence. The jurisprudence of conceptions which had sometimes been given moral aid by the sanction of quasi-natural law was a logical outgrowth of a static positive law. A law which ceased to grow could not be used as a means to achieve contemporary social objectives.

---

[1] See State v. Fire Creek Coal and Coke Co., 33 W. Va. 188 (1889).

[2] See Comm. v. Perry, 155 Mass. 117 (1891); Leep v. Ry. Co., 58 Ark. 407 (1894); State v. Loomis, 115 Mo. 307 (1893).

[3] Brown, *The Bar and the Democratic Process*, 13 Temple L. Quart. 287-295 (1939).

[4] See Pound, *Liberty of Contract*, 18 Yale L. Jour. 454 (1909); Adair v. U. S. 208 U. S. 161, 175 (1907); Coppage v. Kansas, 236 U. S. 1 (1914).

[5] Wright, *American Interpretation of Natural Law* (1931) 316.

C. Causes of the Revival
1. In General

The sterility and ineffectiveness of positivism as a mode of legal and political action became obvious after the consequences of the two world wars. These wars presented a great challenge to the moral convictions of jurists, throughout the world. As a result of those wars, the smug complacency of positivists yielded to the quest for a standard above and beyond the state, based on right reason and the self evident principle of the dignity of the individual. These positivists had been naively relying on the continuation of implicit postulates of a fixed moral order.

Accordingly, the drive to find a formula for political and legal justice became widespread. It led to the revival of natural law jurisprudence. The teleological and practical contributions of the Sociological School, so ably fathered by Rudolf von Jhering in Europe and Roscoe Pound in the United States, were manifestly not adequate to satisfy the juridical demand for non-utilitarian, sociological idealism.

W. Friedmann, Legal Theory pp. 17, 18 (1953—3rd ed.); reprinted by permission of the author and Stevens and Sons, Ltd.

THE PROBLEM OF NATURAL LAW

THE history of natural law is a tale of the search of mankind for absolute justice and of its failure. Again and again, in the course of the last 2,500 years, the idea of natural law has appeared, in some form or other, as an expression of the search for an ideal higher than positive law after having been rejected and derided in the interval. The problem is as acute and as unsolved as ever. With changing social and political conditions the notions on natural law have changed. The only thing that has remained constant is the appeal to something higher than positive law. The object of that appeal has been as often the justification of existing authority as a revolt against it.

Natural law has fulfilled many functions. It has been the principal instrument in the transformation of the old civil law of the Romans into a broad and cosmopolitan system; it has been a weapon used by both sides in the fight between the medieval Church and the German emperors; in its name the validity of international law has been asserted, and the appeal for freedom of the individual against absolutism launched. Again it was by appeal to principles of natural law that American judges, professing to interpret the constitution, resisted the attempt of state legislation to modify and restrict the unfettered economic freedom of the individual.

It would be simple to dismiss the whole idea of natural law as a hypocritical disguise for concrete political aspirations and no doubt it has sometimes exercised little more than this function. But there is infinitely more in it. Natural law has been the chief though not the only way to formulate ideals and aspirations of various peoples and generations with references to the principal moving forces of the time. When the social structure itself was rigid and absolute, as at the time of the Schoolmen, the ideal too would take a static and absolute content. At other times, as with most modern natural law theories, natural law ideals become relative or merely formal, expressing little more than the yearning of a generation which is dissatisfied with itself and the world, which seeks something higher, but is conscious of the relativity of values. It is as easy to deride natural law as it is to deride the futility of mankind's social and political life in general, in its unceasing but hitherto vain search for a way out of the injustice and imperfection, for which so far Western civilisation at any rate has found no other solution but to move between one extreme and another.

The appeal to some absolute ideal finds a response in men, particularly at a time of disillusionment and doubt, and in times of simmering revolt. Therefore natural law theories, far from being theoretical speculations, have often heralded powerful political and legal developments.

Roscoe Pound, Introduction, General Principles of Law by Giorgio Del Vecchio pp. I, VIII, IX (1956); reprinted by permission of the author and the Boston University Press.

IN RECENT YEARS THERE HAS BEEN A REVIVAL of natural law throughout the world. This revival has become well marked in the United States in the past decade.

❖ ❖ ❖ ❖ ❖

In different forms the revived natural law has become strong on the Continent. In France there has been a swing from positivist sociological jurisprudence to Neo-Thomism. In America there is the ethical rationalist natural law of Morris R. Cohen. From many points of view jurists are emphasizing the ideal element in the legal order, in the body of authoritative precepts, or of models or patterns of decision, or of threats of state action, or of predictions of judicial action, as it is variously put, and in the process of judicial decision and administrative determination—in each of the juristic meanings of the term "law" and hence "natural law" in the sense of an ideal system to which we seek to make the legal order, the body of authoritative precepts and the judicial and administrative processes conform. As both a creative ideal and as an ideal basis of criticism, under whatever name it is called and however we arrive at it, a picture of the purpose of the legal order must have a place of real importance in any system of science of law except in the hands of those who deny that there is any reality in systematic application of the force of politically organized society to the controversies and conflicting and overlapping claims and expectations of individuals or of those who consider law nothing but the holding down of the community by a socially or economically dominant class in its own interest. For those who hold such views there is no ideal element. Law is merely organized force.

Joseph P. Witherspoon, Philosophy and the Law, 33 Texas Law Review pp. 321, 341 (1955); reprinted by permission of the author and the Texas Law Review.

Fortunately, the positivist scheme of things has not gone unchallenged. In the twentieth century there has occurred throughout the free world a renascence and remarkable development of the philosophical realism of Aristotle and Saint Thomas Aquinas, which lies at the base of our western cultural heritage. America began to catch up with this development during the second quarter of this century. One facet of this realism is the doctrine of natural law, with which the modern world had lost contact for some three centuries. As Sir Frederick Pollock observed in 1930, the last English writer, until just before the twentieth century, to possess the realist doctrine of natural law as developed by Aquinas was Richard Hooker (1553-1600) who "accordingly stated a consistent and intelligible doctrine."[1] Pollock went on to say: "Much that has been written about the law of nature in modern times is... extremely confused... one cause which would alone be sufficient is the neglect of the scholastic tradition... the schoolmen took some pains to know what they were talking about."[2] The ignorance of writers like Bentham, Austin, and Maine concerning the realist doctrine of natural law is but part of a larger ignorance. As we shall see, the great modern philosophers from Descartes forward have been largely ignorant of our western philosophical heritage. The American legal profession in the twentieth century is in an especially favorable position to familiarize itself with this heritage and must do so if it is to be adequate to the task of dispelling the positivism which pervades so much of our national life. Let us turn to that singular American lawyer who knew the meaning and derivation of positivism as well as our western philosophical heritage. He perhaps can assist other lawyers in finding the road back to the road forward.

The function of the law, the duties of the citizen, and the role of the lawyer in the state have seldom been more acutely perceived and realized in practice than by the lawyers of the American revolutionary era, who played such important roles in the formation of our fundamental legal institutions and in their early administration. One of the most remarkable of these was James Wilson, who helped to shape both of our nation's fundamental documents, particularly the Constitution. * * * * *

The three greatest metaphysicians of all times—Plato, Aristotle, and St. Thomas Aquinas—had no system in the sense in which that term is applicable to the work of the modern idealist philosophers. They did not seek to achieve philosophy once and for all, to construct a system of the world from the inner recesses of thought. Rather, as Aristotle states it, they were concerned to participate in the continuing philosophical experience of mankind, to maintain it and to serve it in their own times. They sought to relate reality to the permanent principles in the light of which the problems of science must be solved.

2. United States

In the twenties and thirties, the movement for a neo-scholastic philosophy of law in the United States was led by certain teachers in law schools under Catholic auspices. In this period, emphasis was placed upon the publication of natural law articles by several law reviews sponsored by such schools as Fordham, Detroit, Marquette, Georgetown, and Notre Dame. This emphasis was continued in the forties and fifties.

In the early thirties, the American Catholic Philosophical Association provided a forum each year for the presentation of papers which applied the principles of scholastic philosophy to current legal problems. A considerable literature grew up as a result of these systematic forums. This literature was further augumented by the Natural Law Institute at Notre Dame, and later by its publication of the Natural Law Forum. In recent years, the St. Thomas More Institute of Legal Research of St. John's University Law School, Brooklyn, began publication of the highly influential "The Catholic Lawyer".

Interest in Natural Law jurisprudence, both scholastic and non-scholastic, became so widespread that beginning in the forties, the pages of the Journal of the American Bar Association became filled with articles pro and con by outstanding authors. Within the past few years, Southern Methodist University gave the movement further impetus by the inauguration of its annual symposium on Natural Law.

Finally, the literature on natural law was expanded by the writings of jurists who were not scholastic, but whose jurisprudence was at least normative. Non-scholastic writers included some of the most influential professors of jurisprudence in the United States. The movement has not lost its momentum.

Miriam Theresa Rooney, *The Movement for a Neo-Scholastic Philosophy of Law in America*, 18 Proceedings of the American Catholic Philosophical Association pp. 185-186, 197-201 (1942); reprinted by permission of the Secretary of the American Catholic Philosophical Association.

THE MOVEMENT FOR A NEO-SCHOLASTIC PHILOSOPHY OF LAW IN AMERICA

SPECIAL REPORT OF THE COMMITTEE ON THE PHILOSOPHY OF LAW AND GOVERNMENT—1932 TO 1942

On the Feast of Saint Thomas of Canterbury, December 29, 1932, the Executive Council of the American Catholic Philosophical Association provided that a Round Table Discussion on the Philosophy of Law be held during the next annual meeting and the Secretary, Dr. Hart, was instructed to complete the final arrangements.[3] In accordance with this provision, the *Proceedings* for the Pittsburgh meeting record that "in the absence of one of the leaders assigned, the Reverend Gerald B. Phelan, the discussion was led by the Reverend William T. Dillon of St. Joseph's College for Women, Brooklyn, who confined the discussion to 'Philosophy of the Common Law in England and America'."[4] This event also took place, perhaps not without significance, on an anniversary of the martyrdom of Saint Thomas à Becket, namely, December 29, 1933. In this simple way was inaugurated a movement which may some day be recognized as one of the most important of this twentieth century, an innovation not only for Catholic philosophers in America, but also for jurists in the English-speaking, or Common Law, world. For lack of a better name it may be called the movement for a Neo-Scholastic Philosophy of Law in America. This year, marking the completion of the first decade of its existence, affords an appropriate time for a brief survey of the movement, noting the situation of the world into which it was born, its youthful achievements, and its promise for future development.

* * * * *

Unfortunately, as Monsignor Dillon brought out in his Pittsburgh address in 1933, "most modern treatises on the law and its history were written by men unsympathetic towards metaphysics and especially towards a spiritual metaphysic, and most especially towards a scholastic metaphysic." [5] The views of most of the authors chosen for translation in the above series, important as they may be for comparative study, are no exception to the latter qualification.

* * * * *

Unhappily the mere launching of the movement, simply providing an opportunity for development, was not sufficient to get it well established at once in spite of the keen grasp of the situation Monsignor Dillon displayed in his excellent paper[6] designed to open discussion on the subject. No provision having been made for a Round Table on legal philosophy for the next meeting in 1934, Dr. Brendan Brown, recently returned from Oxford to resume teaching on the Catholic University Law Faculty, was directed to speak in the name of the Law School in an appeal for further interest in the subject on the part of the Association. The *Proceedings* record that on December 28, 1934,

"The Council was addressed by Dr. Brendan F. Brown, Instructor in the Law School of The Catholic University of America, on the subject of the cooperation of the Association with the efforts of the Law School of The Catholic University of America to build up a Catholic philosophy of law along Scholastic lines. Dr. Brown asked the Council to name a committee of the Association to work with the Law School of The Catholic University of America and any other of the law schools under the direction of Catholic colleges which might care to join with the Catholic University Law School in this regard. The Council accepted the invitation of Dr. Brown, and President Riedl was instructed to appoint such a Committee in the near future."[7]

The Committee on the Philosophy of Law appointed by the President according to the record held its first meeting at Loyola University School of Law, Chicago, on September 14, 1935, those present including the Rev. Linus Lilly, S.J., Rev. Dr. Charles A. Hart, Professor John C. Fitzgerald, and Dr. Brendan Brown. Father Noonan, S.J., of Loyola Law School and Mr. James J. Kearney, now of Notre Dame Law School, also attended.[8] In accordance with the plan adopted, the Secretary of the Association sent 279 letters to professors of law in various Catholic law schools[9] asking their opinions on the subject of a Neo-Scholastic Philosophy of Law and inviting their collaboration. Further communications were sent out October 19, 1935,[10] and November 21, 1935, to the same purpose. The Committee reported to the meeting of the American Catholic Philosophical Association, December 31, 1935, that sufficient interest had been elicited to justify a request in the near future that the Association organize a permanent section on the Philosophy of Law. The signers of the report were Brendan Brown, Acting Chairman, Rev. Timothy L. Bouscaren, S.J., Professor Walter B. Kennedy, Rev. Linus Lilly, S.J., Rev. William T. Dillon, J.D., Dean John C. Fitzgerald, Professor Adam C. Ellis, and Rev. Charles A. Hart. Thereupon the Executive Council, at its meeting, December 31, 1935,[11] appointed a standing committee consisting of Dr. Brown, Father Lilly, and Dr. Mortimer Adler, to conduct a round table on the philosophy of law and government at the next annual meeting.

Notices having been sent to those interested under dates of February 29, June 25, and December 10, 1936, telling them of the work of the Committee, a Round Table discussion was held December 29, 1936, during the Chicago meeting of the Association, at which the Rev. Linus Lilly, S.J., and Professor John W. Curran delivered the principal addresses on the subject,

"Possibilities of a Neo-Scholastic Philosophy of Law in the United States Today."[12]

* * * * *

It was the New York meeting of 1937 which brought assurance that the movement was henceforth to be recognized as of permanent value. At that meeting Monsignor Dillon was President of the Association and his unfailing interest in the subject was disclosed not only in his stirring Presidential Address on "Philosophy in Law and Government"[13] but also in the Round Table Discussion itself, where the late Mr. William P. Moyles, who had written as early as October 3, 1931, in *America*[14] on the intellectual problems facing serious students in our Catholic law schools, presided over the session. Professor Walter B. Kennedy in his paper stressed the fact that "there is here and now in our day and in our land, as well as throughout the world, a direct and purposeful attempt to destroy the common law, and indeed, law in general; and that this movement is centering its gunfire upon the elements of Scholastic jurisprudence which are dominant in that law."[15] And he urged in consequence less the creation of a Neo-Scholastic jurisprudence than its preservation already present in the law.[16] Professor Franklin F. Russell of Brooklyn Law School, whose courses Monsignor Dillon had followed some years earlier, agreed with Professor Kennedy that "Christianity in general and Neo-Scholasticism in particular are already part of the common law, and, therefore, the efforts of this Association should be not to create but to preserve, Neo-Scholasticism in the law."[17]

* * * * *

Since the New York meeting of 1937 established the Committee on the Philosophy of Law and Government on a permanent foundation, a succession of worthwhile discussions have been held during the annual meetings of the Association. In 1938, Dr. Walter Farrell, O.P., and Dean James T. Connor of Loyola, New Orleans, read papers on "The Derivation of Political Authority." In 1939, Dr. Brendan Brown considered the question of "Public Control of Private Property." For the 1940 session, Dr. Miriam Rooney prepared a paper on "Law and the New Logic," which was followed by Dean Daniel J. McKenna's paper on "Some Problems of the Catholic Lawyer." Raoul E. Desvernine, Esq., of New York, and Dr. Frederick J. De Sloovère, formerly of the Catholic University Law Faculty and now Associate Dean of New York University Law School, read eloquent papers at the Philadelphia meeting in 1941. For 1942, for the tenth annniversary observance of the section during the centennial celebration at Notre Dame University, Dean Clarence Manion and Dr. Brendan Brown, recently appointed Acting Dean of Catholic University Law School, were asked to contribute. Their papers, as well as those presented at the previous meetings, published in full in their proper places in the annual volumes of the *Proceedings* of the Association, deserve rereading periodically.

○ ○ ○ ○ ○

Besides the papers relevant to the Neo-Scholastic philosophy of law which have appeared in the *Proceedings* of the American Catholic Philosophical Association, and in the law reviews of Fordham, Notre Dame, Georgetown, the University of Detroit, and Marquette, there are to be included in surveying the literature of the movement to date, the sermons delivered annually at the various "Red Masses" throughout the country, Father Robert White's paper on "Some Opportunities for the Catholic Historian in the Reform and Progress of the Law," in the *Catholic Historical Review* for April, 1935;[18] Professor Kennedy's contributions to the Eighth American Scientific Congress, and the symposium entitled "My Philosophy of Law";[19] articles by Dr. Brown,[20] Dean William F. Clarke, Father Francis Lucey, S.J.,[21] and others, in various law journals, and by Father John C. Ford, S.J., in the Proceedings of the Jesuit Philosophical Society in September, 1941.[22] *New Scholasticism*, under the editorship of Dr. Ignatius Smith, O.P., has featured book reviews in the field of contemporary jurisprudence, as well as articles by Dr. Miriam Rooney and Dr. O. H. Mott.[23] So far there has been nothing done in the way of bibliography and very little in book form.

* * * * *

From this narrative of the establishment and growth of the movement for a Neo-Scholastic Philosophy of Law in America since its formal organization ten years ago, it will be seen that it has a real function to perform in contemporary culture, but that its achievements so far have not yet attained major worth.

3. Latin America

A revival of natural law jurisprudence has also taken place in Latin America, particularly in Argentina and Mexico. This revival represents a sharp reaction against the long standing predominance of the positivism of Comte. It has proceeded approximately along the same paths as it followed in the United States, namely, scholastic and non-scholastic. Non-scholastic natural law jurisprudence has moved principally toward neo-Kantianism.

Josef L. Kunz, Contemporary Latin-American Philosophy of Law: A Survey, 3 The American Journal of Comparative Law pp. 217, 218-219 (1954); reprinted by permission of the Author and the American Journal of Comparative Law.

In contemporary Latin America we see—as in Europe and the United States—a strong revival of natural law philosophy, whether Neo-Thomistic or not. Neo-Thomism, on the strict lines of the *"philosophia perennis"* of St. Thomas of Aquinas, came into being in the whole Catholic world in consequence of the Encyclical *"Aeterni Patris"* of Leo XIII. Leading European Neo-Thomistic thinkers are highly influential in Latin America. But, apart from Neo-Thomism there is, in Latin America as elsewhere, a general revival of natural law thinking. And modern natural law, in Latin America and the rest of the countries of Occidental culture, has many strong connections with modern philosophy and philosophy of law; with the Neo-Kantian Schools of Baden and Marburg; with all "intuitionist" philosophies; Bergson, phenomenology, theory of values, existentialism. Husserl and, particularly Scheler and Hartmann are highly valued also by modern Neo-Thomists. Existentialism, not in the atheist form of Heidegger and Sartre, but in the Christian form, e.g. of Jaspers and Gabriel Marcel finds a ready echo also in Neo-Thomists.

❊ ❊ ❊ ❊ ❊

Even in Brazil, where Comtism was strongest and has lasted longest and where Catholicism in the nineteenth century suffered a period of decadence, there is a revival of Catholic faith and philosophy. The turning point came with Farias Brito (1862-1917), a highly interesting philosopher who is more and more studied.[24] His work in Catholic philosophy of law has been continued by his disciple, Jackson de Figuereida and today by Alceu de Amoros Lima, who writes under the pseudonym of Tristão de Athayde. We must also mention the Professor of Roman Law at the São Paulo Law School, de Correia, who has dedicated many years to a Portuguese translation of the "*Summa Theologiae*" of St. Thomas.

❊ ❊ ❊ ❊ ❊

There are writers on Catholic natural law in all Spanish-American countries, including Argentina (Ismael Quiles, S. J. Alfredo Fragueiro, Manuel Rio) and Mexico—the central figure is Oswaldo Robles—, notwithstanding the rather strong tension between State and Church during some phases of the Mexican Revolution.

The two outstanding Neo-Thomist philosophers of law in contemporary Spanish America are, in this writer's judgment, the Colombian Cayetano Betancour and the Mexican Rafael Preciado Hernández. Betancour's[24] work is symptomatic for modern Neo-

Thomism. He sees in phenomenology a return to the ancient doctrine of Scholasticism and is a fervent admirer of Max Scheler. He has also great merits as the director of the excellent Colombian philosophical Review, "*Ideas y Valores.*"

Preciado Hernández' work, perhaps the most important Neo-Thomistic philosophy of law in contemporary Latin America, is, although strictly Thomistic in an orthodox way, nevertheless a thoroughly modern work. It is modern in the restriction of the contents of natural law, in its opposition to the "Codes" of the Law of Nature of the eighteenth century, in its insistence on the absolute necessity of positive law, in its denial of any rivalry between positive and natural law, in its inclination toward an "integral" philosophy of law, in its recognition of the basically ethical character of the so-called natural law. That "natural law" is ethics, not law, is the solution of this controversy which has lasted for over two thousand years, a solution, hinted at by the Spaniard Luis Legaz y Lacambra, by the German Coing and openly pronounced by the Neo-Thomist theoretician of law of the "School of Louvain," Jean Dabin, who states in clear terms:[25] "*Au binôme: droit naturel—droit positif il faut substituer celui de: morale—droit.*

4. France

Perhaps the vanguard of the movement for a revival of natural law thinking is to be found in France. Even before the outbreak of the first World War, influential French jurists, like Gény, recognized the error of positivism. Roscoe Pound has shown that the present revival of natural law in France is confined to the neo-scholastic and Neo-Kantian.

Roscoe Pound, Introduction, *General Principles of Law* by Giorgio Del Vecchio p. VI (1956); reprinted by permission of the author and the Boston University Press.

In France at the beginning of the present century there was a revival of natural law. At first it took three forms, Neo-Kantian, a revival of juridical idealism, as it was called; Neo-Scholastic, or Neo-Thomist, a social philosophical development of the orthodox philosophy of the Roman church; and sociological, a development of a universal system from a fundamental principle found in the Comtian manner by observation of social phenomena verified by further observation. But this positivist economist natural law is out of the line of development of the ethical-idealist natural law which is reviving today.

5. Germany

The issue of natural law is today in the center of all jurisprudential discussion in Germany. Besides the development of the scholastic doctrine, a neo-Kantian idealism has been emphasized. This idealism has been worked out in several different ways.

Freiherr von der Heydte, Natural Law Tendencies in Contemporary German Jurisprudence, 1 Natural Law Forum pp. 116, 118, 119-121 (1956); reprinted by permission of the Natural Law Forum.

One may distinguish two different currents in the natural law tendencies in postwar German jurisprudence, according to the position from which the question is raised: one group approaches the problem of natural law on the basis of traditional philosophical positions, while the other group approaches it from the basis of the problems and experiences of contemporary thinking.

On the basis of traditional positions Neo-Thomism attempts to solve the problem of natural law. In Germany it has developed a theory usually called the Catholic doctrine of natural law. Its representatives in Germany today are primarily Johannes Messner of Vienna with his voluminous work on natural law,[26] Ernst von Hippel of Cologne,[27] and Günther Küchenhoff of Würzburg.[28] Another member of this group is the Viennese professor Alfred von Verdross, who formerly was strongly influenced by Hans Kelsen. In this connection one must also mention Heinrich Kipp, Arthur Wegner, Adolf Süsterhenn, and Valentin Tomberg, the latter a disciple of Ernst von Hippel. The Catholic natural law theorists see nature above all as the creation of God; and natural law as a law that results from the essence of creation and is recognizable by human reason. Natural law characteristically transcends positive law. Catholic theory conceives this transcending character of natural law as a reference from creation to the Creator: natural law is thus conceived metaphysically. As Wolf has shown, at the core of this doctrine is the problem of the basis of law, and both the faith in and the search after an absolute and timeless law. The doctrine faces the perennial antinomy between timeless natural law and the historical character of positive law.

※ ※ ※ ※ ※

Much greater than the influence of Neo-Hegelianism, in recent years, has been the influence of Neo-Kantianism on German legal philosophy. Neo-Kantian influence appears today in three different schools of thought about natural law. First, Kant's subjective idealism has led to a theory which, following Rudolf Stammler, construes natural law along purely logical lines. This school is today represented by Jürgen von Kempski.[29] Natural law logically construed ultimately coincides, as Erik Wolf has pointed out, with the correct method of legal thinking, the logic of jurisprudence, since it is the quintessence of what is "correctly" thought or known. It transcends positive law in the sense of transcending the historical aspects, ethical principles, psychological compulsions, and sociological conditions which may become the respective content of law; in other words, it is pure form transcending substance, form for which the content is irrelevant.

The central part of such a logically construed natural law is a theory of the fundamental concepts of law; the crucial question is that of what law is logically possible and hence formally correct; the antinomy to be solved is one between actually observed substance and logically correct form. This antinomy originates in the presupposition of a world of being as conflicting with a world of oughtness.

❊ ❊ ❊ ❊ ❊

A second branch of Neo-Kantianism has an utterly different idea, for it construes natural law ethically. On the basis of Kant's philosophy, Rudolf von Laun of Hamburg in his famous address on *Ethics and Law* in 1924 had already predicted a renaissance of natural law theory. The idea which Laun first developed in this address—that the obligation of law could ultimately root only in a norm which the obligated person had in full substance given to himself—is later on consistently developed in Laun's subsequent publications.[30] What he considers natural law is always the autonomously posited and autonomously known law of individual consciousness which alone has obligatory force. Just as many Neo-Hegelians have exaggerated the objectivity of Hegel's idealism, so Laun, who among the Neo-Kantians is the critic closest to Kant himself, pushes the subjectivity of Kant's idealism to its ultimate possibilities. One may well doubt that in Laun's doctrine of natural law there is still a genuine transcendence, since positive law too becomes obligatory, according to Laun, only through the individual consciousness of duty. At most, one may see here the consciousness of duty transcending the actual performance of duty.

Laun's principles of legal theory had already been fully developed before the Second World War. After the war, Helmut Coing of Frankfort[31] sought to reestablish natural law in the sense of Kantian idealism. He leaned on the philosophy of values as developed by Max Scheler and Nicolai Hartmann. Starting with the value consciousness of man, Coing tries to discover a system of supreme ethical values of law and substantive principles of law which would constitute the criteria and legitimation of positive law. Coing's natural law transcends positive law in the sense that the realm of consciousness and conscience transcends the realm of external conduct; but unlike Laun, he does not deny that the positive law outside this realm of consciousness is law; nor does he conceive it as mere projection or as an appeal to the inner sphere.

Despite the many differences between Laun's and Coing's theories, they both have in common not only the basis of Kantian philosophy, but also the conception of natural law as an ethically obligatory order. The centerpiece of this ethically construed natural law is a theory of the fundamental principles of law; the crucial question is which norms are substantively right. The antinomy to be solved is one between the practical concern that exploits the protection of legality and the ethos that seeks the path of morality.

A third Neo-Kantian school of thought is to be found in Gustav Radbruch's last works.[32] Radbruch's starting point is the double thesis that legal norms on the one hand are formed out of the stuff of social facts—which stuff thus enters into the idea of law—and on the other hand have obligatory force only because of the value inherent in these norms—which values legitimize and criticize all positive law. Transpositive law is the sum total of those principles of law which, as the expression of the idea of law, are inherent in and stronger than any positive rule. These principles of law, in Radbruch's view, are not above but within positive law. Any positive rule which does not express the idea of law, i.e., any act that contradicts transpositive law, does not have legal authority for Radbruch. Radbruch is envisaging a transpositive idea of law that transcends social data, factual necessities and purposes. He construes natural law, if we are to give this name to his transpositive law, in ontological terms. The centerpiece of his theory is, therefore, a doctrine of the fundamental structure of law. His chief question is the obligatory force of law. To answer this question, he must of course clarify the previous question of the substance of the idea of law. That substance, for Radbruch, is simply justice, seen in three dimensions as formal justice, the principle of the predictability or calculability of law, and suitability to ideal ends—dimensions among which there is continuous tension. A conflict between them is ultimately a conflict of justice with itself, or rather the inevitable debate of justice with itself which is essential to law. Without this antinomy there can be no law; its solution is the perennial task of law. The principle of predictability (*Rechtssicherheit*) argues in favor of a legal act which in fact may violate formal justice even though it may endeavor to realize that justice. But where there is not even this endeavor, or where the act violates justice in a degree unbearable to the individual conscience, positive law has to give way before transpositive law. The decision about this last question, as we gather from Radbruch, must be made in the realm of the dialectic consciousness and individual conscience.

This last idea is rejected by Hans Welzel of Bonn.[33] Hans Welzel also construes natural law ontologically —in a certain way. His philosophical premises are quite different from those of Radbruch. That is why he does not envisage a dialectic tension between the ontological and the ethical conception of natural law, a tension which Radbruch sees not only in terms of a necessary difference (that much Welzel acknowledges), but also in terms of a necessary and inescapable relation. Welzel rejects the value content of traditional theories of natural law and finally arrives at the assumption of a certain materio-logical structure in the object which he considers the guiding criteria of legal rules limiting the arbitrariness of legislators and embodying eternal truths.

Radbruch and Erik Wolf—somewhat alike in their thinking—already went beyond the starting point of tradition and raised the question of natural law from the point of view of the time, that is from the existence of man, his innermost core and his experience of himself. This latter approach wholly characterizes the work of Erich Fechner of Tübingen,[34] as well as that of Werner Maihofer of Würzburg.[35]

Both approach the problem of natural law from the existentialism of Jaspers and Heidegger; both also have root in the realm of religion; both see the tremendous tension between the static doctrines of classical natural law and the dynamism of time; both are still groping, searching, and trail-blazing rather than quietly observing things from a fixed point of view. Fechner opposes a natural law with a developing substance to a natural law with fixed substance and a natural law with changeable substance. Man participates in this developing natural law through acts of distinction and decision; at the risk of his existence he tries out the tenability of something new. The risky decision on values which again and again confronts man in this developing natural law is, according to Fechner, part of man's essence. The existential necessity of choice springs precisely from the regularities and conditions of the social sphere. Maihofer, one of Erik Wolf's disciples, distinguishes between existential (subjective) and institutional (objective) natural law; he tries to construe natural law as a right of human existence. Thus interpreted, natural law expresses the ego-existence (*Selbstsein*) of an individual in his uniqueness as well as the qua-existence (*Alssein*) of a person in society, inasmuch as he participates in typological situations *qua* father, *qua* husband, *qua* doctor, *qua* judge, *qua* citizen, *qua* neighbor, etc.

This brief survey could cover only the most important currents of natural law theory in contemporary Germany and only the most important theoreticians and their books. But however short, the survey serves to show that the problem of natural law is today the center of the theoretical discussion of law in Germany. If one adds that the highest German courts—the Federal Constitutional Court and the Federal Supreme Court—have adopted natural law ideas in some of their basic decisions, one perceives that Rudolf Laun's prophecy of 1924—that natural law would be reborn in Germany—is about to be fulfilled.

6. Italy

The revived interest in natural law doctrine on the part of Italian jurists may be seen from the increasing number of articles on the subject appearing in their periodicals. The same pattern of revival of natural law thinking as appears in the United States, Latin America, and Germany exists also in Italy. The scholastic movement has been advanced there, as everywhere, by the eloquent and powerful advocacies of the Holy Father. The non-scholastic movement, chiefly neo-Kantian, has been led by Georgio Del Vecchio.

Guido Fasso, Natural Law in Italy in the Past Ten Years, 1 Natural Law Forum pp. 123-125 (1956); reprinted by permission of the Natural Law Forum.

The crisis of idealism showed itself in the dispersion of its old adherents in various contradictory directions, among them that of Catholic spiritualism linked with the fortunes of political Catholicism which seemed to many the surest defense against the menace of communism. This Catholic trend, without declaring itself on the side of Thomistic positions and without therefore embracing the official Catholic doctrine of natural law, could not (because of the central position in its philosophy of the concept of *person* and because of its links with the thought of Antonio Rosmini, during the last century one of the most positive proponents of natural law) fail to be sympathetic with this rebirth of the idea of natural law, in spite of the historical scruples of some of its representatives.

In addition, the renascence of Catholic thought strengthened and spread Neo-Thomism, which had kept alive the Catholic tradition of natural law, even though there are rare signs of it in the prewar period; and in fact Giorgio Del Vecchio began to draw nearer to Thomistic philosophy while yet remaining faithful to the original Neo-Kantian basis of his thought. It was Del Vecchio who had, at the beginning of the century, in the era of dominant positivism, defended the universal value of natural law to whom as early as 1934 Pope Pius XI had written, through the then Cardinal Pacelli, that in his books he pointed out "substantial elements of that *philosophia perennis* which ... is satisfied by the nourishment of the eternal wisdom."[36]

In fact, in the purely philosophical field, in which Catholic spiritualism is accompanied by other active and efficacious currents of thought, from existentialism to Marxism and logical neo-positivism, which now seems in great vogue among youth—currents which all criticize and refute the idea of natural law—this idea appears to arouse less favor than among the jurists: they in turn were in the past no less bitter critics of natural law because of the almost complete domination among them of juridical positivism. The most eloquent proof of this renewed interest on the part of many Italian jurists in natural law can be found by running through the indices of the two officially Catholic law reviews: *Jus*, of the Catholic University of the Sacred Heart in Milan, and *Iustitia*, of the Union of Italian Catholic Jurists. *Jus* frequently prints articles dedicated to natural law; and *Iustitia*, in its first number (1948), opened a discussion of the "basic problem" which faces the conscience of the Catholic jurist when confronted with a law which may not conform to the principles of his faith. Numerous articles on this point anticipated the exhortation made by the Pope to Catholic jurists to examine thoroughly the problem of the conduct of the jurist in regard to unjust laws.

In a discourse directed to the delegates to the first Congress of the Union of the Catholic Jurists, on November 5, 1949, Pius XII drew attention to "the unsolved contrasts between the noble concept of man and law according to Christian principles... and juridical positivism," pointing out the conflict of conscience which arises for the Catholic jurist "who strives to keep faith with the Christian concept of law... particularly when he is in the position of having to apply a law which his own conscience condemns as unjust"; but already in the Encyclical *Summi Pontificatus* (1939) and in the Christmas radio address of 1942 the Pontiff had reaffirmed the eternal validity of natural law, and the Italian Catholic jurists were at that time already turning toward its re-evaluation. Since 1947 one writer has strongly vindicated the juridical quality of natural law, a quality which he on the other hand denied to the laws whose content was opposed to it;[37] and another writer has devoted an entire volume to the problem of the unjust law.[38] Meanwhile, in the review *Iustitia*, the discussion of the same problem was growing intense. This then formed the focal point of the "workshop" held near Varese in June, 1949, by the Union of Catholic Jurists on the theme *Effective Natural Law*, a theme which expressed with polemic evidence a clear-cut point of view.

Both the conclusions of the delegates to the workshop and the writings which appeared from 1948 to 1951 on this point in *Iustitia*, along with the text of the Pope's speech and the article of Del Vecchio mentioned above which serves as an introduction, were collected in a volume published in Rome in 1951 which has as its title the theme of the workshop, *Effective Natural Law*. This is rather useful for anyone who wishes to form an idea of the opinions of the Italian Catholic jurists on this question;[39] it is useful even if the impression which emerges from it is, to use the words of one of the most authoritative participants in the meeting, that among the delegates there exists, in regard to the effectiveness of natural law, "a remarkably surprising disparity of points of view,"[40] and (once again having recourse to the words of another participant in the discussion, the

Jesuit Father Lener[41]) "a profound disorientation" caused by the conflict which is held to be ineluctable between the asserted truth of natural law and the dogmatic principles and practical exigencies of positive jurisprudence. Of the 21 Italian jurists whose opinion is reported in the volume,[42] certainly not all and indeed not many accept what ought to be, according to the title of the volume, the thesis of all of the contributors: that natural law has a vitality of its own, above and beyond law imposed by the State. It would take too long to give here the individual theses, even in the form of syntheses; but certainly while manifestly everyone feels the problem of the duty of the conscience confronted with unjust law to be "a basic problem" (this was the title of the article which first appeared anonymously but in fact written by Santoro Passarelli, which began the discussion in *Iustitia*), it is equally evident that almost all are aware of the danger that would be imminent in basing the principle of verifiability by the citizen of the legitimacy of the laws of the State, with the consequent renunciation of what, at least in continental European countries, is considered an essential requisite of law, its certitude.

And it is significant that, among those who show themselves most troubled about accepting the radical solution of the full effectiveness of natural law, there are a philosopher, a constitutionalist trained in philosophy, and a historian: Giuseppe Capograssi, Carlo Esposito, and Ugo Nicolini, who, better than the jurists themselves, could, although for different reasons, see with great profundity into a problem whose terms seem simple but which excludes any simple solutions (which are, however, not lacking in the volume). Nicolini, in particular, who in several works[43] examined the problem of the unjust law historically, has more concretely and indeed with more historical sense taken up a problem which easily leads to anti-historical solutions.

[1] Sir Frederick Pollock notes to Maine's *Ancient Law* 120-1 (John Murray, New ed. 1930).

[2] *Ibid. Cf.* R. Pound, *An Introduction to the Philosophy of Law* 1-47 (Yale, 1954) and E. Cahn, *The Sense of Injustice* 6-11 N. Y. Univ. Press, 1949).

[3] Proceedings, American Catholic Philosophical Association, 8th annual meeting, 1932, p. 130. (Cited below as Proc. 8th, 1932, etc.)

[4] Proc. 9th, 1933, p. 204.

[5] Proc. 9th, 1933, p. 178.

[6] Proc. 9th, 1933, pp. 175-182.

[7] Proc. 10th, 1934, p. 173.

[8] Proc. 11th, 1935, p. 201.

[9] Proc. 11th, 1935, p. 199.

[10] Proc. 11th, 1935, p. 202.

[11] Proc. 11th, 1935, p. 207.

[12] Proc. 12th, 1936, pp. 111-117.

[13] Proc. 13th, 1937, pp. 1-16.

[14] Moyles, William P., "Our Catholic Law Schools,' 45 *America*, 616-617, Oct. 3, 1931.

[15] Proc. 13th, 1937, p. 186.

[16] *Ibid.*

[17] Proc. 13th, 1937, p. 197.

[18] 21 *Cath. Hist. Rev.*, 49-64, Apr. 1935.

[19] Proceedings of Eighth American Scientific Congress, Washington, D. C., May, 1940, not yet published; cf. 9 Fordham Law Rev. 362-374, Nov. 1940. *My Philosophy of Law*, Boston, Boston Book Co., 1941, pp. 145-160.

[20] See K. N. Llewellyn's acknowledgment of debt to Aquinas in footnote in 9 U. Chi. Law Rev., 247, Feb. 1942, where reference is made to B. F. Brown's article in 15 Notre Dame Lawyer 9, Nov. 1939.

[21] Lucey, F. E., S.J., *Jurisprudence and the Future Social Order*, 16 Social Science (Winfield, Kans.), 211, July 1941.

[22] *Phases of American Culture*, Worcester, Mass., Holy Cross College Press, 1942, pp. 51-83.

[23] Rooney, Miriam Theresa, *Pluralism and the Law*, 13 New Scholasticism, 301-337, Oct. 1939; Mott, Omer Hillman, *Utility as the Norm of Law*, 15 New Scholasticism, 377-390, Oct. 1941.

[24] See Teofilo Cavalcanti, "*A filosofia jurídica de Farias Brito*" (*Revista Brasileira de Filosofia,* Vol. III no. 2 (1953), pp. 225-241, and the two studies, translated into Portuguese, by the above named Spaniard Tejada Spinola, "*Raimundo de Farias Brito na filosofia do Brazil*" (*Revista Portuguesa de Filosofia,* Vol. VI no. 3, Braga (1950) and *As doutrinas politicas de Farias Brito.* São Paulo, 1952.

[24a] He has recently also published an Introduction to the Science of Law (Cayetano Betancour, Introducción a la ciencia del derecho. Bogotá, 1953. p. 366).

[25] Jean Dabin, *Théorie Générale du Droit.* Second ed. Brussels, 1953, p. 324. The text of the first edition is presented in English translation in Vol. IV of the XX Century Legal Philosophy Series.

[26] (2d ed. 1950).

[27] *Rechtsgesetz und Naturgesetz* (2nd ed. 1949) and *Einführung in die Rechtstheorie* (4th ed. 1955).

[28] *Naturrecht und Christentum* (1948).

[29] *Naturrecht und Völkerrecht* (1948); *Das Problem des Rechts und die Ethik,* 9 Zeitschrift für Philosophische Forschung 358-365 (1955).

[30] E.g. *Reden und Aufsätze zum Völkerrecht und Staatsrecht* (1947).

[31] *Die Obersten Grundsätze des Rechts* (1947) and *Grundzüge de Rechtsphilosophie* (1950).

[32] *Gesetzliches Unrecht und Übergesetzliches Recht,* 1 Süddeutsche Juristen Zeitung 105-08 (1946); *Gesetz und Recht,* 12 Stuttgarter Rundschau 5-10 (1947); *Die Natur der Sacheals Juristische Denkform, Festschriff für Rudolf Laun* 157-76 (1948); Rechtsphilosophie (4th ed. 1951).

[33] *Naturrecht und Materiale Gerechtigkeit* (1951).

[34] *Die Soziologische Grenze der Grundrechte* (1954) and *Naturrecht und Existenzphilosophie* (1955).

[35] *Recht und Sein* (1954) and *Vom Sinn menschlicher Ordnung* (1956).

[36] The ideas of Del Vecchio on natural law appear, it may be said, in all his works including the very diffuse *Lezioni di Filosofia del Diritto* and the equally well-known *Giustizia.* Among the recent articles devoted to this point I recall *Dispute e Conclusioni sul Diritto Naturale,* 26 Rivista Internationale di Filosofia del Diritto 155-62 (1949), which had al-

ready appeared in 1 Iustitia 3 (1948) with the title *Le Concezioni Moderne del Diritto Naturale* and which was later included in the volume *Diritto Naturale Vigente*, of which I shall speak later; and *Mutabilità ed Eternità del Diritto*, 5 Jus 1-14 (n.s. 1954), which is without doubt the most valuable writing on natural law inspired by Catholic principles which has appeared in recent years. See in addition *Essenza del Diritto Naturale*, 29 Rivista Internazionale di Filosofia Diritto 18-24 (1952). The thought of Del Vecchio and other authors on natural law is set down by Artana, Contributi alla Rinascita del Diritto Naturale, 26 Rivista Internazionale di Filosofia del Diritto 419-49 (1949); see also Vidal ,*La Filosofia Giuridica di G. Del Vecchio* (Milan 1951), or in shorter form, Aceti, Il *Più Recente Pensiero Filosofico-Giuridico di G. Del Vecchio*, 5 Jus 259-78 (n.s. 1954).

[37] Domenico Barbero, in the work *Diritto e Stato* (Milan 1947), then condensed as an "introduction " in *Sistema Istituzionale del Diritto Privato* (4th ed., Turin (955) with the title "*Diritto e Legge*" and, with the same title, in the volume *Studi di Teoria Generale del Diritto* (Milan 1953). In this last named volume see also the text of the lecture given by the author in 1952 in the Catholic University of Milan, previously printed with the title *Rivalutazione del Diritto Naturale*, 3 Jus 491-507 (n.s. 1952).

[38] Paolo Guidi, *La Legge Ingiusta* (Rome 1948).

[39] The contents of the book have been set down and summarized in the article by G.B.P. (Giorgio Balladore Pallieri), *Diritto Naturale Vigente*, 3 Jus 144-47 (n.s. 1952), and somewhat more amply and critically in the article by Uberto Scarpelli, *Diritto Naturale Vigente?* 9 Occidente 99-123 (1953). For a critical revaluation see Giuseppe Marchello, *Sul Diritto Naturale Vigente*, 18 Annali Della Facoltà Giuridica dell'Università di Camerino 163-77 (1951).

[40] Barbero, *Rivalutazione del Diritto Naturale*, cited in 3 Jus 492 (n.s. 1952).

[41] Salvatore Lener, *La Certezza del Diritto, il Diritto Naturale e il Magistero della Chiesa*, 1 Studi Giuridici in Onore di F. Carnelutti 345-87 (Padua 1950). Such an essay is also noteworthy as a very strictly orthodox manifestation of Catholic thought in this connection.

[42] R. Angeloni, G. Astuti, D. Barbero, G. Bozzetti, G. Capograssi, F. Carnelutti, V. Chieppa, V. Del Giudice, G. Del Vecchio, F. M. Dominedò, F. Di Piazza, M. Elia, C. Esposito,

P. Frezza, G. Graneris, G. Grosso, S. Lener, G. Morelli, U. Nicolini, U. Radaelli, F. Santoro Passarelli.

[43] *Il Principio di Legalità nelle Democrazie Italiana* (Milan 1947); *Certezza del Diritto e Legge Giusta nell'Eta Comunale*, 4 Studi Giuridici in Onore di F. Carnelutti 293-310 (Padua 1950).

PART II. SCHOLASTIC NATURAL LAW JURISPRUDENCE

A. *Plato, Aristotle, and Cicero*

It appears that long before the time of Plato (427-347 B.C.) and Aristotle (384-322 B.C.), there was what may be described as a manifestation of the recognition of natural law in the Oriental World. But the roots of scholastic jurisprudence are to be found in the writings of Greek philosophers, especially the Stoics. This philosophy was followed by Cicero, and in the thirteenth century received further clarification by St. Thomas Aquinas.

The essence of the Stoic-Thomistic doctrine is that man is under an obligation to conform his conduct to a pattern of behavior which originates outside of man. This pattern does not exist solely in the mind of man, but is objective, and is perceived by the reason of man, acting as a telescope, as it were. The obligation of this pattern is based on the authority of reason, and not of revelation. It is the product of philosophy, and not theology.

The Thomistic concept is based on theodicy, which is a branch of philosophy dealing with the knowledge of God obtained by reason alone. The Stoics were uncertain whether the source of this law was a personal Creator, or a pantheistic God. According to the theodicy (not theology) of the scholastics, the source was a personal Creator.

IV Plato, The Dialogues, The Laws, Book X, pp. 457-458, Jowett, 4th Ed. (1953); reprinted by permission of the Clarendon Press, Oxford, England.

Ath. In the first place, my friend, these people would say that the Gods exist not by nature, but by art, and by the laws of states, which are different in different places, according to the agreement of those who make them; and that the honourable is one thing by nature and another thing by law, and that the principles of justice have no existence at all in nature, but that mankind are always disputing about them and altering them; and that the alterations which are made by art and by law have no basis in nature, but are of authority for the moment and at the time at which they are made. These, my friends, are the sayings of wise men, poets and prose-writers, which find a way into the minds of youth. They are told by them that the highest right is might, and in this way the young fall into impieties, under the idea that the Gods are not such as the law bids them imagine; and hence arise factions, these philosophers inviting them to lead a true life according to nature, that is, to live in real dominion over others, and not in legal subjection to them.

II Plato, The Dialogues, The Republic, Book IV, pp. 298-299, Jowett, 4th Edition. (1953); reprinted by permission of the Clarendon Press, Oxford, England.

And in reality justice was such as we were describing, being concerned however, not with a man's external affairs, but with an inner relationship in which he himself is more truly concerned; for the just man does not permit the several elements within him to interfere with one another, or any of them to do the work of others—he sets in order his own inner life, and is his own master and his own law, and at peace with himself; and when he has bound together the three principles within him, which may be compared to the higher, lower, and middle notes of the scale, and any that are intermediate between them—when he has bound all these together, and is no longer many, but has become one entirely temperate and perfectly adjusted nature, then he proceeds to act, if he has to act, whether in a matter of property, or in the treatment of the body, or in some affair of politics or private business; always thinking and calling that which preserves and co-operates with this harmonious condition, just and good action, and the knowledge which presides over it, wisdom, and that which at any time impairs this condition, he will call unjust action, and the opinion which presides over it ignorance.

Aristotle, Politics, Bks. I, III, IV, The Basic Works of Aristotle, McKeon Edition. (1941); reprinted by permission of the Oxford University Press, Inc., Random House, and the Clarendon Press, Oxford, England.

The family is the association established by nature for the supply of men's everyday wants, and the members of it are called by Charondas "companions of the cupboard", and by Epimenides the Cretan, "companions of the manger." But when several families are united, and the association aims at something more than the supply of daily needs, the first society to be formed is the village. And the most natural form of the village appears to be that of a colony from the family, composed of the children and grandchildren, who are said to be "suckled with the same milk." (Bk. I, ch. 2, p. 1128) *** When several villages are united in a single complete community, large enough to be nearly or quite self-sufficing, the state comes into existence, originating in the bare needs of life, and continuing in existence for the sake of a good life. And therefore, if the earlier forms of society are natural, so is the state, for it is the end of them, and the nature of a thing is its end. For what each thing is when fully developed, we call its nature, whether we are speaking of a man, a horse, or a family. Besides, the final cause and end of a thing is the best, and to be self-sufficing is the end and the best.

Hence it is evident that the state is a creation of nature, and that man is by nature a political animal.

And he who by nature and not by mere accident is without a state, is either a bad man or above humanity; he is like the

"Tribeless, lawless, hearthless one,"

whom Homer denounces—the natural outcast is forthwith a lover of war; he may be compared to an isolated piece at draughts. (Bk. I, ch. 2, p. 1129)

*** And it is a characteristic of man that he alone has any sense of good and evil, of just and unjust, and the like, and the association of living beings who have this sense makes a family and a state. (Bk. I, ch. 2, p. 1129)

*** We will therefore restrict ourselves to the living creature, which, in the first place, consists of soul and body: and of these two, the one is by nature the ruler, and the other the subject. But then we must look for the intentions of nature in things which retain their nature, and not in things which are corrupted. And therefore we must study the man who is in the most perfect state both of body and soul, for in him we shall see the true relation of the two; although in bad or corrupted natures the body will ofter appear to rule over the soul, because they are in an evil and unnatural condition. At all events we may firstly observe in living creatures both a despotical and a constitutional rule; for the soul rules the body with a despotical rule, whereas the intellect rules the appetites with a constitutional and royal rule. And it is clear that the rule of the soul over the body, and of the mind and the rational element over the passionate, is natural and expedient; whereas the equality of the two or the rule of the inferior is always hurtful. The same holds good of animals in relation to men; for tame animals have a better nature than wild, and all tame animals are better off when they are ruled by man; for then they are preserved. Again, the male is by nature superior, and the female inferior; and the one rules, and the other is ruled; this principle, of necessity, extends to all mankind. (Bk. I, ch. 5, p. 1132) *** He who bids the law rule may be deemed to bid God and Reason alone rule, but he who bids man rule adds an element of the beast; for desire is a wild beast, and passion perverts the minds of rulers, even when they are the best of men. The law is reason unaffected by desire. (Bk. III, ch. 16, p. 1202)

Hence there are two parts of good government; one is the actual obedience of citizens to the laws, the other part is the goodness of the laws which they obey; they may obey bad laws as well as good. And there may be a further subdivision; they may obey either the best laws which are attainable to them, or the best absolutely. (Bk. IV, ch. 8, p. 1217)

Aristotle, Ethica Nicomachea, Book V, Basic Works of Aristotle, McKeon Edition, (1941); reprinted by permission of the Oxford University Press, Inc., Random House, and the Clarendon Press, Oxford, England.

Of political justice part is natural, part legal,— natural, that which everywhere has the same force and does not exist by people's thinking this or that; legal, that which is originally indifferent, but when it has been laid down is not indifferent, e.g. that a prisoner's ransom shall be a mina, or that a goat and not two sheep shall be sacrificed, and again all the laws that are passed for particular cases, e.g. that sacrifice shall be made in honour of Brasidas, and the provisions of decrees. Now some think that all justice is of this sort, because that which is by nature is unchangeable and has everywhere the same force (as fire burns both here and in Persia), while they see change in the things recognized as just. This, however, is not true in this unqualified way, but is true in a sense; or rather, with the gods it is perhaps not true at all, while with us there is something that is just even by nature, yet all of it is changeable; but still some is by nature, some not by nature. It is evident which sort of thing, among things capable of being otherwise, is by nature; and which is not but is legal and conventional, assuming that both are equally changeable. And in all other things the same distinction will apply; by nature the right hand is stronger, yet it is possible that all men should come to be ambidextrous. The things which are just by virtue of convention and expediency are like measures; for wine and corn measures are not everywhere equal, but large in wholesale and smaller in retail markets. Similarly, the things which are just not by nature but by human enactment are not everywhere the same, since constitutions also are not the same, though there is but one which is everywhere by nature the best. (Bk. V, ch. 7, p. 1014)

Aristotle, Rhetoric, Book I, The Basic Works of Aristotle, McKeon Edition, (1941); reprinted by permission of the Oxford University Press, Inc., Random House, and the Clarendon Press, Oxford, England.

It will now be well to make a complete classification of just and unjust actions. We may begin by observing that they have been defined relatively to two kinds of law, and also relatively to two classes of persons. By the two kinds of law I mean particular law and universal law. Particular law is that which each community lays down and applies to its own members: this is partly written and partly unwritten. Universal law is the law of nature. For there really is, as every one to some extent divines, a natural justice and injustice that is binding on all men, even on those who have no association or covenant with each other. (Bk. I, ch. 13, p. 1370)

First, then, let us take laws and see how they are to be used in persuasion and dissuasion, in accusation and defence. If the written law tells against our case, clearly we must appeal to the universal law, and insist on its greater equity and justice. We must argue that the juror's oath "I will give my verdict according to my honest opinion" means that one will not simply follow the letter of the written law. We must urge that the principles of equity are permanent and changeless, and that the universal law does not change either, for it is the law of nature, whereas written laws often do change. This is the bearing of the lines in Sophocles' *Antigone,* where Antigone pleads that in burying her brother she had broken Creon's law, but not the unwritten law:

> Not of to-day or yesterday they are,
> But live eternal: [none can date their birth.]
> Not I would fear the wrath of any man,
> [And brave Gods' vengeance] for defying these.

We shall argue that justice indeed is true and profitable, but that sham justice is not, and that consequently the written law is not, because it does not fulfill the true purpose of law. Or that justice is like silver, and must be assayed by the judges, if the genuine is to be distinguished from the counterfeit. Or that the better a man is, the more he will follow and abide by the unwritten law in preference to the written. Or perhaps that the law in question contradicts some other highly-esteemed law, or even contradicts itself. Thus it may be that one law will enact that all contracts must be held binding, while another forbids us ever to make illegal contracts. Or if a law is ambiguous, we shall turn it about and consider which construction best fits the interests of justice or utility, and then follow that way of looking at it. Or if, though the law still exists, the situation to meet which it was passed exists no longer, we must do our best to prove this and to combat the law thereby. If however the written law supports our case, we must urge that the oath "to give my verdict according to my honest opinion" is not meant to make the judges give a verdict that is contrary to the law, but to save them from the guilt of perjury if they misunderstand what the law really means. Or that no one chooses what is absolutely good, but every one what is good for himself. Or that not to use the laws is as bad as to have no laws at all. Or that, as in the other arts, it does not pay to try to be cleverer than the doctor: for less harm comes from the doctor's mistakes than from the growing habit of disobeying authority. Or that trying to be cleverer than the laws is just what is forbidden by those codes of law that are accounted best.—So far as the laws are concerned, the above discussion is probably sufficient. (Bk. I, ch. 15, pp. 1374-1375)

Cicero, On the Commonwealth, Book III, chs. 11, 22; Bohn's Classical Library (1853).

*** (If this justice were natural, innate, and universal, all men would admit the same) law and right, and the same men would not enact different laws at different times. If a just man and a virtuous man is bound to obey the laws, I ask, what laws do you mean? Do you intend all the laws indifferently? But neither does virtue permit this inconstancy in moral obligation, nor is such a variation compatible with natural conscience. The laws are, therefore, based not on our sense of justice, but on our fear of punishment. There is, therefore, no natural justice; and hence it follows that men cannot be just by nature.

Are men then to say, that variations indeed do exist in the laws, but that men who are virtuous through natural conscience follow that which is really justice, and not a mere semblance and disguise, and that it is the distinguishing characteristic of the truly just and virtuous man to render every one his due rights? (Bk. III, ch. 11, p. 355)

*** True law is right reason conformable to nature, universal, unchangeable, eternal, whose commands urge us to duty, and whose prohibitions restrain us from evil. Whether it enjoins or forbids, the good respect its injunctions, and the wicked treat them with indifference. This law cannot be contradicted by any other law, and is not liable either to derogation or abrogation. Neither the senate nor the people can give us any dispensation for not obeying this universal law of justice. It needs no other expositor and interpreter than our own conscience. It is not one thing at Rome, and another at Athens; one thing to-day, and another to-morrow; but in all times and nations this universal law must for ever reign, eternal and imperishable. It is the sovereign master and emperor of all beings. God himself is its author, its promulgator, its enforcer. And he who does not obey it flies from himself, and does violence to the very nature of man. And by so doing he will endure the severest penalties even if he avoid the other evils which are usually accounted punishments. (Bk. III, ch. 22, p. 360)

Cicero, On the Laws, Books I, II; Bohn's Classical Library (1853).

Marcus °°° Now, many learned men have maintained that it (right) springs from law. I hardly know if their opinion be not correct, at least according to their own definition; for "law," say they, "is the highest reason implanted in nature, which prescribes those things which ought to be done, and forbids the contrary." And when this same reason is confirmed and established in men's minds, it is then law.

They therefore conceive that prudence is a law, whose operation is to urge us to good actions, and restrain us from evil ones. And they think, too, that the Greek name for law (*nomos*), which is derived from *nemo*, to distribute, implies the very nature of the thing, that is, to give every man his due. The Latin name, *lex*, conveys the idea of selection, *a legendo*. According to the Greeks, therefore, the name of law implies an equitable distribution: according to the Romans, an equitable selection. And, indeed, both characteristics belong peculiarly to law.

And if this be a correct statement, which it seems to me for the most part to be, then the origin of right is to be sought in the law. For this is the true energy of nature,—this is the very soul and reason of a wise man, and the test of virtue and vice. But since all this discussion of ours relates to a subject, the terms of which are of frequent occurrence in the popular language of the citizens, we shall be sometimes obliged to use the same terms as the vulgar, and to call that law, which in its written enactments sanctions what it thinks fit by special commands or prohibitions.

Let us begin, then, to establish the principles of justice on that supreme law, which has existed from all ages before any legislative enactments were drawn up in writing, or any political governments constituted. (Bk. I, ch. 6, pp. 406-407)

*** VII. Marcus.—Do you then grant, my Atticus, (for I know my brother's opinion already,) that the entire universe is regulated by the power of the immortal Gods, that by their nature, reason, energy, mind, divinity, or some other word of clearer signification, if there be such, all things are governed and directed? For if you will not grant me this, that is what I must begin by establishing. (Bk. I, ch. 7, p. 407)

*** Now, the law of virtue is the same in God and man, and in no other disposition besides them. This virtue is nothing else than a nature perfect in itself, and wrought up to the most consummate excellence. There exists, therefore, a similitude between God and man. And as this is the case, what connection can there be which concerns us more nearly, and is more certain? (Bk. I, ch. 8, p. 409)

*** XII. Marcus.—It follows, then, that nature made us just that we might share our goods with each other, and supply each other's wants. You observe in this discussion, whenever I speak of nature, I mean nature in its genuine purity, but that there is, in fact, such corruption engendered by evil customs, that the sparks, as it were, of virtue which have been given by nature are extinguished, and that antagonist vices arise around it and become strengthened.

But if, as nature prompts them to, men would with deliberate judgment, in the words of the poet, "being men, think nothing that concerns mankind indifferent to them," then would justice be cultivated equally by all. For to those to whom nature has given reason, she has also given right reason, and therefore also law, which is nothing else than right reason enjoining what is good, and forbidding what is evil. And if nature has given us law, she hath also given us right. (Bk. I, ch. 12, pp. 412-413)

°°° XV. It is therefore an absurd extravagance in some philosophers to assert, that all things are necessarily just which are established by the civil laws and the institutions of nations. Are then the laws of tyrants just, simply because they are laws? Suppose the thirty tyrants of Athens had imposed certain laws on the Athenians? or, suppose again that these Athenians were delighted with these tyrannical laws, would these laws on that account have been considered just? For my own part, I do not think such laws deserve any greater estimation than that passed during our own interregnum, which ordained that the dictator should be empowered to put to death with impunity whatever citizens he pleased, without hearing them in their own defence.

For there is but one essential justice which cements society, and one law which establishes this justice. This law is right reason, which is the true rule of all commandments and prohibitions. Whoever neglects this law, whether written or unwritten, is necessarily unjust and wicked.

But if justice consists in submission to written laws and national customs, and if, as the same school affirms, everything must be measured by utility alone, he who thinks that such conduct will be advantageous to him will neglect the laws, and break them if it is in his power. And the consequence is, that real justice has really no existence if it have not one by nature, and if that which is established as such on account of utility is overturned by some other utility.

But if nature does not ratify law, then all the virtues may lose their sway. For what becomes of generosity, patriotism, or friendship? Where will the desire of benefitting our neighbours, or the gratitude that acknowledges kindness, be able to exist at all? For all these virtues proceed from our natural inclination to love mankind. And this is the true basis of justice, and without this not only the mutual charities of men, but the religious services of the Gods, would be at an end; for these are preserved, as I imagine, rather by the natural sympathy which subsists between divine and human beings, than by mere fear and timidity. (Bk. I, ch. 15, pp. 416-417)

XVI. But if the will of the people, the decrees of the senate, the adjudications of magistrates, were sufficient to establish rights, then it might become right to rob, right to commit adultery, right to substitute forged wills, if such conduct were sanctioned by the votes or decrees of the multitude. But if the opinions and suffrages of foolish men had sufficient weight to outbalance the nature of things, then why should they not determine among them, that what is essentially bad and pernicious should henceforth pass for good and beneficial? Or why, since law can make right out of injustice, should it not also be able to change evil into good? (Bk. I, ch. 16, p. 417)

*** XVIII. It follows that I may now sum up the whole of this argument by asserting, as is plain to every one from these positions which have been already laid down, that all right and all that is honourable is to be sought for its own sake. In truth, all virtuous men love justice and equity for what they are in themselves; nor is it like a good man to make a mistake, and love that which does not deserve their affection. Right, therefore, is desirable and deserving to be cultivated for its own sake; and if this be true of right, it must be true also of justice. (Bk. I, ch. 18, p. 419)

*** Marcus.—This, then, as it appears to me, has been the decision of the wisest philosophers,—that law was neither a thing contrived by the genius of man, nor established by any decree of the people, but a certain eternal principle, which governs the entire universe, wisely commanding what is right and prohibiting what is wrong. Therefore they called that aboriginal and supreme law the mind of God, enjoining or forbidding each separate thing in accordance with reason. On which account it is, that this law, which the Gods have bestowed on the human race, is so justly applauded. For it is the reason and mind of a wise Being equally able to urge us to good and to deter us from evil.

Quintus.—You have, on more than one occasion, already touched on this topic. But before you come to treat of the laws of nations, I wish you would endeavour to explain the force and power of this divine and celestial law, lest the torrent of custom should overwhelm our understanding, and betray us into the vulgar method of expression.

Marcus.—From our childhood we have learned, my Quintus, to call such phrases as this, "that a man appeals to justice, and goes to law," and many similar expressions, law; but, nevertheless, we should understand that these, and other similar commandments and prohibitions, have sufficient power to lead us on to virtuous actions and to call us away from vicious ones. Which power is not only far more ancient than any existence of states and peoples, but is coeval with God himself, who beholds and governs both heaven and earth. For it is impossible that the divine mind can exist in a state devoid of reason; and divine reason must necessarily be possessed of a power to determine what is virtuous and what is vicious. Nor, because it was nowhere written, that one man should maintain the pass of a bridge against the enemy's whole army, and that he should order the bridge behind him to be cut down, are we therefore to imagine that the valiant Cocles did not perform this great exploit agreeably to the laws of nature and the dictates of true bravery. Again, though in the reign of Tarquin there was no written law concerning adultery, it does not therefore follow that Sextus Tarquinius did not offend against the eternal law when he committed rape on Lucretia, daughter of Tricipitinus. For, even then he had the light of reason deduced from the nature of things, that incites to good actions and dissuades from evil ones; and which does not begin for the first time to be a law when it is drawn up in writing, but from the first moment that it exists. And this existence of moral obligation is co-eternal with that of the divine mind. Therefore, the true and supreme law, whose commands and prohibitions are equally authoritative, is the right reason of the Sovereign Jupiter. (Bk. II, ch. 4, pp. 431-432)

V. Quintus.—I grant you, my brother, that whatever is just is also at all times the true law; nor can this true law either be originated or abrogated by the written forms in which decrees are drawn up.

Marcus.—Therefore, as that Divine Mind, or reason, is the supreme law, so it exists in the mind of the sage, so far as it can be perfected in man. But with respect to civil laws, which are drawn up in various forms, and framed to meet the occasional requirements of the people, the name of law belongs to them not so much by right as by the favour of the people. For men prove by some such arguments as the following, that every law which deserves the name of a law, ought to be morally good and laudable. (Bk. II, ch. 5, p. 432)

*** Marcus.—If, then, in the majority of nations, many pernicious and mischievous enactments are made, which have no more right to the name of law than the mutual engagements of robbers, are we bound to call them laws? For as we cannot call the recipes of ignorant and unskillful empirics, who give poisons instead of medicines, the prescriptions of a physician, so likewise we cannot call that the true law of a people, of whatever kind it may be, if it enjoins what is injurious, let the people receive it as they will. For law is the just distinction between right and wrong, made conformable to that most ancient nature of all, the original and principal regulator of all things, by which the laws of men should be measured, whether they punish the guilty or protect and preserve the innocent. (Bk. II, ch. 5, p. 433)

B. The School Men

In the early stages of Christianity, the emphasis was upon the supernatural law and understandably so. But the inadequacy of the strictly theological approach was ultimately realized since faith and reason are necessarily two sides of the same coin. Hence the problem that confronted the Schoolmen, (i.e.) the teachers in the early medieval schools, was to co-ordinate and correlate the supernatural law, directly communicated from God to man, with the natural law, accepted by unaided reason. A substantial contribution was made by St. Augustine, in the fifth century, and by others. But the work was brought to fruition by St. Thomas Aquinas in the thirteenth century.

1. In General

Heinrich A. Rommen, The Natural Law pp. 35-40, 41-42, 45, 62; reprinted by permission of the author and the B. Herder Book Co. (1947).

The history of the natural-law idea shows that Christianity took it over at a very early date. Paul, the Apostle of the Gentiles, declares that the natural law is inscribed in the hearts of the heathen, who do not have the Law (of Sinai), and is made known to them through their conscience. It is valid both for pagans and for Jews because it is grounded in nature, in the essence of man. (Cf. Rom. 2:12-16).

The Fathers of the Early Church made use of the Stoic natural law, finding in its principles "seeds of the Word," to proclaim the Christian doctrine of the personal Creator-God as the Author of the eternal law as well as of the natural moral law which is promulgated in the voice of conscience and in reason. Thus, for instance, we read in St. John Chrysostom (d. 407): "We use not only Scripture but also reason in arguing against pagans. What is their argument? They say they have no law of conscience, and that there is no law implanted by God in nature. My answer is to question them about their laws concerning marriage, homicide, wills, injuries to others, enacted by their legislators. Perhaps the living have learned from their fathers, and their fathers from their fathers and so on. But go back to the first legislator! From whom did he learn? Was it not by his own conscience and conviction? Nor can it be said that they heard Moses and the prophets, for Gentiles could not hear them. It is evident that they derived their laws from the law which God ingrafted in man from the beginning."[1]

The Fathers also took over the Stoic distinction of a primary and a secondary natural law, which they interpreted in a theological sense. They regarded the former as applying to the state of unimpaired nature or innocence, while they assigned the latter, with the coercive authority of the law, with bondage and slavery, to the theological condition of fallen nature. Nature, somehow wounded indeed but not destroyed, is therefore still able fully to recognize the first principles of morality and law. But the conclusions from the first principles, which were also plainly intelligible in the state of unimpaired nature, are now attainable only by means of deductive reasoning, since the practical reason is also weakened. Accordingly law takes on a harsh, compulsory character, and the state bears a sword. But the state as such was not regarded by the Fathers as some sort of consequence of sin. An age ignorant of tradition has been able to take such a view of the state only on the basis of patristic texts torn from their context and because of a want of understanding of the mental outlook of the Fathers.

The Fathers did not attempt to construct a system of ethics and jurisprudence. Their speculative thinking was wholly taken up with elucidating the truths of faith, which were in danger of being swamped in the upsurge of pseudomystical doctrines characteristic of the numerous mystery cults of declining antiquity.

In addition, their heavy pastoral duties in the period of persecutions, organization, and evangelization left them little leisure for thorough theoretical treatment of questions of moral and legal philosophy.

St. Augustine (d. 430), it is true, forms an exception, and a very brilliant one. In his extremely fertile mind the ideas of ancient philosophy came once again to life and were worked into the new Christian mentality. His talents and the struggles against the Pelagian and Manichaean heresies, as well as the shattering experience of the breakdown of the Roman Empire, of the earthly city, brought ethico-legal problems home to the great bishop of Hippo.

For Augustine the substantial ideas, which Plato had conceived of as dwelling in a heavenly abode, became thoughts of God. The impersonal world reason of the Stoics became the personal, all-wise and all-powerful God. The purely deistic *Nous* of Aristotle became the Creator-God who transcends the world, but who continually sustains it through His omnipotence, directs it through His providence, and governs it according to His eternal law. This eternal law was for Augustine identical with the supreme reason and eternal truth, with the reason of God himself, according to whose laws the inner life and external activity of God proceed and are governed. God's reason is order, and His law rules this ontological order, the order of being, of essences and values. But since this norm is identical with the immutable, immanent nature of God, it does not stand above Him; it is connatural to Him, and it is as unchangeable as He. No power, no chance event, not even the complete collapse of all things can alter it. No obscure, occult fate is any longer enthroned, as in ancient thought, above the personal God.

Through this law God, so far as He produces external effects, directs, guides, and sustains the universe. God, supreme reason, unchangeable being and omnipotent will: this is oneness in its highest form. But the natural moral law and its component part, the *ius naturale,* is precisely this divine law with reference to man, so far as the latter participates in the divine law. The eternal law dwells as blind necessity in irrational nature. As oughtness, as norm of free moral activity, it is inscribed in the heart of man, a rational and free being. It appears in the moral, rational nature of man; it is written into the rational soul. There is no soul, however corrupt it may be, in whose conscience God does not speak, if only it is still capable of rational thought. There are human actions, consequently, which are in themselves good or bad. Bad acts are not qualified as such by force of law, but because they are such in themselves: because they constitute a disturbance of the natural order. Thereupon, because they are such, the lawmaker prohibits them under threat of punishment, which thereby obtains its moral justification. Not the will of the earthly lawgiver, but variance with natural reason is the ground of the intrinsic immorality of determinate actions.

The doctrine of natural law was transmitted to the golden age of Scholasticism not only in the works of the Church Fathers but also through the study of Roman law and through the development of canon law. The classical authors of the *Corpus iuris civilis,* as has been seen, stood in close contact with natural-law thinking. It is not merely in passing that we meet with the natural law in their writings: the natural law is there pronounced valid, unconditionally binding law. Considerably greater, however, was the influence of canon law in the form of Gratian's *Decretum* (*cir.* 1148), especially since during the first period of the flowering of Scholasticism the study of Roman law by theologians was frowned upon and even, for a time, prohibited. Gratian distinguished between *ius naturale* and the mores. The *ius naturale,* which is contained in the Law (i.e., the Decalogue) and the Gospel, is of divine origin. It resides in human nature, it is alike in all men, and it has force independently of human statute. Natural rights and duties may indeed have to be more closely defined by positive law, but they stand as a norm and rule above the positive laws. To Gratian the latter were, like customary law or mores, liable to change according to time, place, and people. In short, Gratian merely set forth what tradition had handed down.

As the great philosophical movement of the Middle Ages, Scholasticism,[2] approached its peak, the natural-law doctrine attained its most masterly expression. It was carried to speculative heights which have never been surpassed in the centuries that followed. Since then the doctrine of natural law has never wholly perished. Even though it might be neglected in the official academic philosophy which has been dominant in the chair of the secular universities, and even though at the close of the nineteenth century and at the opening of the twentieth century jurisprudence might pronounce it dead, the natural-law doctrine has ever found a home and tender care among the adherents of the *philosophia perennis*. These have preserved it even throughout the decades in which legal positivism held fullest sway. Moreover, they carried it over, as Christian natural law, into an environment that is once again more favorable to the idea of natural law. For World War I and its consequences, to say nothing of World War II and its effects (which promise to be still more fateful), have brought men to recognize more and more openly the questionableness of a philosophy without metaphysics, of an epistemology without certainty of truth, of a jurisprudence without an idea of right.

The history of the natural-law idea exhibits a uniform doctrinal development from the first Scholastics down to the able leaders of the scholastic revival of recent times. Its two culminating points were the synthesis of St. Thomas Aquinas and, following the heaviest assault made inside Scholasticism by the Occamists on the idea of natural law, the work of Vittoria, Bellarmine, Suarez, Vasquez, and De Soto (to mention only the most distinguished of the Late Scholastics). And the period after World War I again produced more understanding and esteem for a uniform doctrinal development that has been substantially independent of fashionable philosophies and of a jurisprudence with special sociological or political ties.

Scholasticism has dealt exhaustively with the problem of natural law. Not one of its exponents has failed to treat of the natural law, either in general in connection with the discussion of the virtues or in particular under such headings as *De legibus* or *De iure et iustitia*. And with the *lex naturalis* they handled, though not always with the aid of special distinctions, the *ius naturale* and *ius gentium* in the sense of the traditional formulas of Roman law. This holds true from Alexander of Hales to Thomas Aquinas, and thence down to the great masters of Late Scholasticism. It further holds good for the theologians and philosophers of the *philosophia perennis*, whether they were contemporaries of Pufendorf and Thomasius or of Savigny, down to the increasingly esteemed representatives of the scholastic revival which set in at the close of the nineteenth century.

* * * * *

Relativism in ethics, legal positivism, the theory of will in public and international law, nominalism and agnosticism in epistemology and metaphysics form down to the present a united front with the mysticism of a biological positivism appearing in natural-law dress. On the other side stands the conviction of unalterable principles of morality and law, of the idea of right as object of a philosophy of right, of the natural law, of the possibility of knowing the nature of things, of objective values and an ultimate unity of being and oughtness as well as the possibility of a true theodicy, or natural theology. And this antithesis continues on, in an ever more acute form, into the domain of constitutional theory and practice. The powerful position, in Anglo-Saxon countries, of the judiciary which understands and interprets (functions of the intellect) in contrast to the enactment of law through the will of the legislature rests ultimately upon the philosophical view that law is reason, not will. This means that right is discernible in the nature of the case or lies in the legal institution regulated by law, not in the will of the legislator: not, that is to say, in the wording of the law representing such a will or command. Such formulas as those found in the administration of justice in Anglo-Saxon countries (especially in the United States), where formal natural-law thinking has never disappeared among judges, are continually recurring even today.[3]

It was not with St. Anselm of Canterbury (1033-1109), often called the first of the Schoolmen, that Scholasticism began to concern itself more seriously with the natural law, but rather with the first great author of a *Summa*, Alexander of Hales (d. 1245). Deeper interest in it thus arose first and foremost from the philosophical preoccupation with laying a solid foundation for ethics, for law and the social forms of family and state, for a doctrine of society and the state. This interest was considerably heightened, however, in connection with the exegesis of certain passages in the Old Testament.

*   *   *   *   *

St. Thomas (1225-74) starts from the likeness of human nature to the divine nature. Understanding and free will are the most essential marks that distinguish man from every other earthly creature. It is precisely through them that man is in a special degree the image and likeness of God. Man's intellect and free will constitute the closest image of God in the material universe, His creation. St. Thomas, indeed, is fond of setting out from the notion of analogy of being: namely, that all created being, though of an altogether different kind from the divine Being, is an image of the latter and a participation in it—from merely inanimate being of inorganic nature up to man, whom God created after His own image.

Here teleology, the doctrine of ends or final causes, enters the scene.[4] The essences of things, which are exemplifications of the ideas conceived by the divine intellect, constitute at the same time the end or goal of the things themselves. The perfection or fulfillment of the things is their essence: formal cause and end are one (*causa finalis* is ultimately identical with *causa formalis*). Accordingly in the essential nature of the created world, as it came forth in conformity with the will of the Creator, are imbedded also the norms of its being. In the essential nature is likewise founded essential oughtness, the eternal law, which is God's wisdom so far as it directs and governs the world as first cause of all acts of rational creatures and of all movements of irrational beings. The eternal law, then, is the government of the world through God's will in accordance with His wisdom. * * * Thus it came about that nearly every scholar of the time composed treatises entitled *De legibus and De iure et iustitia*.

The task of the Late Scholastics was, then, as Petavius so well pointed out, to work out further, to develop fully and completely, what the thinkers of the golden age of Scholasticism, in particular St. Thomas Aquinas, had taught implicitly and in outline. They saw and carried out this task in the case of the natural-law doctrine, too. The decline of the doctrine of natural law set in only after them. So competent a scholar as Joseph Kohler has heald that "if, then, a natural law is to be fashioned today, it must be attached to these Spaniards of the age of Spain's greatness, not to Hugo Grotius."

2. In Particular

St. Thomas Aquinas

St. Thomas Aquinas elaborated a complete science of philosophy and theology and coordinated both in his famous *Summa Theologica*. He used materials from many sources, particularly Aristotle to whom he refers as "the philosopher." He also used the scriptures and contemporary authorities. He regards the natural law as that part of the eternal law, proceeding from the reason and will of God, which is applicable to man. It does not relate to animal or vegetable life, or to inanimate matter. These forms of creation come under the eternal law, exclusive of the natural law.

The fuller significance of the Stoic concept of natural law was presented by Aquinas. Thus the *jus naturale* of the Stoic became the *lex naturalis* of Aquinas. This semantic change had conceptual implications. It indicates that Aquinas regarded the *jus naturale,* or the discovered law of conduct formulated by the Stoics, as a statute (*lex*) originating from a personal divine Law-giver.

The influence of Aquinas on jurisprudence is enormous, particularly since his writings still constitute the starting point for discussions concerning the perennial Stoic-Thomistic natural law. Unfortunately his writings were ignored by certain influential jurists after the Reformation in the sixteenth century. This was largely so because his writings were erroneously identified exclusively with Roman Catholic theology. Only now is there a growing realization of the fact that his philosophy of a natural law stands on its own two feet, and is not essentially dependent upon the authority of such theology.

St. Thomas Aquinas, Summa Theologica, Part II (First Part), first complete American Edition in three volumes, literally translated by Fathers of the English Dominican Province, Vol. I, (1947); reprinted by permission of Benziger Brothers, Inc.

*** Law is a rule and measure of acts, whereby man is induced to act or is restrained from acting: for *lex* (law) is derived from *ligare* (to bind), because it binds one to act. Now the rule and measure of human acts is the reason, which is the first principle of human acts, as is evident from what has been stated above; since it belongs to the reason to direct to the end, which is the first principle in all matters of action, according to the Philosopher (*Phys.* ii.). Now that which is the principle in any genus, is the rule and measure of that genus: for instance, unity in the genus of numbers, and the first movement in the genus of movements. Consequently it follows that law is something pertaining to reason. (p. 993)

*** Reason has its power of moving from the will, as stated above: for it is due to the fact that one wills the end, that the reason issues its commands as regards things ordained to the end. But in order that the volition of what is commanded may have the nature of law, it needs to be in accord with some rule of reason. And in this sense is to be understood the saying that the will of the sovereign has the force of law; otherwise the sovereign's will would savour of lawlessness rather than of law. (p. 994)

*** As stated above, the law belongs to that which is a principle of human acts, because it is their rule and measure. Now as reason is a principle of human acts, so in reason itself there is something which is the principle in respect of all the rest: wherefore to this principle chiefly and mainly law must needs be referred.—Now the first principle in practical matters, which are the object of the practical reason, is the last end: and the last end of human life is bliss or happiness, as stated above. Consequently the law must needs regard principally the relationship to happiness. Moreover, since every part is ordained to the whole, as imperfect to perfect; and since one man is a part of the perfect community, the law must needs regard properly the relationship to universal happiness. (p. 994)

***Actions are indeed concerned with particular matters: but those particular matters are referable to the common good, not as to a common genus or species, but as to a common final cause, according as the common good is said to be the common end.

°°° Just as nothing stands firm with regard to the speculative reason except that which is traced back to the first indemonstrable principles, so nothing stands firm with regard to the practical reason, unless it be directed to the last end which is the common good: and whatever stands to reason in this sense, has the nature of a law. (p. 994)

°°° A law, properly speaking, regards first and foremost the order to the common good. Now to order anything to the common good, belongs either to the whole people, or to someone who is the viceregent of the whole people. And therefore the making of a law belongs either to the whole people or to a public personage who has care of the whole people: since in all other matters the directing of anything to the end concerns him to whom the end belongs. (p. 995)

°°° Thus from the four preceding articles, the definition of law may be gathered; and it is nothing else than an ordinance of reason for the common good, made by him who has care of the community, and promulgated. (p. 995)

°°° Now it is evident, granted that the world is ruled by Divine Providence, as was stated in the First Part, that the whole community of the universe is governed by Divine Reason. Wherefore the very Idea of the government of things in God, the Ruler of the universe, has the nature of a law. And since the Divine Reason's conception of things is not subject to time but is eternal, according to Prov. viii. 23, therefore it is that this kind of law must be called eternal. (p. 996)

°°° As stated above, law, being a rule and measure, can be in a person in two ways: in one way, as in him that rules and measures; in another way, as in that which is ruled and measured, since a thing is ruled and measured, in so far as it partakes of the rule or measure. Wherefore, since all things subject to Divine providence are ruled and measured by the eternal law, as was stated above; it is evident that all things partake somewhat of the eternal law, in so far as, namely, from its being imprinted on them, they derive their respective inclinations to their proper acts and ends. Now among all others, the rational creature is subject to Divine providence in the most excellent way, in so far as it partakes of a share of providence, by being provident both for itself and for others. Wherefore it has a share of the Eternal Reason, whereby it has a natural inclination to its proper act and end: and this participation of the eternal law in the rational creature is called the natural law.

*** As stated above, a law is a dictate of the practical reason. Now it is to be observed that the same procedure takes place in the practical and in the speculative reason: for each proceeds from principles to conclusions, as stated above. Accordingly we conclude that just as, in the speculative reason, from naturally known indemonstrable principles, we draw the conclusions of the various sciences, the knowledge of which is not imparted to us by nature, but acquired by the efforts of reason, so too it is from the precepts of the natural law, as from general and indemonstrable principles, that the human reason needs to proceed to the more particular determination of certain matters. These particular determinations, devised by human reason, are called human laws, provided the other essential conditions of law be observed, as stated above. (p. 997)

*** The human reason cannot have a full participation of the dictate of the Divine Reason, but according to its own mode, and imperfectly. Consequently, as on the part of the speculative reason, by a natural participation of Divine Wisdom, there is in us the knowledge of certain general principles, but not proper knowledge of each single truth, such as that contained in the Divine Wisdom; so too, on the part of the practical reason, man has a natural participation of the eternal law, according to certain general principles, but not as regards the particular determinations of individual cases, which are, however, contained in the eternal law. Hence the need for human reason to proceed further to sanction them by law.

*** Human reason is not, of itself, the rule of things: but the principles impressed on it by nature, are general rules and measures of all things relating to human conduct, whereof the natural reason is the rule and measure, although it is not the measure of things that are from nature.

*** The practical reason is concerned with practical matters, which are singular and contingent: but not with necessary things, with which the speculative reason is concerned. Wherefore human laws cannot have that inerrancy that belongs to the demonstrated conclusions of sciences. Nor is it necessary for every measure to be altogether unerring and certain, but according as it is possible in its own particular genus. (p. 998)

*** Just as in every artificer there pre-exists a type of the things that are made by his art, so too in every governor there must pre-exist the type of the order of those things that are to be done by those who are subject to his government. And just as the type of the things yet to be made by an art is called the art or exemplar of the products of that art, so too the type in him who governs the acts of his subjects, bears the character of a law, provided the other conditions be present which we have mentioned above. Now God, by His wisdom, is the Creator of all things, in relation to which He stands as the artificer to the products of his art, as stated in the First Part. Moreover He governs all the acts and movements that are to be found in each single creature, as was also stated in the First Part. Wherefore as the type of the Divine Wisdom, inasmuch as by It all things are created, has the character of art, exemplar or idea; so the type of Divine Wisdom, as moving all things to their due end, bears the character of law. Accordingly the eternal law is nothing else than the type of Divine Wisdom, as directing all actions and movements. (p. 1003)

*** As stated above, the law denotes a kind of plan directing acts towards an end. Now wherever there are movers ordained to one another, the power of the second mover must needs be derived from the power of the first mover; since the second mover does not move except in so far as it is moved by the first. Wherefore we observe the same in all those who govern, so that the plan of government is derived by secondary governors from the governor in chief; thus the plan of what is to be done in a state flows from the king's command to his inferior administrators: and again in things of art the plan of whatever is to be done by art flows from the chief craftsman to the under-craftsmen who work with their hands. Since then the eternal law is the plan of government in the Chief Governor, all the plans of government in the inferior governors must be derived from the eternal law. But these plans of inferior governors are all other laws besides the eternal law. Therefore all laws, in so far as they partake of right reason, are derived from the eternal law. (p. 1005)

*** We must speak otherwise of the law of man, than of the eternal law which is the law of God. For the law of man extends only to rational creatures subject to man. The reason of this is because law directs the actions of those that are subject to the government of someone; wherefore, properly speaking, none imposes a law on his own actions. Now whatever is done regarding the use of irrational things subject to man, is done by the act of man himself moving those things, for these irrational creatures do not move themselves, but are moved by others, as stated above. Consequently man cannot impose laws on irrational beings, however much they may be subject to him. But he can impose laws on rational beings subject to him, in so far as by his command or pronouncement of any kind, he imprints on their minds a rule which is a principle of action.

Now just as man, by such pronouncement, impresses a kind of inward principle of action on the man that is subject to him, so God imprints on the whole of nature the principles of its proper actions. And so, in this way, God is said to command the whole of nature, according to Ps. cxlviii. 6: *He hath made a decree, and it shall not pass away*. And thus all actions and movements of the whole of nature are subject to the eternal law. Consequently irrational creatures are subject to the eternal law, through being moved by Divine providence; but not, as rational creatures are, through understanding the Divine commandment.

*** The impression of an inward active principle is to natural things, what the promulgation of law is to men: because law, by being promulgated, imprints on man a directive principle of human actions, as stated above. (p. 1006)

*** As stated above, the precepts of the natural law are to the practical reason, what the first principles of demonstrations are to the speculative reason; because both are self-evident principles. Now a thing is said to be self-evident in two ways: first, in itself; secondly, in relation to us. Any proposition is said to be self-evident in itself, if its predicate is contained in the notion of the subject: although, to one who knows not the definition of the subject, it happens that such a proposition is not self-evident. For instance, this propposition, *Man is a rational being*, is, in its very nature, self-evident, since who says *man*, says *a rational being:* and yet to one who knows not what a man is, this proposition is not self-evident. Hence it is that, as Boethius says (*De Hebdom.*), certain axioms or propositions are universally self-evident to all; and such are those propositions whose terms are known to all, as, *Every whole is greater than its part*, and *Things equal to one and the same are equal to one another*. But some propositions are self-evident only to the wise, who understand the meaning of the terms of such propositions: thus to one who understands that an angel is not a body, it is self-evident that an angel is not circumscriptively in a place: but this is not evident to the unlearned, for they cannot grasp it.

Now a certain order is to be found in those things that are apprehended universally. For that which, before aught else, falls under apprehension, is *being*, the notion of which is included in all things whatsoever a man apprehends. Wherefore the first indemonstrable principle is that *the same thing cannot be affirmed and denied at the same time*, which is based on the notion of *being* and *not-being*: and on this principle all others are based, as is stated in *Metaph.* iv, text 9. Now as *being* is the first thing that falls under the apprehension simply, so *good* is the first thing that falls under the apprehension of the practical reason, which is directed to action: since every agent acts for an end under the aspect of good. Consequently the first principle in the practical reason is one founded on the notion of good, *viz.*, that *good is that which all things seek after*. Hence this is the first precept of law, that *good is to be done and pursued, and evil is to be avoided*. All other precepts of the natural law are based upon this: so that whatever the practical reason naturally apprehends as man's good (or evil) belongs to the precepts of the natural law as something to be done or avoided.

Since, however, good has the nature of an end, and evil, the nature of a contrary, hence it is that all those things to which man has a natural inclination, are naturally apprehended by reason as being good, and consequently as objects of pursuit, and their contraries as evil, and objects of avoidance. Wherefore according to the order of natural inclinations, is the order of the precepts of the natural law. Because in man there is first of all an inclination to good in accordance with the nature which he has in common with all substances: inasmuch as every substance seeks the preservation of its own being, according to its nature: and by reason of this inclination, whatever is a means of preserving human life, and of warding off its obstacles, belongs to the natural law. Secondly, there is in man an inclination to things that pertain to him more specially, according to that nature which he has in common with other animals: and in virtue of this inclination, those things are said to belong to the natural law, *which nature has taught to all animals,* such as sexual intercourse, education of offspring and so forth. Thirdly, there is in man an inclination to good, according to the nature of his reason, which nature is proper to him: thus man has a natural inclination to know the truth about God, and to live in society: and in this respect, whatever pertains to this inclination belongs to the natural law; for instance, to shun ignorance, to avoid offending those among whom one has to live, and other such things regarding the above inclination. (pp. 1009-1010)

* * * Now each thing is inclined naturally to an operation that is suitable to it according to its form: thus fire is inclined to give heat. Wherefore, since the rational soul is the proper form of man, there is in every man a natural inclination to act according to reason: and this is to act according to virtue. Consequently, considered thus, all acts of virtue are prescribed by the natural law: since each one's reason naturally dictates to him to act virtuously. But if we speak of virtuous acts, considered in themselves, i.e., in their proper species, thus not all virtuous acts are prescribed by the natural law: for many things are done virtuously, to which nature does not incline at first; but which, through the inquiry of reason, have been found by men to be conducive to well-living. (p. 1010)

* * * As stated above, to the natural law belongs those things to which a man is inclined naturally: and among these it is proper to man to be inclined to act according to reason. Now the process of reason is from the common to the proper, as stated in *Phys. i.* The speculative reason, however, is differently situated in this matter, from the practical reason. For, since the speculative reason is busied chiefly with necessary things, which cannot be otherwise than they are, its proper conclusions, like the universal principles, contain the truth without fail. The practical reason, on the other hand, is busied with contingent matters, about which human actions are concerned: and consequently, although there is necessity in the general principles, the more we descend to matters of detail, the more frequently we encounter defects. Accordingly then in speculative matters truth is the same in all men, both as to principles and as to conclusions: although the truth is not known to all as regards the conclusions, but only as regards the principles which are called common notions. But in matters of action, truth or practical rectitude is not the same for all, as to matters of detail, but only as to the general principles: and where there is the same rectitude in matters of detail, it is not equally known to all.

It is therefore evident that, as regards the general principles whether of speculative or of practical reason, truth or rectitude is the same for all, and is equally known by all. As to the proper conclusions of the speculative reason, the truth is the same for all, but is not equally known to all: thus it is true for all that the three angles of a triangle are together equal to two right angles, although it is not known to all. But as to the proper conclusions of the practical reason, neither is the truth or rectitude the same for all, nor, where it is the same, is it equally known by all. Thus it is right and true for all to act according to reason: and from this principle it follows as a proper conclusion, that goods entrusted to another should be restored to their owner. Now this is true for the majority of cases: but it may happen in a particular case that it would be injurious, and therefore unreasonable, to restore goods held in trust; for instance if they are claimed for the purpose of fighting against one's country. And this principle will be found to fail the more, according as we descend further into detail, *e.g.*, if one were to say that goods held in trust should be restored with such and such a guarantee, or in such and such a way; because the greater the number of conditions added, the greater the number of ways in which the principle may fail, so that it be not right to restore or not to restore.

Consequently we must say that the natural law, as to general principles, is the same for all, both as to rectitude and as to knowledge. But as to certain matters of detail, which are conclusions, as it were, of those general principles, it is the same for all in the majority of cases, both as to rectitude and as to knowledge; and yet in some few cases it may fail, both as to rectitude, by reason of certain obstacles (just as natures subject to generation and corruption fail in some few cases on account of some obstacle), and as to knowledge, since in some the reason is perverted by passion, or evil habit, or an evil disposition of nature; thus formerly, theft, although it is expressly contrary to the natural law, was not considered wrong among the Germans, as Julius Caesar relates (*De Bello Gall.* vi.). (p. 1011)

* * * As stated above, man has a natural aptitude for virtue; but the perfection of virtue must be acquired by man by means of some kind of training. Thus we observe that man is helped by industry in his necessities, for instance, in food and clothing. Certain beginnings of these he has from nature, *viz.*, his reason and his hands; but he has not the full complement, as other animals have, to whom nature has given sufficiency of clothing and food. Now it is difficult to see how man could suffice for himself in the matter of this training: since the perfection of virtue consists chiefly in withdrawing man from undue pleasures, to which above all man is inclined, and especially the young, who are more capable of being trained. Consequently a man needs to receive this training from another, whereby to arrive at the perfection of virtue. And as to those young people who are inclined to acts of virtue, by their good natural disposition, or by custom, or rather by the gift of God, paternal training suffices, which is by admonitions. But since some are found to be depraved, and prone to vice, and not easily amenable to words, it was necessary for such to be restrained from evil by force and fear, in order that, at least, they might desist from evil-doing, and leave others in peace, and that they themselves, by being habituated in this way, might be brought to do willingly what hitherto they did from fear, and thus become virtuous. Now this kind of training, which compels through fear of punishment, is the discipline of laws.

*** Men who are well disposed are led willingly to virtue by being admonished better than by coercion: but men who are evilly disposed are not led to virtue unless they are compelled. (pp. 1013-1014)

*** As Augustine says (*De Lib. Arb. i. 5*), *that which is not just seems to be no law at all:* wherefore the force of a law depends on the extent of its justice. Now in human affairs a thing is said to be just, from being right, according to the rule of reason. But the first rule of reason is the law of nature, as is clear from what has been stated above. Consequently every human law has just so much of the nature of law, as it is derived from the law of nature. But if in any point it deflects from the law of nature, it is no longer a law but a perversion of law.

But it must be noted that something may be derived from the natural law in two ways: first, as a conclusion from premises, secondly, by way of determination of certain generalities. The first way is like to that by which, in sciences, demonstrated conclusions are drawn from the principles: while the second mode is likened to that whereby, in the arts, general forms are particularized as to details: thus the craftsman needs to determine the general form of a house to some particular shape. Some things are therefore derived from the general principles of the natural law, by way of conclusions; *e.g.*, that *one must not kill* may be derived as a conclusion from the principle that *one should do harm to no man:* while some are derived therefrom by way of determination; *e.g.,* the law of nature has it that the evil-doer should be punished; but that he be punished in this or that way, is a determination of the law of nature.

Accordingly both modes of derivation are found in the human law. But those things which are derived in the first way, are contained in human law not as emanating therefrom exclusively, but have some force from the natural law also. But those things which are derived in the second way, have no other force than that of human law. (pp. 1014-1015)

*** Whenever a thing is for an end, its form must be determined proportionately to that end; as the form of a saw is such as to be suitable for cutting (*Phys.* ii, text. 88). Again, everything that is ruled and measured must have a form proportionate to its rule and measure. Now both these conditions are verified of human law: since it is both something ordained to an end; and is a rule or measure ruled or measured by a higher measure. And this higher measure is twofold, *viz.,* the Divine law and the natural law, as explained above. Now the end of human law is to be useful to man, as the jurist states. Wherefore Isidore in determining the nature of law, lays down, at first, three conditions; *viz.,* that it *foster religion* inasmuch as it is proportionate to the Divine law; that it be *helpful to discipline,* inasmuch as it is proportionate to the natural law; and that it *further the common weal,* inasmuch as it is proportionate to the utility of mankind. (p. 1015)

*** As stated above, law is framed as a rule or measure of human acts. Now a measure should be homogeneous with that which it measures, as stated in *Metaph.* x, text. 3, 4, since different things are measured by different measures. Wherefore laws imposed on men should also be in keeping with their condition, for, as Isidore says (*Etym.* v. 21), law should be *possible both* *according to nature, and according to the customs* of the country. (p. 1018)

*** Laws framed by man are either just or unjust. If they be just, they have the power of binding in conscience, from the eternal law whence they are derived, according to Prov. viii. 15: *By Me kings reign, and lawgivers decree just things.* Now laws are said to be just, both from the end, when, to wit, they are ordained to the common good,—and from their author, that is to say, when the law that is made does not exceed the power of the lawgiver,—and from their form, when, to wit, burdens are laid on the subjects, according to an equality of proportion and with a view to the common good. (p. 1019)

> Brendan F. Brown, The Influence of St. Thomas Aquinas on Jurisprudence, 3 The Catholic Lawyer pp. 358-359, 363-364 (1957); reprinted by permission of The Catholic Lawyer.

Greek philosophers had reached a primitive notion of the natural law as embodied in the expression *jus naturale*.[5] They had observed the recurring phenomena of nature about them, and everywhere they had beheld a maintenance or ordering principle. They concluded that such a principle was also necessary for human society if cosmos therein was to be attained and anarchy avoided.[6]

The ordering principle of the universe was called *jus* because it was law which was discovered or perceived by the individual person. Unlike *lex*, it was not man-made. It was called *naturale* because it was ordained by nature, and hence beyond the reach of caprice and human will.[7]

The concept of the *jus naturale* was a most important contribution to rational science, postulating, as it did, the existence of an eternal and immutable body of objective principles of moral right and wrong. It justified a doctrine of inalienable rights and was conducive to the dignity of the human personality. It exerted great influence in shaping the destiny of the

Roman law, beginning approximately in the third century, B.C.[8]

But the genius of the Stoics was incapable of solving the difficult problems of the source of this law, its consequences, and its full implications. This was to be expected since they did not have the benefit of divine positive law. Hence many of them believed that the *jus naturale* was derived from nature in the sense of a pantheistic universe. Many were of the opinion that it was a law of instinct, identical with that which moves non-rational creation.

The concept of the natural law was not fully developed even in the period between the Stoics and St. Thomas. Even at the time of Justinian, in the sixth century, A.D., approximately, when Christianity was exerting wide influence in Rome, the distinction between the eternal law and the natural law, and between animal instinct and human reason, was not clearly understood. Thus in the *Institutes of Justinian*, the natural law is amorphously defined as "that which nature has taught to all animals, for this law is not peculiar to the human race, but applies to all creatures which originate in the air, or the earth, and in the sea."[9]

It remained for the Angelic Doctor to make the full, final transformation of the rudimentary Stoic concept of the *jus naturale* into the *lex naturalis*, or the divine enactment of a Personal Lawgiver. In doing this, he clarified the meaning of the writings of St. Albert the Great and St. Isidore of Seville, and worked them into an original synthesis so as to carry forward the tradition of natural law philosophy to its highest possible pinnacle of development, consistent with the political and sociological experience of the thirteenth century.[10] This tradition enjoyed universal acceptance throughout Christendom until the sixteenth century. It then had to compete with a philosophy which detached human law from both divine positive law and objective natural law.

ST. THOMAS PERFECTED THE KNOWLEDGE OF THE RELATION OF THE NATURAL LAW TO THE JUS GENTIUM AND THE JUS CIVILE

St. Thomas placed special emphasis upon human positive law in formulating his brilliant synthesis of legal theory. He has described human law in terms of its relation to the natural law. He postulates that "every human law has just so much of the nature of law, as it is derived from the law of nature." [11] He wrote that "it is from the precepts of the natural law, as from general and indemonstrable principles, that the human reason needs to proceed to the more particular determinations of certain matters." [12] These determinations, devised by human reason, are called human laws, provided the other essential conditions of law are observed.[13] These conditions demand that the law be ordained to the common good. It must be made by the whole people, or their public representatives who have rightful authority over them. Moreover, it must be promulgated.

Human law is necessary for man. It is essential for the proper direction of the community and for the attainment of the common good. Human lawmakers must reinforce the primary and necessary conclusions of the natural law, because otherwise some men might not be sufficiently aware of them, or else inclined to disobey.[14] An example would be the criminal law which forbids murder. Secondly, these lawmakers are obliged to decide upon certain rules which the natural law leaves undetermined, as for example, the precise type of capital punishment.[15] Changing sociological factors will affect their determination.

An enactment contrary to the natural law is not law.[16] The force of a law depends upon the extent of its justice. This in turn is determined by the law's reasonableness: ". . . [T]he first rule of reason is the law of nature."[17] Unjust enactments do not bind in conscience. An enactment will be contrary to the natural law if it is not ordained to the common good, or if the lawmaker exceeds his legislative authority, or if the burden of the law is not properly distributed among the people.[18] But prudence may dictate obedience to certain types of unjust law to avoid public disturbance.[19] Manifestly, St. Thomas had in mind an unjust law which took away a person's right to do the thing forbidden, but did not oblige him to do something intrinsically wrong.[20]

* * * * *

Custom perhaps played an even more important role in English, than in Roman, legal history in integrating positive law and morals. Thus, *lex*, or imperative law, and *jus*, or traditional law which produced custom, were considered together in the works of Glanvill and Bracton, two celebrated English jurists of the twelfth and thirteenth centuries, respectively.[21] They were much preoccupied with customary law, as well as later English jurists. The whole Law Merchant, which Lord Mansfield absorbed into the English Common Law in the eighteenth century, was founded on mercantile custom over the centuries.[22]

Equity transformed the Roman and English laws into world systems. Before the impact of equity, these systems were on the road to decay. They were morally sterile. They could not adjust themselves to the newly rising problems of justice which society created. They resisted change.

Equity compelled the creation of new courts, with new procedures, the Court of the *Praetor Peregrinus* in Rome, and the Court of Chancery in England. In these courts, the positive law was again placed in proper relation to the natural law. Positive law again became a means toward an end. The individual person was recognized as the unit upon which the legal order operated, rather than arbitrary classes of men.

Positive law resulted which premised an objective body of moral principles. These were applicable to all men everywhere. Adherence to these principles is the secret of the survival of the Roman law, with all its civil law derivatives, and of the Anglo-American legal system.

ST. THOMAS AQUINAS HAS PROFOUNDLY AFFECTED THE COURSE OF JURISPRUDENCE DURING THE PAST SEVEN CENTURIES.

The genius of St. Thomas reached its highest point of creative power in its capacity to communicate order to what seemed to be chaos. He synthesized what was apparently contradictory and irreconcilable. This always followed an exhaustive analysis of the facts of the problem at hand. By his synthesis of natural law with the eternal law, and with positive law, both divine and human, he set in motion one of the two great parallel lines of juridical development. Modern legal science began in the twelfth century with the revival of the study of Roman law in the newly founded European universities, such as Bologna. Thereafter this science advanced in two ways, first by the analytical method, and secondly, by that of scholastic natural law.[23] The former was sponsored by the lawyers, and the latter by the philosophical jurist-theologians. These were the schoolmen. The greatest of them all was St. Thomas Aquinas.

The superiority of the natural law method over the analytical is manifest. The analytical approach postulated the supremacy of all temporal authority in any particular community. It was primarily concerned with human positive law as an end in itself.

The analytical activity consisted in making notes or commentaries, marginal and interlinear, on the texts of the Roman or civil law, such as the *Corpus Juris Civilis* of Justinian. These notes clarified the meaning of difficult words or obscure passages. These notes or glosses were compiled, arranged and classified. But no attempt was made to evaluate them in the light of reason or justice. Accursius was perhaps the most famous Glossator.[24] He was to the analytical technique what St. Thomas was to the natural law method. Accursius is just a name to the legal historian. But the writings of St. Thomas have endured as a living force in the administration of justice.

St. Thomas conclusively demonstrated that the true philosophy of the natural law could reconile *lex* and *jus*. In the thirteenth century and thereafter, the late imperial Roman idea, which found expression in codification, imposed the duty on every political ruler to make law. This idea competed with the English concept that the sovereign must rule under God and the law. This concept was emphasized by Bracton, the father of the English Common law.[25] St. Thomas demonstrated that there was no conflict between these two legal theories. The state was subordinate to the natural law, which was the foundation of *jus*, but not to the positive law, which it made. But the state is not exempt from the directive force of just positive law. It is the duty of the state to fulfill the law on its own free initiative. If the state makes law which is actually just and for the common good, this *lex* will reinforce rather than destroy *jus*.

In conclusion, the Thomistic concept of the natural law avoids both a jurisprudence of conceptions and an uninhibited philosophy of utility. St. Thomas rejected a psychological relativism which would admit of no objective norms of right and wrong. He repudiated the theory that all ideas a person may hold have cosmic validity. At the same time, he accords a reasonable weight to the useful and the practical. Jhering, one of the founders of the Sociological School of Jurisprudence, in the second edition of his classic book, *Der Zweck im Recht*, or *Law as a Means to an End*, published in 1886, stated with regard to St. Thomas:

> Now that I have come to know this vigorous thinker, I cannot help asking myself how it was possible that truths such as he has taught should have been so completely forgotten among our Protestant scholars. What errors could have been avoided if people had kept

these doctrines! ... For my part, if I had known them earlier, I probably would not have written my whole book; for the fundamental ideas which I have treated here are found expressed in full clarity and in a convincing manner by this powerful thinker.

John C. H. Wu, Fountain of Justice pp. 41-43 (1955); reprinted by permission of Sheed and Ward.

Even from a purely phenomenological point of view, Kant's dualism is an oversimplification of things. It was John Dewey who said: "We live in a world which is an impressive and irresistible mixture of sufficiencies, tight completeness, order, recurrences, which make possible prediction and control, and singularities, ambiguities, uncertain possibilities, processes going to consequences as yet indeterminate. They are mixed not mechanically, but vitally like the wheat and tares of the parable."[26] This comes close to the Thomistic view of *empirical* reality, which "is neither a kind of solid homogeneous mass which has the same sense throughout, nor a swarm of profoundly unrelated particles, but nuanced and differenced from within."[27] Thus the Thomistic position in the philosophy of experience is *pluralistic* rather than dualistic.

Such, too, is juridical reality. Jurisprudence must face the whole juridical reality and tackle it with a true scientific temper. It must not arbitrarily isolate that part of juridical reality which can be reduced to neat and clear-cut categories and build itself an ivory tower. A jurist with a true scientific temper will not deal with the law as if it belonged to speculative reason. He will deal with his data as they are, not as he wishes them to be. He will not call justice an irrational ideal, simply because it does not fit in with "pure reason" in the Kantian sense.

Among the Neo-Kantians there are two main schools, represented by Stammler[28] and Kelsen.[29] The former treated the problem of justice with the method of pure reason. The latter, who seems to have a more objective understanding of Kant's system, especially of the implications of Kant's conception of practical reason—which is really no reason, but sentiment—dropped the problem of justice as an irrational idea,[30] and dismissed it from jurisprudence, which must be rational. I have a high respect for both. They have made lasting contributions to jurisprudence, each in his own field. I think Stammler's theory of the Right Law keeps legal speculation from degenerating into sheer positivism; and Kelsen's theory of different stages of the legal order and a hierarchy of juridical norms is a valuable contribution to analytical jurisprudence. But because both Stammler and Kelsen accepted uncritically Kant's naive bifurcation of pure reason and practical reason, the results have been affected by the erroneous starting point. Stammler's system is a revised rationalism, under the flag of critical idealism, while Kelsen's "pure theory of law" is sheer positivism, excluding from the domain of jurisprudence the "irrational" idea of justice as mere emotion. One wonders whether it is justice or rather its exclusion from the concept of law that is irrational.

It was Goethe who said, "He who shies away from the idea finally does not even have the concept." [31] Stammler would understand this much better than Kelsen. To my mind, "the idea" has to do with the *essential*, while "the concept" has to do with the *existential*. Legal positivists, who shy away from the *essential*, will end by missing even the *existential*.

Thomism furnishes the answer to both rationalism and irrationalism, or voluntarism. To the former it says that law does not belong to speculative reason, which deals with causes and effects, but to practical reason, which deals with means and ends. The one has to do with natural phenomena, which are called "necessary things" because they cannot be otherwise than they are. The other has to do with human actions, which are called "contingent matters" because human beings are endowed with free will as well as with reason, and they differ from each other both in the valuation of the ends and in the choice of the means thereto. In the case of speculative reason, there is necessity both in the generalities and in the particularities. But in the case of practical reason, there is necessity only in the general principles, and the more we descend to the matters of detail the less necessity we find. If men were angels, or if Adam had not fallen, this might have been different. As it is, probability must be the guide of life in matters of detail.

To the irrationalists, on the other hand, Thomism would say that practical reason is still reason, and not an inarticulate judgment or blind volition, and that although "general propositions do not decide concrete cases," [32] they are nevertheless the indispensable foundation on which the judicial edifice must be built. Although, as St. Thomas says, there is no absolute rectitude in matters of detail, there is still a relative rectitude. In these matters he does not speak in terms of all reason or no reason, but in terms of the "more or less reasonable." "In the dealings of man, you cannot attain demonstrable and infallible proof, but it is sufficient that you attain a certain conjectural probability, such as an orator would use in his art of persuasion." [33] St. Thomas is realistic through and through, empirically as well as ontologically. As Heinrich Rommen has pointed out, the difference between empiricism and philosophical realism lies in the fact that while the former remains content with what is in the foreground, the latter, with its delight in knowledge, pierces beyond the cheerfully affirmed actuality to that which is in the background.[34]

Christopher St. Germain

Christopher St. Germain (about 1460-1540) was a barrister of the Inner Temple, learned in Canon and English Common law. He "has exercised as great an influence upon the development of modern equity as Bracton's treatise has exercised upon the development of the common law," according to Sir William S.

Holdsworth, the great English legal historian. He did this by the application of the principles and implications of the natural law, as understood by Aquinas, to the positive law-making process. The excerpt below is from one of the two celebrated dialogues which he wrote.

Christopher Saint Germain, The Doctor and Student, Chapters I, II, IV, V, VII, (1518); revised and corrected by William Muchall, Cincinnati, 1874.

THE DOCTOR AND STUDENT
OR DIALOGUES BETWEEN A DOCTOR OF DIVINITY AND A STUDENT IN THE LAWS OF ENGLAND

Christopher Saint Germain[14]

CHAP. I—Of the law eternal.

Doct. This law eternal no man may know, as it is in itself, but only blessed souls that see God face to face. But Almighty God of his goodness sheweth of it as much to his creatures as is necessary for them, for else God should bind his creatures to a thing impossible; which may in no wise be thought in him. Therefore it is to be understood that three manner of ways Almighty God maketh this law eternal known to his creatures reasonable. *First*, by the light of natural reason; *secondly*, by heavenly revelation; *thirdly*, by the order of a prince, or any other secondary governor that hath power to bind his subjects to a law.

And when the law eternal or the will of God is known to his creatures reasonable by the light of natural understanding, or by the light of natural reason, that is called the *law of reason*: and when it is shewed by heavenly revelation in such manner as hereafter shall appear, then it is called the *law of God*: and when it is shewed unto him by the order of a prince, or of any other secondary governor that hath a power to set a law upon his subjects, then it is called the *law of man,* though originally it be made of God. (p. 4.)

CHAP. II—*Of the law of reason, the which by doctors is called the law of nature of reasonable creatures.*

[Doct.] First it is to be understood, that the *law of nature* may be considered in two manners, that is to say, generally and specially. When it is considered generally, then it is referred to all creatures, as well reasonable as unreasonable: for all unreasonable creatures live under a certain rule to them given by nature, necessary to them for the conservation of their being. But of this law it is not our intent to treat at this time. The law of nature specially considered, which is also called the *law of reason*, pertaineth only to creatures reasonable, that is, man, which is created to the image of God.

And this law ought to be kept as well among Jews and Gentiles, as among christian men: and this law is always good and righteous, stirring and inclining a man to good, and abhorring evil. And as to the ordering of the deeds of man, it is preferred before the law of God, and it is written in the heart of every man, teaching him what is to be done, and what is to be fled; and because it is written in the heart, therefore it may not be put away, ne it is never changeable by no diversity of place, ne time: and therefore against this law, prescription, statute nor custom may not prevail: and if any be brought in against it, they be not prescriptions, statutes nor customs, but things void and against justice. And all other laws, as well the laws of God as to the acts of men, as other, be grounded thereupon. (p. 5.)

Doct. Though the law of reason may not be changed, nor wholly put away; nevertheless, before the law written, it was greatly lett and blinded by evil customs, and by many sins of the people, beside our original sin; insomuch that it might hardly be discerned what was righteous, and what was unrighteous, and what was good, and what evil. Wherefore it was necessary, for the good order of the people, to have many things added to the law of reason, as well by the church as by secular princes, according to the manners of the country and of the people where such additions should be exercised. * * *

Doct. The law of reason teacheth, that good is to be loved, and evil is to be fled: also that thou shalt do to another, that thou wouldest another should do unto thee; and that we may do nothing against truth; and that a man must live peacefully with others; that justice is to be done to every man; and also that wrong is not to be done to any man; and that also a trespasser is worthy to be punished; and such other. Of the which follow divers other secondary commandments, the which be as necessary conclusions derived of the first. (p. 6.)

CHAP. IV.—*Of the law of man.*

[Doct.] The *law of man* (the which sometime is called the *law positive*) is derived by reason, as a thing which is necessary, and probably following of the law of reason and of the law of God. And that is called *probable,* in that it appeareth to many, and especially to wise men to be true. And therefore in every law positive well made, is somewhat of the law of reason, and of the law of God; and to discern the law of God and the law of reason from the law positive is very hard. And though it be hard, yet it is much necessary in every moral doctrine, and in all laws made for the commonwealth. And that the law of man be just and rightwise, two things be necessary, and that is to say, wisdom and authority. Wisdom that he may judge after reason what is to be done for the commonalty, and what is expedient for a peaceable conservation and necessary sustentation of them; authority, that he have authority to make laws. For the law is derived of *ligare,* that is to say, to bind. But the sentence of a wise man doth not bind the commonalty, if he have no rule over them. Also to every good law be required these properties: that is to say, that it be honest, rightwise, possible in itself, and after the custom of the country, convenient for the place and time, necessary, profitable, and also manifest, that it be not captious by any dark sentences, ne mixt with any private wealth, but all made for the commonwealth. (pp. 9, 10.)

[Doct.] For laws of man not contrary to the law of God, nor to the law of reason, must be observed in the law of the soul: and he that despiseth them, despiseth God, and resisteth God. And furthermore, as Gratian saith, because evil men fear to offend, for fear of pain; therefore it was necessary that divers pains should be ordained for divers offences, as physicians ordained divers remedies for several diseases. And such pains be ordained by the makers of laws, after the necessity of the time, and after the disposition of the people. And though that law that ordained such pains hath thereby a conformity to the law of God, (for the law of God commandeth that the people shall take away evil from among themselves;) yet they belong not so much to the law of God, but that other pains (standing the first principles) might be ordained and appointed therefore. That is the law that is called most properly the *law positive*, and the *law of man*. (p. 11.)

Francisco Suarez

One of the greatest exponents of the Stoic-Scholastic natural law after Aquinas was Suarez. His contributions to the science of law were made in the late sixteenth and early seventeenth centuries. Perhaps his most significant contribution was the application of the natural law to the problems of justice created by the emergence of the new political entities in the sixteenth century. These entities arose as a result of the fragmentation and shattering of political unity in the Western World. They were the beginnings of the modern states which claimed moral sovereignty, as well as legal and political. Suarez subjected these entities to the imposed obligations of the natural law through the creation of an international positive law.

He derived this law from legal concepts common to the nations by analogy with the *Jus Gentium*. His contributions together with those of other Spanish jurists of his time furnished important materials which were used later by Grotius in the writing of his epochal book, *De Jure Belli ac Pacis* (The Law of War and Peace.)

Francisco Suárez, De Legibus ac De Legislatore, (1619). Quoted by J. B. Scott, 22 Georgetown L. J. pp. 405-406 (1934); reprinted by permission of the Georgetown Law Journal.

DE LEGIBUS AC DEO LEGISLATORE
By Francisco Suárez

Strictly and absolutely speaking, only that which is a measure of rectitude, viewed absolutely, and consequently, only that which is a right and virtuous rule, can be called law.

The eternal law has first place, on account of its dignity and excellence, and because it is the source and origin of all laws.

Natural law is the first system whereby the eternal law has been applied or made known to us. * * *

The natural law is made known to men in a twofold way, first through natural reason, and secondly, through the law of the Decalogue written on the Mosaic tablets. * * *

The *jus gentium* is the most closely related to the natural law.

All the precepts written by God in the hearts of men, pertain to the natural law, a fact which may be gathered from the words of Paul [*Romans*, chap. II (vs. 14-15)]: and all precepts which may clearly be inferred by reason from natural principles are written in [human] hearts; therefore, all such precepts pertain to the natural law.

The commands relating to the restitution of the property of another, or the return of a deposit, or observing good faith, in telling the truth, and to similar matters * * * pertain in the highest degree to the province of the natural law.

It should be further noted that, among the precepts of natural law, there are certain ones, dealing with pacts, agreements, or obligations, which are introduced through the will of men. Such are the laws relating to the observance of vows and of human promises, whether these be made in simple form or confirmed by oath; and the same is true of other contracts, according to the particular characteristics of each; and true, also, of the rights or duties arising therefrom.

In the case of any contract or commercial agreement * * * the observance of the contract after it has been made * * * pertains to the natural law. * * *

Likewise, treaties of peace and truces may be placed under the head of the *jus gentium* in the strict sense of the term; not in so far as relates to the obligation to observe them after they are made, since this obligation pertains rather to the natural law; but in so far as [offers to make] such treaties should be needed, and not refused, when duly presented, and for a reasonable cause. * * *

With regard * * * to peace, truces and ambassadors, * * * all the [rules] on these points have their foundation in some human agreement, in which both the power to contract [a treaty or convention] and the obligation arising from that treaty or convention and demanding good faith and justice, have regard to the law of nature. Only the exercise [of these powers] may be termed a part of the *jus gentium* owing to the accord of all nations with respect to the exercise of such faculties, generally speaking. And this actual use [of the powers in question] is the effect of law, and not law itself; for the law under discussion does not spring from such use; on the contrary, the use has its source in the law.

---

[1] *Ad pop. Ant.*, XII, 4 (Migne, PG, Vol. CXXXII), quoted by Stanley Bertke, *The Possibility of Invincible Ignorance of the Natural Law*. The Catholic University of America Studies in Sacred Theology, No. 58 (Washington, D. C.: The Catholic University of America Press, (1941), p. 8, where also (pp. 5-11)

the views of the other Church Fathers on the natural law are conveniently presented in summary fashion. Bertke's study is a real contribution to the whole problem of the natural law.

[2] Scholasticism, which follows the main lines of Aristotle's thought, in part "advocates a natural dualism of God and creature, mind and matter, thought and thing, as against monism and pantheism; it defends a moderate realism, as against ultrarealism, nominalism, and conceptualism, in the problem of the universals; it is spiritualistic and not materialistic, experimental and not aprioristic, objectivistic and not subjectivistic; in sense-perception it is presentational and not agnostic or representational or idealistic; concerning intellectual knowledge it defends a moderate rationalism, as against sensism, positivism, and innatism; it is common-sense knowledge critically examined and philosophically vindicated" (Celestine N. Bittle, O. M. Cap., *Reality and the Mind* [Milwaukee: The Bruce Publishing Co., 1936], p. 146).

[3] Cf. Charles Grove Haines, The Revival of Natural Law Concepts (Cambridge: Harvard University Press, 1930), pp. 104-234; Benjamin Fletcher Wright, Jr., American Interpretations of Natural Law (Cambridge: Harvard University Press, 1931), especially pp. 292-306.

[4] For an excellent discussion of the all-important and universal metaphysical principle of finality, "every agent acts for an end," see R. Garrigou-Lagrange, O.P., God: His Existence and His Nature, trans. by Bede Rose, O.S.B. (2 vols., St. Louis: B. Herder Book Co., 1934-36), I, 199-204; also K. F. Reinhardt, A Realistic Philosophy, pp. 87-89.

[5] See Brown, Natural Law and the Law-Making Function in American Jurisprudence, 15 Notre Dame Law. 9 (1939).

[6] Ibid.

[7] Ibid.

[8] Brown & Cormack, The Stoic Philosophy and the Roman Law, 16 Bullettino d'Istituto Di Diritto Romano 451-58 (1937).

[9] Institutes of Justinian, Book I, Title II.

[10] James, Some Historical Aspects of St. Thomas' Treatment of the Natural Law, 24 Proceedings of the American Catholic Philosophical Association 147 (1950).

[11] Summa Theologica, I-II, q. 95, art. 2, concl.

[12] Id., I-II, q. 91, art. 3, concl.

[13] Ibid.

[14] Id., I-II, q. 95, art. 1, concl.

[15] Id., I-II, q. 95, art. 2, concl.

[16] Ibid.

[17] Ibid.

[18] Id., I-II, q. 96, art. 4, concl.
[19] Ibid.
[20] See Foreword by Brown, Del Vecchio, Philosophy of Law XVI (1953).

[21] Lex and Jus appear in the titles of their principal works. Bracton's great book was entitled De Legibus et Consuetudinibus Angliae. Glanvill's monumental work was Tractatus de Legibus et Consuetudinibus Regni Angliae.
[22] 1 Holdsworth, A History of English Law 568-72 (1931).
[23] Pound, Outlines of Lectures on Jurisprudence 6-7 (5th ed. 1943).
[24] 2 Holdsworth, A History of English Law 146 (1936).
[25] Id., at 252-56.
[26] Experience and Nature, p. 47.
[27] Gilby, Between Community and Society, p. 14.
[28] Rudolf Stammler (1856-1938) was generally considered the greatest legal philosopher of the present century. Of him Pound wrote: "Stammler has undoubtedly been the strongest influence in philosophical jurisprudence in the present century" (Harvard Law Review, Vol. 51, p. 448). The importance of his position lies in the fact that he was writing at a time when positivism was at its height and natural law was at its lowest ebb, and that he advocated, by adapting the method of Kant, the universal validity of the fundamental principles of justice, which he classified into two categories: (1) the principles of respect, (2) the principles of participation. His system was transcendental idealism, not transcendental realism. His idea of "universal validity" was confined to the human mind. He did not claim any ontological basis for the idea of justice. In the early twenties, I was studying under him as a private pupil. I already felt that his system was a half-way house between reality and the mind. I had difficulties with what seemed to me an excessive formalism in his system. I wrote an article in which I maintained that the concept of law presupposed the law as a thing in itself, and therefore one could not know the law completely through conceptual knowledge alone. Perception was just as important as conception, and over and above conception and perception, we needed to resort to "intellectual intuition." In one word, it took the *whole* mind to know the law. To my immense surprise, my great teacher said, "This is so far the most formidable criticism that my philosophy has met with!"

But Stammler's contribution to jurisprudence cannot be

gainsaid. He was combatting the prevailing positivism in a language that it could understand.

His best-known book was Die Lehre vom dem richtigen Rechts (1902), ("The Theory of Right Law"), which was translated into English and published in 1925 in the "Modern Legal Philosophy Series" under the title The Theory of Justice.

Similar in tendency but a little more metaphysically inclined is the Italian jurist Giorgio Del Vecchio. Although generally labeled a Neo-Kantian, he is in fact a humanist pure and simple. His Philosophy of Law has recently been translated into English and published by the Catholic University of America Press (1953). In his foreword to the book, Dr. Brendan Francis Brown has very ably brought out the inadequacies of Del Vecchio's system, which "does not reach the scholasticism of François Gény." One cannot help wishing that the works of Gény and the other great French jurist, Georges Ripert, be translated into English.

[29] Hans Kelsen desires "to free the concept of law from the idea of justice" (General Theory of Law and State, [Harvard, 1945], p. 5). As an orthodox Kantian dualist, Kelsen sees only two alternatives: either identify law with justice or isolate law completely from justice; and he chooses the latter course. To my mind, the statement of these alternatives is purely arbitrary. Law is neither identical with justice nor separable from it. When the very *Fragestellung* (or the way of presenting the question) is wrong, all discussions pro and con are like talking to the wind.

[30] See Kelsen's essay "The Metamorphoses of the Idea of Justice" in Paul Sayre, Interpretations of Modern Legal Philosophers (Oxford, 1947), pp. 390 ff.

[31] Quoted in Gustav Radbruch, "Legal Philosophy," in The Legal Philosophies of Lask, Radbruch, and Dabin (Harvard, 1950), p. 72.

[32] Justice Holmes dissenting in Lochner v. New York (1905), 198 U. S. 45 at 74.

[33] S. T., I-II, 105. 2. ad 8.

[34] Heinrich Rommen, The Natural Law (Herder, 1947), p. 166.

C. Continuation of Scholastic Thinking After the Reformation by Non-Catholics

After the Reformation, influential non-Catholic writers like Blackstone continued to advocate natural law thinking. The view has long prevailed that these jurists had emancipated jurisprudence from theology and hence could not be classified as scholastics, in any sense. In the opinion of this Editor, such a view is erroneous and is based on a misconception of the essence of scholastic natural law. He is aware of the controversial character of this statement.

As a matter of fact, Aquinas did not intend to disturb the rational basis of Aristotelian-Stoic natural law. In his *Summa Theologica*, Aquinas placed the emphasis upon the relation of philosophy to the theology of the Catholic Church. It is primarily a work of theology and not philosophy, relative to theodicy and natural law. It is unfortunate for the clarity of his views toward natural law that Aquinas, who died at the age of forty-nine (or forty-seven), did not live longer so as to be able to elaborate the full implications of his philosophy of the natural law.

Aquinas was writing about natural law from the point of view of a person who has accepted the theology of the Catholic Church. But the particular theological persuasion of a natural law jurist is not part of the doctrine of natural law. Nor is the Thomistic conclusion that the Catholic Church has the authority to determine the content of the natural law when reasonable men disagree about it derived from natural law according to Aquinas.

Non-Catholic jurists, like Blackstone, did not accept Catholic theology. But this is beside the point. It would have been equally irrelevant if they had believed only in the Old Testament or in the Koran. But they did believe in a divine personal Law-giver, known by reason, Who is the Source of the natural law. Hence they are properly classified as scholastic jurists in a certain sense. This would not have been so if they believed in the existence of a pantheistic God only, or if they were agnostic as to the existence of God.

1. In General

Rev. Thomas E. Davitt, S. J. St. Thomas Aquinas and the Natural Law in Origins of the Natural Law Tradition p. 39 (1954) reprinted by permission of the author and the Southern Methodist University Press.

Hence at this point a somewhat prevalent misconception of St. Thomas' concept of the Natural Law may well be pointed out. Many seem to have the impression that the Natural Law refers to certain basic truths that may be known either from the use of reason *or from revelation.* Revelation is here taken to mean, for instance, the Ten Commandments. While it may be true that there is a coincidence between the content of the commands known by faith in the authority of Sacred Scripture and the demands of a man's basic inclinations known connaturally, nevertheless this coincidence is entirely beyond any consideration of the Natural Law as such. If the word "natural" means anything at all, it refers to the nature of a man, and when used with "law", "natural" must refer to an ordering that is manifested in the inclinations of a man's nature and to nothing else. Hence, taken in itself, there is nothing religious or theological in the "Natural Law" of Aquinas—if by religion and theology are meant truths to which the mind assents because of the authority of the word of God as revealed in the Sacred Scriptures. If it is based on this kind of revelation, then Natural Law is not natural; it is supernatural. No, the truths of the Natural Law are assented to by the human mind simply because of the evidence that is observable in a man's natural inclinations: the evidence of an ordering that ultimately is recognized as a law.

Brendan F. Brown, Book Review of the Philosophy of Law in Historical Perspective, by Carl Joachim Friedrich, 48 Georgetown Law Journal 192, 194-196 (1959); reprinted by permission of the Georgetown Law Journal.

This scholarly book is substantially an English version of a work which Professor Friedrich [1] published in Munich under the title *"Die Philosophie des Rechts in historischer Perspektive."* This work appeared in the *Enzyklopadie der Rechts-und Staatswissenschaft.*[2] But significant variations and additions have been made in the English edition. An example of a major shift of view is the statement of the author in chapter vi that he no longer regards his former opinion "that Thomas Aquinas favored monarchy as a form of government, regardless of constitutional limitations", as tenable.[3] Other changes[4] have been made, particularly in chapter xi, which deals with law as a command, in the sense understood by Hobbes and the utilitarians. The same is true of chapters xx-xxiv, where the author has expressed his most recent philosophical convictions.

* * * * *

Indeed, "justice needs to be comprehended within the context of politics".[5] Only natural law thinking can justify the author's contention "that the will even of the majority must be related to the 'higher reason' of a system of values—values that are not seen as purely subjective preference".[6] Such thinking alone can account for the author's opinion that justice must be related "to the complex value system of a man, a community, or mankind."[7] His high regard for the Thomistic concept of natural law is evidenced by his broad conclusion that there is "the need for a standard of justice by which to evaluate the positive law, a standard firm and yet not subject to the criticism which destroyed the older natural-law doctrines."[8] He adds that "this is a broad philosophical problem to which only the Catholic tradition has a coherent metaphysical answer."[9]

But unfortunately the author may have unintentionally beclouded the true meaning of the Thomistic doctrine of the natural law by the use of an ambiguous nomenclature. Thus, in describing this doctrine, Professor Friedrich has employed such phrases as "rational theology,"[10] "Christian natural law,"[11] "philosophical natural law,"[12] and theological reason."[13]

These phrases may fail to communicate the fact that Thomas Aquinas did not disturb the rational basis of the Aristotelian-Stoic concept of natural law. This law is known to be divine, not in the sense that it is prescribed by a particular theology, but only because reason discovers a divine Law-giver Who is the Source of the natural law. Reason perceives the difference between moral good and moral evil as it is related to human behavior. Obligation attaches to the doing of the good and the avoiding of the evil.

Good is almost immediately associated with that type of human conduct which is conducive to the supreme value of man, as an individual and as a member of society. Evil is almost immediately related to actions which violate man's rational nature. Almost self evident is the goodness of the behavior dictated by such ethical norms as are found in the Ten Commandments.

Up to this point there is nothing characteristically pagan, Christian, or agnostic about the existence or content of the natural law. As yet, supernatural or divine positive law or theology, in the sense of law which has been immediately revealed by God and accepted on faith, has not entered the picture because there is unanimity, generally speaking, among all men whose rational faculty is freely operating. It is reason alone which recognizes that the natural law is divine, and hence immutable, universal and more than subjective or even transpersonal, according to Thomas Aquinas.

Acceptance of a specific supernatural law by a jurist or legal philosopher becomes relevant only when more detailed behavior is examined to ascertain whether it is part of the content of the natural law. Men of good will, of equal intellectual attainments, and similar educational backgrounds will disagree only in that area of the natural law which is not self evident, or almost so, but which is reached only after considerable induction and deduction.

For example, jurists who believe in natural law as

the promulgation of a divine Law-giver, through reason, may and do disagree as to whether divorce, followed by remarriage during the lifetime of the divorced spouse, is contrary to the natural law. But they will not disagree as to the necessity of some kind of a marital institution for the protection and rearing of the human species. A natural law jurist who is a Catholic will have the benefit of certitude resulting from an insight afforded him by Catholic theology, which teaches that such a marriage is contrary to the will of Almighty God. But the non-Catholic natural law jurist may continue to adhere to his position, i.e. that such a marriage is not divinely prohibited. This disagreement as to detailed human behavior, however, will not make the natural law Catholic or non-Catholic, although jurists who accept the doctrine of the scholastics may be Catholic or non-Catholic. Indeed, scholastic jurists who are Catholics disagree among themselves as to more remote applications of the natural law, for example, the Right to Work legislation, since theology and the divine teaching authority of the church are silent on this point.

The tenet that the Catholic Church, through its divine mission, has the right and duty to decide the content of the natural law when reasonable men disagree is not a part of the natural law but of the supernatural law. In fact, if a person is convinced in good faith by an unbiased and completely informed reason that a part of the content of a particular law which is alleged to be of supernatural origin conflicts with his concept of the natural law, he must be guided by his interpretation of the latter. Thus Aztec theology, which dictated human sacrifice, should have yielded to the test of the natural law.

Sir William Blackstone, Commentaries on the Laws of England, Section 2, Cooley Edition, 1872 pp. 38-41.

This will of his Maker is called the law of nature. For as God, when he created matter, and endued it with a principle of mobility, established certain rules for the perpetual direction of that motion, so, when he created man, and endued him with free-will to conduct himself in all parts of life, he laid down certain immutable laws of human nature, whereby that free-will is in some degree regulated and restrained, and gave him also the faculty of reason to discover the purport of those laws.

Considering the Creator only as a being of infinite *power*, he was able unquestionably to have prescribed whatever laws he pleased to his creature, man, however unjust or severe. But as he is also a being of infinite *wisdom*, he has laid down only such laws as were founded in those relations of justice, that existed in the nature of things antecedent to any positive precept. These are the eternal immutable laws of good and evil, to which the Creator himself, in all his dispensations, conforms; and which he has enabled human reason to discover, so far as they are necessary for the conduct of human actions. Such, among others, are these principles: that we should live honestly, should hurt nobody, and should render to every one his due; to which three general precepts Justinian has reduced the whole doctrine of law. (Book I, pp. 39, 40.)

But if the discovery of these first principles of the law of nature depended only upon the due exertion of right reason, and could not otherwise be obtained than by a chain of metaphysical disquisitions, mankind would have wanted some inducement to have quickened their inquiries, and the greater part of the world would have rested content in mental indolence, and ignorance, its inseparable companion. As, therefore, the Creator is a being not only of infinite *power*, and *wisdom*, but also of infinite *goodness*, he has been pleased so to contrive the constitution and frame of humanity, that we should want no other prompter to inquire after and pursue the rule of right, but only our own self-love, that universal principle of action. For he has so intimately connected, so inseparably interwoven the laws of eternal justice with the happiness of each individual, that the latter cannot be attained but by observing the former; and, if the former be punctually obeyed, it cannot but induce the latter. In consequence of which mutual connection of justice and human felicity, he has not perplexed the law of nature with a multitude of abstracted rules and precepts, referring merely to the fitness or unfitness of things, as some have vainly surmised, but has graciously reduced the rule of obedience to this one paternal precept, "that man should pursue his own true and substantial happiness." This is the foundation of what we call ethics, or natural law; for the several articles into which it is branched in our systems amount to no more than demonstrating that this or that action tends to man's real happiness, and therefore very justly concluding that the performance of it is a part of the law of nature; or, on the other hand, that this or that action is destructive of man's real happiness, and therefore that the law of nature forbids it.

This law of nature, being coeval with mankind, and dictated by God himself, is of course superior in obligation to any other. It is binding over all the globe, in all countries, and at all times; no human laws are of any validity, if contrary to this; and such of them as are valid derive all their force and all their authority, mediately or immediately, from this original.

But, in order to apply this to the particular exigencies of each individual, it is still necessary to have recourse to reason, whose office it is to discover, as was before observed, what the law of nature directs in every circumstance of life, by considering what method will tend the most effectually to our own substantial happiness. And if our reason were always, as in our first ancestor before his transgression, clear and perfect, unruffled by passions, unclouded by prejudices, unimpaired by disease or intemperance, the task would be pleasant and easy; we should need no other guide but this. But every man now finds the contrary in his own experience; that his reason is corrupt, and his understanding full of ignorance and error. (Book I, pp. 40, 41.)

* * * * *

Upon these two foundations, the law of nature and the law of revelation, depend all human laws; that is to say, no human laws should be suffered to contradict these. There are, it is true, a great number of indifferent points in which both the divine law and the natural leave a man at his own liberty, but which are found necessary, for the benefit of society, to be restrained within certain limits. And herein it is that human laws have their greatest force and efficacy; for, with regard to such points as are not indifferent, human laws are only declaratory of, and act in subordination to, the former. To instance in the case of murder: this is expressly forbidden by the divine, and demonstrably by the natural law; and, from these prohibitions, arises the true unlawfulness of this crime. Those human laws that annex a punishment to it do not at all increase its moral guilt, or superadd any fresh obligation, *in foro conscientiae*, to abstain from its perpetration. Nay, if any human law should allow or enjoin us to commit it, we are bound to transgress that human law, or else we must offend both the natural and the divine. But, with regard to matters that are in themselves indifferent, and are not commanded or forbidden by those superior laws,—such, for instance, as exporting of wool into foreign countries,—here the inferior legislature has scope and opportunity to interpose, and to make that action unlawful which before was not so. (Book I, pp. 42, 43.)

FOOTNOTES TO SECTION II—C

[1] Dr. Friedrich is the Easton Professor of the Science of Government at Harvard University.

[2] Friedrich, The Philosophy of Law in Historical Perspective vii (1958).

3 Id. at 43, footnote 2.
4 Id. at vii.
5 Id. at 198.
6 Id. at 203.
7 Id. at 199.
8 Id. at 188.
9 Ibid.
10 Id. at 44.
11 Id. at 56.
12 Ibid.
13 Id. at 54.

D. *Impact of Scholastic Natural Law Jurisprudence on Positive Law*

Natural law thinking has had wide influence on positive law, both international and national, particularly the Roman and Anglo-American legal systems. Indeed the character of these two great legal systems would have been different if they had not felt the impact of scholastic natural law over the centuries. This applies to both public and private law.

1. Public Law
a. *International Law*

Joseph B. Keenan and Brendan F. Brown, *Crimes against International Law* [Tokyo War Crimes Trial], pp. 72-73 (1950).

For the Prosecution, the extrinsic facts of specific legislative codification, judicial recognition, or enforcement were not essential elements of law.[1] But for the Defense, law might be challenged on the grounds that it lacked these elements. For the Defense, law existed only if it had sanction of a physical character.

Manifestly the same difference of jurisprudential faith between Prosecution and Defense obtained as to international law. This is so because the law of nations is a *species* of the *genus* law. Prosecution and Defense were agreed that there is a body of international law. They were disagreed, however, as to its origin, essence and attributes, as well as its function, although both sides agreed that it was not strictly legislative.

The Prosecution postulated an objectively existing moral order as the final medium of international social control.[2] A common morality applies to the individual person, to the nation, and to the community or family of nations [3]—a morality rooted in the spiritual dignity, worth, and value of all men, who constitute a universal brotherhood under the fatherhood of God. This common morality is made up of intrinsic and immutable concepts of right and wrong.[4] The fundamental philosophy of the Prosecution was that customary law and international law exist partly in the form of these concepts, as consented to consciously, sooner or later, by reasonable men, when occasion so justifies.[5] The principles included in these concepts become the basis of customary action. This action is not judicial at first, but later it is.[6] Extrajudicial customary law later becomes judicial customary law.

The Prosecution rejected, as unsound, socially dangerous and anarchic, the theory of the Defense that all rules must be agreed to and participated in by all the countries of the world, if they are to be universal and universally applicable.[7] This theory conceives international law entirely as the product of human consent. But men, not being gods, are not morally free and able to convert any principle whatsoever into law, or deliberately to refrain from transforming certain principles into law. The ethical obligation or binding force of an international custom, (i.e.) an observance of certain rules by part of or all of the international community, so that these rules become part of international law, does not arise entirely from the consent of men, but also from the natural law.[8] If the rule in question is contrary *per se* to the natural law, no period of human recognition could give it the force of law, customary or otherwise. If the rule is in accord with the fundamental dictates of natural law, it has the force of law despite the length of the period of consent and recognition. It has moral force regardless of any human consent.

b. National Law

Edward S. Corwin, The Natural Law and Constitutional Law, 3 University of Notre Dame, Natural Law Institute Proceedings p. 79 (1949); reprinted by permission of the author and the University of Notre Dame.

How are we to assess the importance of the Natural Law concept in the development of American Constitutional Law? What it all simmers down to is essentially this: while that distinctive American institution, judicial review, is regarded today as stemming from the principle of popular sovereignty, it sprang in the first instance from "common right and reason," the equivalent with men of law in the Sixteenth Century England of "Natural Law." What is more, popular sovereignty in the last analysis is itself a derivative from the Natural Law postulate, being neither more nor less than a sort of *ad hoc* consolidation of the natural right of human beings to choose their own governing institutions.

Edward S. Corwin, The "Higher Law" Background of American Constitutional Law, 42 Harvard Law Review, pp. 152-153, 166 (1928); reprinted by permission of the author and the Harvard Law Review Association. Copyright 1928 by Harvard Law Review Association.

THE "HIGHER LAW" BACKGROUND OF AMERICAN CONSTITUTIONAL LAW

The attribution of supremacy to the Constitution on the ground solely of its rootage in popular will represents, however, a comparatively late outgrowth of American constitutional theory. Earlier the supremacy accorded to constitutions was ascribed less to their putative source than to their supposed content, to their embodiment of essential and unchanging justice. The theory of law thus invoked stands in direct contrast to the one just reviewed. *There are, it is predicated, certain principles of right and justice which are entitled to prevail of their own intrinsic excellence, altogether regardless of the attitude of those who wield the physical resources of the community. Such principles were made by no human hands; indeed, if they did not antedate deity itself, they still so express its nature as to bind and control it. They are external to all Will as such and interpenetrate all Reason as such. They are eternal and immutable. In relation to such principles, human laws are, when entitled to obedience save as to matters indifferent, merely a record or transcript, and their enactment an act not of will or power but one of discovery and declaration*[9].

*   *   *   *   *

The sweep and majesty of the medieval conception of a higher law as at once the basis and test for all rightful power is emphasized by the German historian, von Gierke. Natural law constrained the highest earthly powers. It held sway over Pope and Emperor, over ruler and sovereign people alike, indeed over the whole community of mortals. Neither statute (*Gesetz*) nor any act of authority, neither usage nor popular resolve could break through the limits which it imposed. Anything which conflicted with its eternal and indestructible principles was null and void and could bind nobody. Furthermore, while there was no sharp disseverance of natural law from morality, yet the limits thrown about the legitimate sphere of supreme power should by no means, von Gierke insists, be regarded as merely ethical principles. Not only were they designed to control external acts and not merely the ruler's internal freedom, but they were addressed also to judges and to all having anything to do with the application of the law, who were thereby bound to hold for naught not only any act of authority but even any statute which overstepped them. They morally exonerated the humblest citizen in defiance of the highest authority; they might even justify assassination.[10]

Read in the light of Austinian conceptions, these words may easily convey a somewhat exaggerated impression. Yet the outstanding fact is clear, that the supposed precepts of a higher law were, throughout the Middle Ages, being continually pitted against the claims of official authority and were being continually set to test the validity of such claims.

Harold G. Reuschlein, Jurisprudence—Its American Prophets pp. 26-27, reprinted by permission of the author and Bobbs Merrill Co., Inc.

In Fletcher v. Peck, a decision under the contract clause, we find Marshall not content with a constitutional peg alone upon which to hang his decision, but admitting the availability of the constitutional provision, adding to the authority of the express provision, the alluring authority of higher law as well:

"It may well be doubted whether the nature of society and of government does not prescribe some limits to the legislative power; and if any be prescribed, where are they to be found, if the property of an individual, fairly and honestly acquired, may be seized without compensation. * * *

It is, then, the unanimous opinion of the court, that in this case, the estate having passed into the hands of a purchaser for a valuable consideration, without notice, the state of Georgia was restrained, either by general principles which are common to our free institutions, or by the particular provisions of the Constitution of the United States from passing a law whereby the estate of the plaintiff in the premises so purchased could be legally impaired." [11]

Nor did the employment of the natural law concept as a basis for judicial decisions cease with Marshall. One may find it stalking in full vigor in the opinions of Chase,[12] Miller,[13] Field,[14] Brewer,[15] Harlan[16] and Pitney.[17] Indeed, we are told that in substance the concept still lives in American constitutional law under a name more acceptable to our day—"due process."[18]

Viscount Kilmuir, The Lord High Chancellor of Great Britain, Address at the Opening Ceremony in Westminster Hall of the London Meeting of the American Bar Association in 1957, 43 American Bar Association Journal pp. 886-888 (1597), reprinted by permission of Viscount Kilmuir and the American Bar Association Journal.

Chief Justices, Attorneys General, Presidents, my Lords, Ladies and Gentlemen:

It is thirty-three years since the American Bar Association last held its annual conference in London, and assembled in this famous hall to be welcomed by the Lord Chancellor and His Majesty's Judges.

* * * * *

In 1924, a young lawyer such as I thought of the rule of law as something unassailable: we imagined that the horrors and sacrifices of the First World War had not been futile, and that mankind had at last learnt its lesson and would henceforth live in accordance with reason and with that need for harmony and peace which is instinctive in us all.

What happened to these fond imaginings? Every single belief which we held was furiously assailed; every hope that we nursed was disappointed; reason was once more dethroned; one brutalizing dogma after another was propagated and bore dreadful fruit. The house that we thought to be empty, swept and garnished, was entered by seven other devils more wicked, and the last state of man appeared indeed worse than the first.

In those times many felt with the great Irish poet that,

> The best lack all conviction, while the worst
> Are full of passionate intensity.[19]

In this situation some lost their nerve and in the years of tyranny that seemed to have been loosed upon the world took comfort in doctrines that exalted authority. They lost confidence in the free legal and political systems which are the heritage and pride not only of our two nations but of the Western World, and of all those countries in Asia and Africa that have been nurtured in the noble and fruitful ways of the common law.

However, as it turned out, there was no need to have been so alarmed, or so doubtful about democracy's power to survive. One fact that has been made abundantly clear during the terrible period of trial (for that is how I regard it) through which we have been passing is that (to put it at its lowest) a tyrannical society is much less efficient than a society which is free. We had always hoped that this was so because we had been brought up to dislike tyranny, and in these small islands had spent much blood, over the centuries, in resisting it. But there were moments when the loud noises which tyranny made and the formidable façade which it presented to the world unnerved those who had forgotten, or were unaware of, the inherent weaknesses of authoritarian rule. History has taught us, time and time again, that no society can for long endure which is not based on morality and order.

* * * * *

This great hall in which we are now assembled was built 858 years ago by a Norman—William Rufus, the son of the Conqueror. *** These venerable walls have echoed the voices of the famous judges and pleaders whose names are as much a household word to you as to us. St. Thomas More, one of the greatest and certainly the best of my predecessors, whenever he came to this hall made a typically graceful gesture. His father was a puisne judge of the King's Bench and St. Thomas More, on his way to take his seat as Lord Chancellor, always stopped at his father's court and bowed. Peter the Great of Russia visited the hall in 1697. He was astonished to learn that all the busy men in wigs and gowns hurrying about the hall were lawyers. "Lawyers!" he exclaimed, "Why, I have but two in my whole dominion and I believe I shall hang one of them the moment I get home."

All this great past we share with you, yet there is a doctrine which we both share with a wider community even than that of the common law, but which has, for various reasons, become a little dusty and old-fashioned in recent years, and which I myself should like to see refurbished and restored to the position which it once used to occupy. I refer to the doctrine of the law of nature, one of the noblest conceptions in the history of jurisprudence. Lord Bryce, once British Ambassador in Washington, who is believed to be the only Englishman (and I have heard a typically generous American say the only human being) who has ever understood the American Constitution, described the doctrine as it appeared to the Roman jurists thus: "... the Law of Nature represented to the Romans that which is conformable to Reason, to the best side of Human Nature, to an elevated morality, to practical good sense, to general convenience. It is Simple and Rational, as opposed to that which is Artificial or Arbitrary. It is Universal, as opposed to that which is Local or National. It is superior to all other law because it belongs to mankind as mankind, and is the expression of the purpose of the Deity or of the highest reason of man. It is therefore Natural, not so much in the sense of belonging to man in his primitive and uncultured condition, but rather as corresponding to and regulating his fullest and most perfect social development in communities, where they have ripened through the teachings of Reason." [20]

Our two nations, socially and legally, are highly evolved and the law of nature is so firmly embedded in our jurisprudence that it only occasionally shows above the surface, as in the inherent power of our own courts here to avoid a judicial or quasi-judicial decision on the grounds that it is "contrary to natural justice"—a phrase of which everyone knows the meaning but which no one, thank heaven, has finally defined. But although, as I have said, our system of law is highly evolved we need always to remind ourselves that the law cannot stand still, that it must, in Bryce's words, always be "conformable to Reason, to the best side of Human Nature, to an elevated morality, to practical good sense, to general convenience". There lies our duty as lawyers.

And there is another side to the law of nature that we must not forget. "You may throw out Nature with a pitchfork," said a Latin poet who was also a good gardener, "but she will always come back." *Naturam expelles furca, tamen usque recurret*. What we are seeing now in some parts of the world where it was least expected is, I am convinced, a spontaneous expression of that timeless longing, inseparable from the human condition, for justice, for the acceptance and fulfillment of the requirements of natural law which recognize that man is born to die and has but a little time to fulfill himself and to care for those to whom he is bound by ties of friendship and love. That the young in those countries, blinkered and intellectually constricted from birth, should nevertheless express these needs is, in my belief, yet another manifestation of the working of the law of nature or, as it became known in medieval times, the law of God.

Therefore let us be of good heart. The ideals which underlie the laws of our two countries have outlasted many tyrannies and have seen the decay and death of many specious theories. The reason why that anvil has broken many hammers is (once more in Bryce's sober words) that these ideals are "conformable to the best side of Human Nature" and an "expression of the highest reason of man". Moreover, our laws are not static any more than society or human nature is static. Their roots, well grounded in history and watered by wisdom, are constantly putting out fresh branches and leaves for the comfort of mankind. The vitality of our institutions is demonstrated by such a great gathering as this, of professional men and women seeking constantly to improve that contribution to the well-being of the community which it is their duty and vocation to make.

Rev. William J. Kenealy, S.J., The Majesty of the Law, 5 Loyola Law Review (New Orleans) pp. 106-109, 112-113 (1949-1950); reprinted by permission of the author and the Loyola Law Review.

The battle is on, make no mistake about it. Our modern legal pragmatists pooh-pooh the very notion of the natural law as a medieval fiction, which served a useful purpose in its day, but is now obsolete and never had any objective existence. To them, therefore, inalienable rights are so much metaphysical nonsense. There are no duties in conscience because morality, in its last analysis, is merely current good taste. There are no principles; there are merely prevailing formulae of expediency. Above all, there are no absolutes; no absolutes, that is, except pragmatic public policy—which means the absolute state. If it works, it's true; if it works, it's right. A rudderless philosophy which leads, logically and psychologically, to the philosophy of force. Do you think I overdraw the picture? That I exaggerate the danger?

Such alien and corrosive ideas have so far eaten their way into the fabric of modern American legal thought that even the late Mr. Justice Holmes, idol of the profession and deity of the schools, could write:

> "The first requirement of a sound body of law is that it should correspond with the actual feelings and demands of the community, whether right or wrong.... But it is clear to me that the *ultima ratio,* not only *regum,* but of all private persons is force...." [21]

This was written in 1881. In 1926, forty-five years later, with the intellectual consistency characteristic of all his writings, Holmes wrote to his friend Dr. John C. H. Wu: "I don't believe that it is an absolute principle or even a human ultimate that man is always an end in himself—that his dignity must be respected, etc. We march up a conscript with bayonets behind to die for a cause he doesn't believe in. And I feel no scruples about it. Our morality seems to me only a check on the ultimate domination of force, just as our politeness is a check on the impulse of every pig to put his feet in the trough. When the Germans in the late war disregarded what we called the rules of the game, I don't see there was anything to be said except: we don't like it and shall kill you if we can. So when it comes to the development of a *corpus juris* the ultimate question is what do the dominant forces of the community want, and do they want it hard enough to disregard whatever inhibitions may stand in the way." [22]

Now Holmes was an honest and a logical man. Believing the essence, the *ultima ratio,* of law was simply physical force, he was logical in defining law as merely "a statement of the circumstances in which the public force will be brought to bear upon men through the courts." [23] He was logical in defining the study of law as the study of "prediction, the prediction of the incidence of the public force through the instrumentality of the courts." [24] He was logical in sarcastically defining a right as the "hypostasis of a prophecy"[25] a

SCHOLASTIC—JURISPRUDENCE

prophecy, that is, of what the courts will in fact do about it. He was logical in defining a duty as "nothing but a prediction that if a man does or omits certain things he will be made to suffer in this or that way by the judgment of the court."[26] And he was logical in stating that "the duty to keep a contract at common law means a prediction that you must pay damages if you do not keep it—and nothing else."[27]

This philosophy of Holmes flowed from his fundamental skepticism concerning the nature of truth, the nature of man, and the nature of human life. In his repudiation of the natural law he wrote: "I used to say when I was young that truth was the majority vote of the nation that could lick all others ... and I think that the statement was correct in so far as it implied that our test of truth is a reference to either a present or an imagined future majority in favor of our view."[28] Holmes was an intellectually honest man, to whom pussy-footing was an abomination. Hence he could write to Sir Frederick Pollock: "I see no reason for attributing to man a significance different in kind from that which belongs to a baboon or a grain of sand."[29] And again to Sir Frederick Pollock, when he wrote cynically: "Functioning is all there is—only our keenest pleasure is in what we call the higher sort. I wonder if cosmically an idea is any more important than bowels."[30] With these views of life and of human nature, it is small wonder that, in 1920, he could write to his English friend: "I do think that the sacredness of human life is a purely municipal ideal of no validity outside the jurisdiction. I believe that force, mitigated so far as may be by good manners, is the *ultima ratio*...."[31] To which Sir Frederick replied: "My dear Holmes: ... As to the sanctity of human life, I quite agree with you that there is too much fuss about it."[32] In 1924, at the age of eighty-three, he wrote, somewhat pathetically I think, "If I were dying my last words would be: Have faith and pursue the unknown end."[33] Two years later, he gave it as his opinion that the human personality was merely "a cosmic ganglion." [34] And in 1929, a few years before his death, he penned this *nunc dimittis*: "I may work for a year or two but I cannot hope to add much to what I have done. I am too skeptical to think that it matters much, but too conscious of the mystery of the universe to say that it or anything else does not. I bow my head, I think serenely and say, as I told someone the other day, O Cosmos—Now lettest thou my ganglion dissolve in peace." [35]

So much for the philosophy of Mr. Justice Holmes! It is of tremendous importance to students of the law and to the legal profession because, as Mr. Justice Frankfurter has said, Holmes "above all others has given the directions of contemporary jurisprudence."[36] Roscoe Pound asserted that Holmes "has done more than lead American juristic thought of the present generation. Above all others he has shaped the methods and ideas that are characteristic of the present as distinguished from the immediate past."[37] And, according to the late Mr. Justice Cardozo: "He is today for all students of the law and for all students of human society the philosopher and seer, the greatest of our age in the domain of jurisprudence and one of the greatest of the ages."[38]

Now Mr. Justice Holmes was indeed a great jurist, an eminent legal scholar, a fascinating stylist, a vibrant personality, and a masterful champion of many just and liberal causes—causes which deserved support from sounder premises. But I, for one, rejoice that his philosophy did not often determine his judicial decisions. I have cited his words merely for the purpose of illustrating the current trend of legal philosophy. I believe this trend constitutes a grave menace to American liberties, because it is cutting away at the foundations of American jurisprudence. I fear that, if it is not checked, it may topple the superstructure which we are proud and happy to call our American way of life.

Do you think that philosophy has not within itself the awful power to make and destroy and re-make civilization? Approach the question from a practical viewpoint. Look back eight or nine years to the time when mankind was in the grip of one of the greatest catastrophes of human history. The armies of totalitarian states were shattering the civilization of Europe and drenching her peoples in human blood.

*****

The ideological attack has caught us unprepared, confused, divided and uncertain about the essential principles of our own democracy, about fundamental premises of our own exalted American philosophy of life and of government. Before we can hope to win the ideological war, upon which the peace and civilization of the whole world depends, we must have an intellectual and spiritual leadership convinced, united and vocal, about the true American idea of life, of law, and of government. Today we have no such conviction, no such union, no such voice. If we do not achieve such leadership in the reasonably near future, then we will lose the war of ideas. And, if that happens, American blood will be spilled again and again —or American liberty will be lost. No philosopher in history has ever pointed out another alternative between the natural law and physical force. It will be one or the other.

If man is essentially no different from "a baboon or a grain of sand"; if we are simply "cosmic ganglia"; if "functioning is all there is"; if truth is merely "the majority vote of the nation that can lick all others"; if "the sacredness of human life is a purely municipal ideal, of no validity outside the jurisdiction"; if the *"ultima ratio"* of law is simply physical force:—if these things are true, as Mr. Justice Holmes thought they were true, then we have no rational defense against the philosophy of totalitarianism; we have fought a war in vain; and American democracy is doomed to extinction. And if the thought of the legal profession and the teaching of the law schools are to follow Holmes, "the greatest of our age in the domain of jurisprudence", then our profession and our schools will play a tragic part in the distintegration of American society.

But if, on the other hand, "all men are created equal"; if "they are endowed by their Creator with certain inalienable rights" beyond the reach of any government; if all governments derive "their just powers from the consent of the governed"; if truth is something more than a counting of ballots or bullets; if ideas are worth more than bowels; if the sanctity of human life is always to be respected; if the essence of law is not mere force, but reason based upon man's moral nature:—if these things are true, as the Founders of our Republic solemnly declared, and as the philosophers of the natural law believe them to be true, then totalitarianism has no rational defense against the American philosophy of law; there was a point to World War II; and democracy will survive. And if the schools and leaders of the legal profession follow the philosphy of the natural law, rather than the philosophy of force, then they will play a glorious part in the preservation and betterment of our society.

The philosophy of the natural law is the *"philosophia perennis"*, as old as the thought of civilized man. It has been shaped by the noblest thoughts of some of the best minds in history, Sophocles, Plato, Aristotle; Cicero, Tertullian, Justinian; Jerome, Ambrose, Augustine, Albertus Magnus, Aquinas, Vittoria, Suarez, Bellarmine; Bracton, Langton, Coke, Blackstone, Edmund Burke; James Wilson, Marshall, Chase, Storey, Cooley, Kent and a host of others have contributed to its development. It is the American philosophy in the sense that, for the first time in history, a great people incorporated it expressly into the written charter of their government.

The philosophy of the natural law is not specifically Catholic, or Protestant, or Jewish. It is the philosophy which is logically antecedent to the theology of every religion. It is the philosophy of the pagan—in the

SCHOLASTIC—JURISPRUDENCE

classical sense of the word pagan, namely, one who worships Almighty God albeit without the benefit of supernatural revelation.

This philosophy maintains that there is in fact an *objective moral order* within the range of human intelligence, to which human societies are bound in conscience to conform, and upon which the peace and happiness of personal, national and international life depend. The mandatory aspect of the objective moral order we call the natural law. In virtue of the natural law, fundamentally equal human beings are endowed by their Creator with certain natural rights and obligations, which are *inalienable* precisely because they are God-given. They are antecedent, therefore, both in logic and in nature, to the formation of civil society. They are not granted by the beneficence of the state; wherefore the tyranny of a state cannot destroy them.

Charles S. Rhyne, The Magna Carta Memorial Ceremonies: Runnymede, 43 American Bar Association Journal pp. 904-905 (1957); reprinted by permission of the author and the American Bar Association Journal.

We meet at Runnymede representing the legal profession of two great nations to commemorate one of legal history's most momentous events, the sealing of the Magna Carta in 1215.

Much of the language of Magna Carta seems curious to us today and alien to the twentieth century. But some of its words still move and inspire us. Men still rely upon the Great Charter's solemn promise that "to no one will we sell, to no one will we refuse or delay, right or justice" and that powerful provision that no freeman is to be proceeded against except by "the law of the land". These words are revered and cherished by the people of the United States as well as by the people of the British Commonwealth. For both of us they are the taproot of our way of life. Thus, the Constitution of the United States assures every citizen that the Government cannot deprive him of his life, liberty, or property except by "due process of law". Our Supreme Court has declared that the words "due process of law" are equivalent to the words "law of the land" in the Magna Carta.

As Lord Evershed has emphasized, Magna Carta has been more important in the broad sweep of history for its implications than for its specific provisions. When King John sealed Magna Carta he assented to a principle which is basic to the constitution of every state in which men are free—the principle that the law, and not the state, is supreme, that every man has natural rights even as against the King. The struggle to establish the rule of law did not begin at Runnymede, nor was it ended here. Tyranny did not disappear with the sealing of the Magna Carta; indeed it has not disappeared yet. But Runnymede was a turning point; it established a precedent which the English people were never to forget and which tyrants were to forget at their peril. "Magna Carta," Lord Coke was to declare in the seventeenth century, "is such a fellow that he will have no sovereign."

* * * * *

Mere mention of Magna Carta stirs the Anglo-American pulse like a battle cry against oppression and tyranny. From generation to generation its pledges of liberties and rights, constantly repeated, have been a powerful force in the formation of national character. From it, more than from any other single source, we draw our shared tradition of fundamental and inalienable rights and liberties common to all men. Those thousands of American lawyers who have contributed to this memorial did so in the realization that every American citizen would be less than he is but for the privileges of Magna Carta.

The world today is at a crucial point in the struggle between freedom and tyranny. On the one side are those who stand in the tradition of Magna Carta and defend the right of men to be free. On the other side stand the forces of darkness, who would deny freedom and exalt the state. This monument dramatizes the fundamental difference between our system of government, with its recognition of individual rights, and the Communist system, which denies such rights. This is the basic difference between Communism and the free world: we hold to the principle of individual human freedom under the rule of law as the inherent right of every man, while Communism rejects that concept and would destroy it.

Wherever Communism prevails, the very existence of freedom under law is aggressively denied. All life, all government, all law, and whatever justice there may be, is subordinated to the concept of a supreme state, vested with all power, to which every individual owes complete obedience, and against which no person may lay a demand or raise a defense based on any asserted right not granted by the all-powerful State.

There are men today who profess to see no great difference between Communist and anti-Communist regimes. They do not perceive what this monument represents and what Communism stands for. That difference is measured by the phrase: Freedom under law.

What do we mean by freedom under law? We mean a great deal more, surely, than mere obedience to written laws. We mean acknowledgement of the fact that there are moral limitations on civil power. We mean that human beings have rights, *as human beings,* which are superior to what may be thought to be the rights of the state or of society. This is the truth which all men of good will must some day see. It is the truth exemplified in the Magna Carta and in the American Declaration of Independence and Bill of Rights. This is the truth to which we must cling, the truth we must never permit to become trite with dull repetition, the truth we must proclaim and proclaim again and again until it echoes and re-echoes not only in that half of the world which is free, but also in that half of the world which is enslaved. This is the truth which is the crux of our heritage of freedom, which has made mighty nations of both Britain and America, the truth which is at once the sword and the shield of the Free World in its battle against the alien tyranny of Communism.

Freedom can be won only in struggle; and once won, no matter how ably recorded in writing for posterity, it can never be assured to any new generation not willing to fight for it. When freedom becomes ingrained in the civilization of a people, when they understand it, cherish it, and guard it, when their institutions bespeak it and their daily lives are guided by it, when they love it more than life and covet it not merely for themselves but for each other, then only is it truly theirs.

Mere love of country will not suffice without understanding devotion to its true ideals. Compromise between what we know is good and what we know is wholly evil can produce no good. Each generation that would pass on to its children the heritage of freedom must be honestly and intelligently ready to live or to die for human liberty. It must count no personal ambition, no private gain, no popular cause or national slogans for a single instant more important than the freedom of man.

We honor here an idea; not the idea of a man, but the idea of a people, and an idea *for* all people; the idea of a permanent law of the land preserving and safeguarding the fundamental rights and liberties of every individual.

We Americans thank God and England for the origin and development of that body of law and those principles of government which were the foundation and have been the inspiration of America's legal system and of the great basic guaranties of individual liberty and self-determination which underlie our constitutional structure.

Lord Evershed, Master of the Rolls, The Magna Carta Memorial Ceremonies: Runnymede, 43 Ameri-

can Bar Association Journal p. 902-903 (1957); reprinted by permission of the author and the American Bar Association Journal.

You, Mr. Smythe Gambrell, recalled the terms of King James' first charter to the Virginian colonists 350 years ago. I am proud that as Master of the Rolls I have been able to send for exhibition to Jamestown, by consent of Her Majesty, the confirmation of Magna Carta by King Edward I in 1297, which came to the Public Record Office by gift of Her late Majesty Queen Victoria. It was in fact that confirmation which was first inscribed upon the Statute Roll of England.

The principles enshrined in Magna Carta were regarded as their birthright by the American colonists. These same principles, and in many cases the terms of the articles themselves, exercised a profound effect upon the constitutions of the states of the Union and also upon the Federal Constitution itself, notably the Fifth and Fourteenth Amendments. In the Revolution which cut—at the time—the political cord that tied the colonists to the United Kingdom, the colonists relied upon and asserted the rights which they so inherited, under the law, in common with Englishmen. What they repudiated was the power of the Parliament and Government of the United Kingdom to override those rights. So is it that the Great Charter, the progenitor and exemplar of later constitutional documents, justifies the conception that government involves a trust; and justifies also the view inherent in the Constitution of the United States that limitations may be placed not only upon the executive but also upon the legislative power. It has been said that the crowning achievement of the Supreme Court of the United States, that great Court, "independent of party, independent of power, independent of popularity", whose prestige is something won, not merely conferred, may be in having given—with the assistance, let us not forget, of the Bar—continuity of life and expression to the high ideals of the founders of the Union.

But still, for all of us, English and American alike, the true, the almost sacred value of the Great Charter lies not in the terms of its diverse sixty-three articles but in its implications. As Lord Bryce said on a somewhat similar occasion, its influence has been far deeper than that of a single constitutional document.

* * * * *

Now here at Runnymede has been raised a monument to our common heritage of the rule of law and to the proposition that:

We must be free who speak the tongue
That Shakespeare spake; the faith and morals hold
That Milton held.

For, as I suggest, the two characteristics of our English law which have given to it perseverance and a title to fame, and even supremacy, are, first, that being essentially practical, it is part of our way of life itself; and, second, that it recognizes and reflects, in some degree at least, the moral law as well.

2. Private Law

a. *The Family*

Brendan F. Brown, *The Natural Law, the Marriage Bond, and Divorce,* 24 Fordham Law Review pp. 83-87, 92-94 (1955); reprinted by permission of the Fordham Law Review.

I

THE NATURAL LAW DICTATES MONOGAMY

Natural law is that objective, eternal and immutable hierarchy of moral values, which are sources of obligation with regard to man because they have been so ordained by the Creator of nature. This Law conforms to the essence of human nature which He has created. It is that aspect of the eternal law which directs the actions of men.[39] Although this law is divine in the sense that it does not depend on human will, nevertheless, it is distinguishable from divine positive law, which has been communicated directly from God to man through revelation, for natural law is discoverable by reason alone.[40] Natural law has been promulgated in the intellect. At least as regards its more fundamental principles it is knowable proximately through the conscience.[41]

The most basic ideal of this law, namely, that every man must live in accordance with his rational nature, so that he will do good and avoid evil, is self-evident to all. No reasoning is required to reach a knowledge of this ideal.[42] But other parts of the natural law are not perceivable with an equal degree of facility. Varying gradations and types of reasoning are necessary to ascertain the sub-norms of that law.[43] Some of these are discoverable by an immediately derived deduction, which is almost obvious, such as the requirement of *some* form of marriage or contractual agreement before a man and a woman can lawfully have sexual relations. But other sub-norms are ascertainable only after observation, study, and experience, both individual and sociological. Examples are the secondary goal of marriage, and the precise means for the just and adequate effectuation of the primary and secondary purposes of marriage.[44]

The necessity of some kind of marriage, either polygamous or monogamous, dissoluble or indissoluble, is obviously deducible from the basic ideal of the natural law, since without propagation and the rearing of children the human race would become extinct.[45] This ideal demands some form of abiding union between man and woman, even if it be only for a limited period. All men realize that there must be some fixed, definite, and settled arrangement, which will enable man and woman not only to procreate, but also to protect the offspring until they are capable of looking after themselves. It is self-evident that marriage differs from the mating of animals, to the extent that will and reason are distinguishable from blind instinct.[46] No demonstration is needed to show that marriage must uphold the unique dignity of human personality.

The study of cultural anthropology reveals the historical fact that practically all peoples have attached an inherently sacred and religious character to marriage, which they have expressed by special and symbolic rites of a public and solemn kind. These rites became part of their traditions, customs, and laws, which recognized that marriage is not of human, but of divine, origin, in which man does not create life, but only cooperates with Divinity in its transmission.[47]

Man is obliged in his choice of institutions to select only those which are in agreement with the natural law. This is particularly true of marriage since it is one of the most important, affecting, as it does, the spiritual and temporal welfare of the whole human race by determining the status of the family which is the foundation of society.[48] According to the natural law, there is an obligation to adopt that form of marriage which will best achieve not only the almost self-evident objective of satisfying the urge toward propagation, and care for the physical needs of children, and their moral and educational training, but also the secondary purpose, namely, the mutual assistance of the spouses, physical, mental and spiritual, and the allaying of concupiscence.[49]

But the *precise* form of marriage which is commanded by the natural law is not immediately apparent and known to all, for it does not pertain directly to the primary inclination of that law. The prescribed type of marriage is not a primarily derived deduction from the basic ideal of the natural law, as are the prescriptions of the Decalogue, for example.[50] This explains why there is more agreement that murder is against the natural law than there is that divorce is morally wrong.

The characteristics of unity and indissolubility in regard to marriage are secondary conclusions from the natural law, like the right of a worker to a living wage. They are not readily obvious because they relate to the secondary end of marriage, and to ways

SCHOLASTIC—JURISPRUDENCE

and means for best reaching the primary and secondary goals.[51] Reasoning and study are required to distinguish between perfect and imperfect means, and to recognize the secondary objective of marriage, but not in regard to the abnegation of means altogether. Lifelong monogamy is morally necessary for the attainment of man's ethical life, and the aims and functions of marriage.[52] This becomes clearer when it is contrasted with the only other type of marital relationship, namely, polygamy.

It is manifest that polyandry, (i.e.) that type of polygamy found in history in which one woman has two or more husbands at the same time, is the worst possible matrimonial arrangement, for if it does not entirely suppress the primary end of marriage, at best it places obstacles to its realization.[53] Polyandry contravenes the most important purpose of marriage, for it curtails generation, casts doubt on paternity, and interferes with the proper upbringing of children. It is not necessary to have recourse to the rational faculty of deduction and induction, to any considerable extent, to know that polyandry, like murder, may never be reconciled with any part of the natural law under any circumstances.[54]

Neither polygyny, (i.e.) that form of polygamy, where one man has more than one wife at the same time, nor successive polygamy, which results from the exercise of the right of re-marriage after divorce, when the former spouse, either husband or wife, is still alive, entirely suppresses or prevents the attainment of the primary end. But neither perfectly achieves the primary goal, and both are directly opposed to the secondary.[55] Both attain the secondary goal better than polyandry,[56] and, strictly speaking, may be reconciled with the essential demands of nature, in those exceptional situations which are sanctioned by supernatural law.[57] But only indestructible monogamy will adequately make possible the complete fulfillment of all the duties which have been imposed on husband and wife by the natural law. Hence, marriage under the natural law may be defined as a lawful, exclusive, and lifelong contract between a man and a woman by which is mutually given and accepted a right to those physical functions for the performance of acts which are mutually apt for the generation of children, resulting in a status primarily intended for the care and education of children, and secondarily for the mutual help of the spouses and the allaying of concupiscence.

* * * * *

IV
THE STATE HAS A LIMITED JURISDICTION OVER MARRIAGE

But while reason does not positively enable man to discover the supernatural law in regard to the marriage bond, it will make known that marriage is a social institution, so that civil authority, exercised by the State, has some jurisdiction over the natural bond in the case of the unbaptized.[58] The State is the only social authority available for the unbaptized. They are not under the authority of the Church. Hence, the competence of the State may extend not only to the material aspects of their marriage, such as property rights, but also into the field of morals and natural religion with certain limitations.[59] Natural law sets the minimum requirements of a juridical institution, authorizing Church and State to establish additional reasonable requirements in the light of specific social conditions of the time and place.

The State has the right and duty to create a juridical institution of marriage for the unbaptized, and also for the baptized insofar as the purely civil effects are concerned.[60] Manifestly the State has authority over the strictly temporal effects of marriage.[61] These are separable from the essence of marriage. Examples would be the determination of property rights, such as dower or testamentary succession.

The State is competent to establish reasonable diriment impediments, and to grant separation from bed and board, provided it follows the principles of the natural law.[62] But it has no power to dissolve the marriage bond, which is never civil, but either natural or supernatural.[63] Every positive law which purports to confer authority to grant divorce, except in cases coming within the operation of the supernatural law, is contrary to the natural law, and therefore lacks the element of juridicity. This does not mean, of course, that those who avail themselves of such laws are subjectively culpable, if they act in ignorance and good faith.

According to the natural law, all marriages are either valid or invalid from the beginning, on the objective plane, with no human discretion capable of declaring void what was once a valid marriage.[64] Natural law does not admit of a voidable contract of marriage, as does the law of New York, for example, which distinguishes between a voidable marriage, as where one of the parties is under the age of eighteen, and a void marriage, as where a brother and sister have endeavored to marry. In the first case, the voidable marriage may be declared void, or annulled, at the suit of the party under the proper age, in the discretion of the court. In the second instance, the marriage is void and the court must declare it a nullity.[65] The New York statutes have blurred the concept of annulment as understood by the natural law, by referring to the annulment of a voidable marriage which was originally valid, because annulment according to the natural law declares that a marriage never existed.[66] The concept of voidable marriage attaches, to an objectively valid marriage, a divesting condition subsequent in the form of a discretion, on a subjective and psychological level, and accordingly deviates from the standard of the natural law which knows only conditions precedent completely invalidating a marriage.[67]

These conditions precedent relate to deficiencies in the matter of the internal factors of will and reason, and the external element of form. The State is under an obligation to construct a juridical institution of marriage, applicable to the unbaptized, which will incorporate these conditions precedent into its positive law. Only in this way will the correct line be drawn between valid and void marriage, and consequently between the relevance of divorce or annulment in a particular case.

b. Contracts, Torts, Property, Criminal Law and Procedure, Corporations, Law Merchant, and Equity

Brendan F. Brown, *The Natural Law Basis of Juridical Institutions in the Anglo-American Legal System*, 4 *The Catholic University of American Law Review* pp. 82-86, 87, 88-89, 90-39 (1954), reprinted by permission of the Catholic University of America Law Review.

The Anglo-American Common law doctrine of consideration did conform to a philosophy of natural law, but only imperfectly and haltingly. The blight which had fallen on the Common law in virtue of that strange phenomenon of the fourteenth century, making the writ the starting point by severing it from the moral order, and enshrining the mechanical and analytical criterion of *stare decisis*, affected all its doctrines, including that of consideration. Yet, in the first decade of the seventeenth century, the Common law took the revolutionary step in *Slade's Case*,[68] of irrevocably treating the individuals involved in a transaction of sale as human beings with the capacity to will freely, and with the obligation to exercise their will so as to assume responsibility. Hence *Slade's Case* may be evaluated as a long delayed response to that dictate of the natural law which prescribes that the will-factor must be related to every just juridical arrangement. The volitional element was thus given recognition by the action of *Indebitatus Assumpsit*.

But evidence of the reason-factor, also required by the natural law, was limited by the Common law to proof of an exchange of something for something, in a materialistic sense, (i.e.) consideration. It was considered *reasonable* by the Common law to enforce only those agreements which were based upon consideration. This identification of reasonableness with consideration was due to raising the specific fact situation in *Slade's Case* to the level of an exclusive universal. But it was only accidental that this case involved a sale, and that it was the action of *Indebitatus Assumpsit*, which was broadened by the inclusion of the consensual element. Legal elements derived from the law of procedure, debt and sales obscured the necessary factor of reason in the Common law doctrine of consideration. But that doctrine was an imperfect attempt to follow a requirement of the natural law, although the Common law was not concerned with moral obligation as such.

Long before *Slade's Case*, however, while the Common law was still struggling to evolve a law of contracts from the delictual writs and actions, the ecclesiastical Chancellors had formulated a law of contracts based on the idea of *causa*, as elaborated by the Canon law. This idea, which the Roman law used to express the element of reason in willed obligations, had made possible the specific performance of certain types of agreements in Chancery. The moral test of enforcement of certain kinds of agreements was more reasonable than the principally mechanical criterion of consideration. In the beginning, Chancery followed the conception of Canonical *causa*, which was the reason which the law considered as sufficient for the creation of a legally enforceable agreement. But ultimately, the structure of the doctrine of consideration in Chancery became similar to that of the Common law, with lessening emphasis upon the philosophy of natural law. That philosophy was later vindicated, however, even though under the disguise of fiction and doubtful logic, by the numerous modifications of the Common law doctrine of consideration, and by arbitrarily expanding the sphere of contract law so as to make it include such equitable concepts as those of unilateral contract, promissory estoppel, and injurious reliance.

The law of torts is one of the most normative in the curriculum, highly dependent upon the natural law. But even the greatest authorities on tort law have tended to camouflage its moral content by the use of subtle terms and definitions in texts and case-books, indoctrinating students with a preference for the amoral approach. Thus they have emphasized the word "interests," in the presentation of the law of torts, as contrasted with "rights" and "equities". The word "interests", which the Sociological and Realist Schools of Jurisprudence introduced to supersede "rights" and "equities" as descriptive of the most fundamental substratum with which the legal order is concerned, stresses the psychological and materialistic claims and appetites of man regarded as a non-moral entity.

By their definition of a tort, even such eminent authorities as the late Dean Wigmore and Professor Kocourek have contributed willingly or unwillingly to the obscurity of the ethical premise upon which the law of torts rests. Thus Dean Wigmore has defined a tort as the violation of an irrecusable nexus, (i.e.) a relationship which may not be denied or rejected. But he does not disclose the reason, which causes the law to impose an inescapable duty. Nor does Professor Kocourek, who has described a tort in terms of physical science, as the breach of an unpolarized private duty, explain the cause of this obligation. These authorities do not correlate their definitions with the historical fact that the English Common law began, and continued for centuries, to enforce duties in the field of delict because they resulted from an objective natural law.

The development of the law of torts from the actions of trespass and trespass on the case assumes jurisprudential significance, when these actions are appraised as attempts to carry into effect the natural law. Originally, these two actions were merely crude and perhaps subconscious efforts to do this, doctrinally stressing the physical differences of certain fact-situations, (i.e.) whether the injury was direct or indirect. Although considerable time was required before it was recognized that the direct injury remedied by the action of trespass constituted a distinct category because of the will-factor involved, and that the indirect injury covered by the action of trespass on the case was actionable because it was the result of negligence, or conduct contrary to right reason, however unintentional, nevertheless, these two actions sought to redress moral wrongs under the natural law. The law of torts began to assume its modern appearance, however, only after the specific sources of human culpability, according to that law, namely will and reason, began to be related to trespass and trespass on the case.

The doctrine of "liability without fault" responds to a natural law critique in the determination of its proper limits. In the stage of all primitive law, including the English, there is legal liability without moral fault, because of the predominantly materialistic, impersonal and objective attitude of the positive law toward the damage or loss in question, which is connected only with the proximate cause. Slowly but surely, as the social need of integrating law and morals is realized and satisfied, by the infiltration of the persuasive norms of the natural law into the thought processes of judges and legislators, legal liability becomes identified more and more with the moral fault of the individual. This takes place in an era which is primarily concerned with private, as distinguished from public and social, rights and duties and continues until the sociological period is reached.

Some authorities on the law of torts contend that there was a return to the old formula of liability without fault, in this sociological period, as exemplified by the case of *Rylands v. Fletcher*,[69] and the enactment of such statutes as the Workmen's Compensation Acts. The impression may be left with the student that the law of torts lost its moral and natural law content when this occurred, if the change is presented as an adoption of the principle of a balancing of the social interest against that of the individual, and of the intrinsic absolute value of the social solidarity, apart from the members of society, as advocated by certain sociological jurists. It is important that this change be interpreted as an extension of the concept of justice from commutative to social, rather than as a shift from the doctrine of liability only if there is moral fault to that of liability without fault. Justification of the change must be sought in the balancing of equities or moral interests, and in the support of the social claim, given by the natural law. Thus in the instance of the Workmen's Compensation Acts, it is a question of social justice, not simply whether the rich employer should be compelled to pay, since he is the one best able to do so.

The standard of the reasonable man, which has enabled judges and law-makers to introduce into the law of torts numerous ethical principles, supplied a criterion which was objective, and in ultimate analysis, absolute and immutable. The reasonable man, so indispensable for the creation of tort law, affords an objective measure of moral and legal conduct, unlike the subjective tests, furnished by the individual conscience, which were advanced by certain post-Reformational theories of natural law. In this respect, the criterion of the reasonable man conforms to the idea of natural law, as understood by Stoic and Scholastic. Conformity may also be found in the absolute and immutable character of the test of the reasonable man, which is derived from intrinsic reasonableness, not from human will, or economic utility.

The development of tort law may be traced roughly in terms of the expanding application of the natural

SCHOLASTIC—JURISPRUDENCE

law which attaches moral culpability to unjustified interference with the morally free will, and to behavior contrary to that of a reasonable man. The emergence of such torts as duress, deceit and fraud evidenced the efforts of tort law to make actionable the overcoming of another's morally free will by force, or the hampering of its operation by the suppression or twisting of essential facts. As soon as the ethical consequences of motive were accepted by the legal order, a new series of torts arose, grounded on the mental factor of purpose, such as the tort of malicious prosecution.

* * * * *

The principles of property law, embodied in the decisions of the Chancellors, were logical extensions of the philosophy of St. Thomas Aquinas, as expressed in his SUMMA THEOLOGICA, wherein he upheld the right of private property and its just exercise on both utilitarian and idealistic grounds. Chancery supplemented the Common law of real property with numerous devices to provide greater recognition of the inalienable right of each individual in society to acquire, retain, and transfer a reasonable amount of property. Thus it allowed married women certain property rights in land, denied by the Common law at one time, because of the fiction of the unity of marriage and the amoral absorption of the personality of the wife into that unity, represented only by the husband. Sensitive to the natural law, Chancery corrected this situation by recognizing the ownership of land by married women when made equitable by the vesting of the legal estate in trustees.

* * * * *

The numerous restrictions which have been placed by law upon the exercise of the right of private property, beginning in the United States, the latter part of the nineteenth century, are compatible with the premise that scholastic philosophy does not ordain the preservation of any particular property *status quo*. These restrictions, exemplified by the growth of administrative law and the establishment of the great federal commissions, as well as by the limitations placed upon the individual in the matter of acquiring, using and disposing of property, may be scholastically interpreted as efforts by the legal order to compel the property owner to fulfill his moral obligations towards others in the societal relationship. These obligations are rooted in the natural law, which has always been alert to the sociological implications of private property. Any other justification of the socialization of private property, which has taken place within recent years, may conceivably open the door to theories, counseling the serious impairment, or even the destruction, of the right to such property.

A philosophy of natural law, through the media of Admiralty, Canon and Roman laws, produced the essential characteristics of the law of agency in England. Mariners, citizens of the world, and hence free to follow the dictates of natural law in the selection of juridical institutions, wrote the Rhodian Sea Law, the genesis of the law of Admiralty. The Rhodian Sea Law contained the rudiments of a law of agency, pertaining to both contracts and torts. This law was incorporated into the Digest, constituting part of the CORPUS JURIS CIVILIS of Justinian, the great legal monument of the sixth century, A.D. The example of the Canon law, which had borrowed the Roman concept of agency, and applied it to the conduct of the affairs of religious corporations, such as monasteries and convents, supplied experience for the construction of an English law of agency. It is true, of course, that, in England, the idea of representation was fitted into the feudal survival of status, found first in the relation of master and slave, and thereafter, in that of lord and vassal, lord and serf, and lastly, master and servant.

The Anglo-American criminal law rests upon an assumed moral order which may be historically demonstrated to be scholastic. It emerged as a distinct category of delict with the gradual recognition of offenses against the social interest. This moral order was, at first, clothed with customary law, later with judicial positive law, and finally with legislation, which defined various classes of crime and prescribed specific punishments. In its evolutionary quest for progressively greater effectuation of this moral order, the lode star of the English criminal law was social justice, transcending the concept of merely commutative justice, referable to the commission of certain offenses, which grossly exceeded the injustice of those wrongs, now known as civil, and hence called for social punishment.

But punishment does not make crime, nor does the extent of the punishment determine the gravity of the crime, although that may be the impression left with students of criminal law by the common definition of a felony, as an offense punishable by death or by imprisonment in the penitentiary, and of a misdemeanor as an act, calling for lesser punishment. It is the duty of the scholastic teacher to insist that these definitions reflect the position of the analytical, not the natural law, School of Jurisprudence, and that they conceal the true essence of crime.

* * * * *

The course on Constitutional law makes available a fertile field for the consideration of the scholastic conception of society, the state and government, and their relation to the legal order under the Constitution, intended as a bulwark against the invasion of the rights of the individual by the sovereign. The Constitution of the United States is neither objective natural law, nor a mere algebraic equation, describing an equilibrium of economic pressures and political compromises. But it is a manifestation of objective natural law in the same sense as were the *Magna Charta* and the American Declaration of Independence.

It was not until the time of Henry VIII, in the sixteenth century, and thereafter, that the philosophy of force, relative to the ascertainment of the legitimate limits of state action, was given currency in England. This philosophy was formally elaborated in the analytical or imperative theory of Hobbes. In English and American constitutional theory, this philosophy competed for acceptance with the older English conception of the nature and function of the state, which had been in accord with the state-limitation doctrine of scholastic philosophy.

Thus far the philosophy of force has prevailed in English constitutional theory. A Parliamentary Bill of Attainder may today be unjust, but never illegal. The test of the juridicity of a statute or enactment of Parliament is to be found in the will and physical power of the sovereign, not in the sphere of morals.

But the philosophy of an objective natural law has been accepted, for the most part, in American constitutional theory, as manifested by the doctrine of judicial supremacy. This doctrine upholds the opinions expressed in *Bonham's Case*[70] and *Calvin's Case*,[71] that an act of a legislature which is contrary to the natural law does not have the force of law, although it may have the appearance of such. As far back as the American Declaration of Independence, however, the philosophy of an objective natural law was obliged to compete with belief in the moral supremacy of the authority of the people, as expressed in their highest legislative assembly. That Declaration simultaneously asserted the natural law principle of self evident, inalienable rights, springing from an immutable, objective order of morality, and the subjective proposition that governments derive their just powers from the consent of the governed. For the scholastic jurist, the foundation of the natural law is not the will of a majority of the people at any particular time, although there is a reliable, but rebuttable, presumption that the will of the people, freely expressed, with a knowledge of the facts, is the voice of God.

A considerable analytical influence appears in most treatises on the law of Corporations. The view presented in these treatises is that a corporation is a fiction, and that only the State has the right to originate this fiction. The fiction theory of the corporation exalts the absolute sovereignty of the State and ignores the natural law right of association, which precedes the State. This theory may be invoked to justify the State's seizure of the corporation's property, as ownerless, should the State erase the fiction.

The fiction theory of the corporation is contradicted by the scholastic view which is that the corporation is a metaphysical entity, and that the State does not create the underlying moral personality, which is incorporated, as it were, by the natural law, but only gives it legal recognition, and determines, in a reasonable manner, the scope of its operation. The essence of a corporation results from the natural law right of association, and from the metaphysical and conceptual relation of the persons, who form the corporation, to the central entity.

It was the influence of natural law thinking, which corrected the original concepton of a mortgage, as an outright conveyance of the full ownership of land, to be forfeited upon failure to pay a sum of money at a future split second of time. The Court of Chancery, applying moral principles, obtained jurisdiction over the mortgage by preventing injustices arising from failure to pay the money at the specific time, caused by accident, mistake, *vis major*, or Act of God. The course of development of the device of the mortgage was determined by natural law, which communicated the idea that the true purpose of a mortgage was to provide security for a debt. The mortgaged property thus became simply collateral, or a means to an end. The mortgagee no longer owned the land, subject to a condition subsequent, but either held legal title to the property as a quasi-trustee, or had a lien on the land to the extent of the debt.

The Law Merchant is of special concern and interest for the natural law jurist, because he finds, therein, an historical vindication of the capacity of men, when freed from totemism and taboo, and from the inhibiting effect of provincial environments, to create just customary law inspired by natural law, for the authoritative settlement of disputes. The formation of legal categories, new even to the Roman law, resulting from the invention and the use of bills and notes and from the idea of negotiability, by merchants, who were cosmopolitans, evidenced the creative power of a notion like *bona fides* taken from the natural law. The Law Merchant supports the thesis that custom may have the force of law, as a means of social discipline, although it does not rest on the will of the political sovereign, but on objective standards of reason.

It is well known that the moral content in the subject of "Equity" and its historical natural law foundation have been progressively concealed for many years by some teachers and authors. Much evidence attests this fact. Thus the name of the subject was changed from "Equity Jurisprudence" to "Equity". Less and less attention was paid to the maxims, (i.e.) moral generalizations, reflecting the spirit of ethical idealism. Lords Nottingham, Hardwicke and Eldon were hailed as the greatest of the Chancellors, because they were chiefly responsible for the transference of moral principles into positive rule. Finally, within the past few years, some of the "prestige" law schools have abolished "Equity" as a separate course.

It is the duty of the scholastic jurist to resist this trend and make specific efforts to expose its Realist implications. If this is not done, the law student will be denied his educational birthright, which includes the knowledge that the equity administered in the English Court of Chancery was not emotion, not the changing moral conscience of the time and place, nor the caprice of the Chancellor, but rather that body of transcendental principles of right and wrong, existing in the metaphysical order, which may be identified as natural law.

* * * * *

Extrinsic or transcendental equity has provided ideals which have been transfused into the empty categories of "due process," equal protection of the laws, and the like, of the Federal Constitution, and made possible the development of American Constitutional law. It has produced norms for the interpretation of ambiguous statutes. It has been indispensable in all those fields, wherein justice is administered without law. It has been employed in effecting settlements by mediation and arbitration, and adjudicating issues in administrative tribunals. It is the only medium of international social control in the absence of developed juridical institutions in the world order.

Intrinsic equity, or the casuistic application of transcendental equity in the judicial, administrative, or legislative process, historically followed the employment of fictions as a means of modifying or abolishing old law, and creating new law. The equitable method produced new law, with no fictional changing of the facts, by reliance on certain principles, which dominated the choice of the major premise by the law-maker, because of their internal reasonableness. Intrinsic equity may be expelled from a legal system, for a while, but the history of both Roman and English law shows that when this happens, it becomes necessary eventually to construct a new court for the restoration of applied equity.

Rev. Francis E. Lucey, S.J. Liability without Fault and the Natural Law, 24 Tennessee Law Review pp. 960-962, (195); reprinted by permission of the author and the Tennessee Law Review.

Where unforeseeable and hence unavoidable harms come to others in the individual's exercise of morally lawful activities, Natural Law moralists do not require restitution or what we call damages. In such cases commutative justice is not violated and hence grounds for restitution are absent. In some cases of this kind there may be a duty in charity, but charity is not a basis in morals for the imposition of restitution. However, Natural Law moralists do hold that where society, for the good of all, in a court of law, requires an individual to recompense the one innocently harmed, the judgment debt must be paid. The civil law can convert what otherwise would be only a duty in charity into a legal duty. As we all know it has been doing so and is doing so in an increasing manner. And so the law may require us to notify proper authority or take other steps so that an injured party may be aided by society or by private persons. If the welfare of each or all is involved the law can, in a sense, make each of us his brother's helper and keeper. This is one form of what we call social justice. In short liability without fault is not foreign to nor incompatible with Natural Law doctrine.

For the purpose of philosophical analysis or explanation it may be helpful in this article to divide all liability without fault into two classes. In the first category fall those cases involving types of conduct which are purely or chiefly for the benefit of the actor himself. In general this would include cases where no sale of a product or service is contemplated. In the second category fall those cases where a sale of consumer goods or services is the intended object of the activity. In the first class *Rylands v. Fletcher*[72] would be in point. The second class would include such groups as producers, suppliers, manufacturers, employers, broadcasting companies and publishers. These two classes cover important and critical areas of the field and any justification applicable to them should apply to remaining areas.

Is there any justifiable grounds for attaching liability without fault to the first class? In this class there is no cost that may be passed on and distributed among others. There are two justifiable possibilities here, as the writer sees it. Society may absolutely prohibit the conduct or activity. On the other hand, if after weighing the tangible or intangible benefits of the activity to the members of society, and the incidence of unforeseeable harms, society deems the activity permissible, the writer sees no reason why it cannot condition its exercise on the payment of damages for unforeseeable harms to unforeseeable plaintiffs. It seems to the writer, at least, that the imposition of the burden falls within the scope of social justice. It would seem to follow from the fact that as society has the right and duty to protect the rights of each and all, where the good of each and all is at stake, society also has a right to allocate the burdens in a way that is socially fair. Between two innocent parties a choice must be made. In such a situation where no fault is involved, the social value of the allocation of the burden should be a determining factor.

The second class of cases seem to me less difficult. The justification given for the first class would apply here also. But in addition, there seems to be another ground for justification. Are not damages for unforeseeable harms just as much an element in the cost of the goods or services provided as is the cost of providing safeguards against foreseeable harms, insurance, and capital depreciation? Is it not an element in the cost of the benefit conferred? If it may be considered as an element in the cost of the benefit conferred, the justification for the increased cost to the consumer or recipient of services would not be that the consumer can pay, but that *it is fair to make him pay* the necessary increase in cost. If society, on the grounds of social justice, has upped the expense of production for the producer or supplier, then it would seem, to the writer at least, that the increase should be an element in the price charged. As between producer or supplier and the consumer or recipient of services, the relationship would be more akin to one involving commutative justice. Whether or not we may justly consider the damages for unforeseeable harms an element of cost, it still remains reasonable that for the purposes of social justice, society may put the burden on one of the innocent parties instead of the other as it does in workman's compensation acts.

1 Keenan, Joseph B., address read at the annual convention of the American Bar Association, Atlantic City, N. J., October 29, 1946.

2 Phleger, Herman, "Nuernberg—A Fair Trial?" April 1946, 177 Atlantic Monthly, No. 4, 60 at p. 63. Gentili, De jure belli, Book I, c. I in The Classics of International Law, 1933, Carnegie Endowment for International Peace. Suarez, De legibus, Book II, c. xxii, sec. 3, (2 Law, the State and the International Community, 1939, Scott, James B.) at p. 69.

3 Sophocles, Antigone, Lines 450-59, (2 Law, the State and the International Community, 1939, Scott, James B.), at p. 68. Justinian, Institutes, I, ii, 11 (Ibid.) at p. 68, Nuernberg Transcript, January 17, 1946, 2868, M. Francois de Menthon, Chief Prosecutor, for the Republic of France.

4 St. Thomas Aquinas, Summa Theologica, II-II, qu. 80.

5 Nuernberg Transcript, July 26, 1946, 14,447, Shawcross, Sir Hartley, Chief Prosecutor, for Great Britain and Northern Ireland. Pollock, Sir Frederick, "The Sources of International Law," 1902, 2 Columbia Law Review at pp. 511, 512.

6 Tokyo Transcript, June 4, 1946, 406-410, Keenan, Joseph B.

7 Tokyo Transcript, April 29, 1946, 126, Mr. Ichiro Kyose, for the Defense.

8 Gratian, Decretum, Part I, Dist. v. para. 1 (2 Law, the State and the International Community, 1939, Scott, James B.), at p. 68.

9 For definitions of law incorporating this point of view, see Holland, op. cit. supra note 7, at 19-20, 32-36. Cf. I Bl. Comm. Intro.

10 Gierke, op. cit. supra note 46, 75-76, 85; Gierke, Althusius 272, and n. 22, where Aquinas, Occam, Baldus, Alliacus, Cusanus, Gerson, and others are cited; ibid. 275-76 and notes 30 and 31. The doctrine was stated that when the Emperor acted against the law he did not act as emperor ("non facit ut imperator"). Bartolus and his followers attributed greater authority to statutes than to judicial judgments, but held none the less that even statutes contrary to natural law were void.
* * *

11 6 Cranch 87, 135, 139 (U. S. 1810), 3 L. ed. 162.

12 See Chase, J. in Calder v. Bull, 3 Dall. 386, 388 (U. S. 1798, 1 L. ed 648. See also the language of Chase, C. J. many years later in the License Tax Cases, 5 Wall. 462, 469 (U. S. 1866), 18 L. ed. 499.

[13] See Loan Association v. Topeka, 20 Wall. 655, 662 (U. S. 1874, 22 L. ed. 455.

[14] See Butcher's Union Co. v. Crescent City Co., 111 U. S. 746, 756, 28 L. ed. 585, 591, 4 Sup. Ct. 652, 660 (1884); see also his dissent in the Slaughter House Cases, 16 Wall. 36, 105 (U. S. 1873), 2 L. ed. 394.

[15] Comments on the Philosophy of Mr. Justice Brewer are found in Haines, Revival of Natural Law Concepts, 201, (1930).

[16] Adair v. United States, 208 U. S. 161, 174, 52 L. ed. 436, 442, 28 Sup. Ct. 277, 280, (1908).

[17] Coppage v. Kansas, 236 U. S. 1, 59 L. ed. 441, 35 Sup. Ct. 240, (1915).

[18] Fuller, C. J. stated that the Fourteenth Amendment required that the powers of the states be "exerted within the limits of those fundamental principles of liberty and justice which lie at the base of all our civil and political institutions. Undoubtedly the Amendment forbids any arbitrary deprivation of life, liberty or property, and secures equal protection to all under like circumstances in the enjoyment of their rights." In re Kemmler, 136 U. S. 436, 448, 34 L. ed. 519, 524, 10 Sup. Ct. 930, 934 (1890). Thus was the transition from natural rights to the rights of due process effected.° ° °

[19] W. B. Yeats, "The Second Coming".

[20] Bryce, Studies in History and Jurisprudence, Volume II, page 589.

[21] Holmes, The Common Law (1881) 41, 44.

[22] Shriner, Justice Oliver Wendell Holmes: His Book Notices and Uncollected Papers and Letters (1936) 187.

[23] American Banana Co. v. United Fruit Co., 213 U. S. 347, 356, 29 Sup. Ct. 511, 512, 53 L. ed. 826, 827 (1909); quoted in Shriner, Justice Oliver Wendell Holmes, etc. (1936) 157.

[24] Holmes, The Path of the Law, Collected Legal Papers (1920) 167.

[25] Holmes, The Natural Law, Collected Legal Papers (1920) 313.

[26] Holmes, The Path of the Law, Collected Legal Papers (1920) 169.

[27] Holmes, The Path of the Law, Collected Legal Papers (1920) 175.

[28] Holmes, The Natural Law, Collected Legal Papers (1920) 310.

[29] 2 Holmes-Pollock Letters (1941) 252.

30 2 Holmes-Pollock Letters (1941) 22.

31 2 Holmes-Pollock Letters (1941) 36.

32 2 Holmes-Pollock Letters (1941) 39.

33 Shriner, Justice Oliver Wendell Holmes, etc. (1936) 175.

34 Shriner, Justice Oliver Wendell Holmes, etc. (1936) 185.

35 Shriner, Justice Oliver Wendell Holmes, etc. (1936) 202.

36 Frankfurter, The Early Writings of O. W. Holmes, Jr. (1931) 44 Harv L. Rev. 717, 723.

37 Pound, Judge Holmes' Contributions to the Science of Law (1921) 34 Harv. L. Rev. 449.

38 Cardozo, Mr. Justice Holmes (1931) 44 Harv. L. Rev. 682, 684.

39 Aquinas, St. Thomas, Summa Theologica, Treatise on Law, Q. 90-97 inclusive, Review by Brown, Brendan F. (1952) 1 De Paul Law Review 312-318.

40 Ibid.

41 Sheedy, Very Rev. Charles E., C.S.C., Letter, October 10, 1954, to Brendan F. Brown.

42 Connell, Very Rev. Francis J., C.SS.R., Outlines of Moral Theology (1953) 30.

43 Sheedy, Very Rev. Charles E., Materials for Legal Ethics 10 (1950) edited notes of Right Reverend Monsignor William J. Doheny, C.S.C., J.U.D., judge of the Roman Rota.

44 Joyce, Rev. George Hayward, S.J., M.A. (Oxon.), Christian Marriage (1948) 6-8.

45 See Petrovits, Rev. Joseph J. C., The New Church Law on Matrimony (1921). On page 1, he writes: "*Marriage in General.* The word matrimony is a compound derived from the two Latin words, namely, *matris munium* meaning the *office of the mother.* The burdens inherent in gestation, the pain accompanying parturition, and the numerous anxieties subsequent to child birth, being indicative of the most intimate relationship between mother and child, are generally adduced as the reason why the word mother in preference to the word father has been embodied in the name of this sacrament."

46 Pope Pius XI, Encyclical Letter, *Christian Marriage (Casti Connubii),* December 31, 1930, Translation published by the National Catholic Welfare Conference, Washington, D. C. (1931), 5. This Encyclical elaborates and emphasizes certain points in the Encyclical *Arcanum* of Pope Leo XIII, published fifty years previously, namely, on February 10, 1880. The chief purpose of *Casti Connubii* was to reaffirm the basic thought of *Arcanum* in the light of conditions which adversely affected the society of the family at the beginning of the

SCHOLASTIC—JURISPRUDENCE 151

thirties. See also Pope Pius XII, *Address to the Italian Catholic Union of Midwives*, October 29, 1951, *Translation included* in *Moral Questions affecting Married Life*, Discussion Outline by Rev. Edgar Schmiedeler, O.S.B., Ph.D., Director, N.C.W.C. Family Life Bureau, National Catholic Welfare Conference, 18 parag. 49.

[47] Pope Pius XI, Encyclical Letter, Christian Marriage, op. cit. supra note 8 at p. 28; Ayrinhac, Very Rev. Henry A., S.S., D.D., D.C.L., Marriage Legislation in the New Code of Canon Law (revised and enlarged by Rev. P. J. Lydon, D.D.) (1952) 234; and Bouscaren, Rev. Timothy Lincoln, S.J., LLB., S.T.D. and Ellis, Rev. Adam C., S.J., M.A., J.C.D., Canon Law, A Text and Commentary (2nd ed. 1953) 453, 454.

[48] Pope Pius XI, Encyclical Letter, Christian Marriage, op. cit. supra note 46 at p. 3, and Pope Pius XII, Address to the National Congress of the "Family Front" and the Association of Large Families, November 26, 1951, Translation included in Moral Questions affecting Married Life, supra note 46 at p. 24, parag. 1.

[49] Pope Pius XI, Encyclical Letter, Christian Marriage, op. cit. supra note 46 at p. 21; Canon 1013 parag. 1 of the Code of Canon Law.

[50] It should be noted that there is another nomenclature to express the varying gradations of the natural law. Thus sometimes the basic or most universal principle is called the primary precept, while an immediate deduction is referred to as a secondary precept rather than as a primary deduction. According to this nomenclature, a more remote conclusion would be called a tertiary precept of the natural law rather than a secondary conclusion. See Connell, Very Rev. Francis J., C.SS.R., Outlines of Moral Theology (1953) 29, 30; Sheedy, Very Rev. Charles E., C.S.C., The Christian Virtues (1951) 33-35, and Letter, October 10, 1954, to Brendan F. Brown.

The marriage bond is the *formal* cause of marriage; man and woman, the *material* cause; the wills of the parties, the *proximate efficient* cause, the natural appetites, the *remote efficient* cause; and the procreation and education of children and the natural aid of spouses are the *final* cause: See Ryan, Rev. Louis A., O.P., Philosophy of Marriage and the Family, in Marriage and Family Relationships (edited by Dr. Alphonse H. Clemens) (1950) 42 at pp. 49-54.

[51] Pope Pius XI, Encyclical Letter, Christian Marriage, op. cit. supra note 46 at pp. 36, 37; Canon 1013, parag. 2.

[52] Davis, Rev. Henry, S.J., 4 Moral and Pastoral Theology

(1936) 49: "Marriage is the lawful contract between man and woman by which is given and accepted the exclusive and perpetual right to those mutual bodily functions which are naturally apt to generate offspring." Ryan, Rev. Louis A., O.P., Philosophy of Marriage and the Family in Marriage and Family Relationships, op. cit. supra, note 50 at p. 54: "The matrimonial bond is indissoluble because it is ordained to a function which is not arbitrary or temporary, but durable and permanent." Vermeersch, Rev. A., S.J., A Catechism arranged according to the Encyclical "Casti Connubii" of Pope Pius XI (trans. by Timothy Lincoln Bouscaren, S.J.), under title What is Marriage (1950) 7 and following. See Canon 1110.

[53] Individual Ethics and Social Ethics, a Digest of Lectures for Students of Fordham University, 59, 60.

[54] Bouscaren, Rev. Timothy Lincoln, S.J., and Ellis, Rev. Adam C., S.J., op. cit. supra note 47 at p. 457.

[55] Individual Ethics and Social Ethics, a Digest of Lectures for Students of Fordham University, 60, 61.

[56] Joyce, op. cit. supra note 44 at pp. 18-21.

[57] Idem, pp. 26-31.

[58] Bouscaren and Ellis, op. cit. supra note 47 at pp. 529-530: The State may temporarily restrain the exercise of the right of marriage when one is afflicted with a contagious disease, provided it puts "itself in agreement with the competent authority, which, in the case of baptized persons, is the Church." But the laws "enacted in several states requiring health certification as a condition for the issuance of the marriage license" fail to "recognize this limitation upon the power of the state."

[59] Idem at pp. 462-463: All persons have the right to marry from the natural law, but not the duty. This right precedes the State. But the State may reasonably regulate the exercise of this right or even suspend it for a while for a private or a common good. The State may establish reasonable impediments with regard to the marriages of citizens who are not baptized, but not such as will in effect alienate the right itself. Of course the State has no authority over the sacramental bond resulting from marriages between two baptized persons. See Madden, Joseph W., Handbook of the Law of Persons and Domestic Relations (1931) 38, 39. See Brown, Brendan F., The Canon and Civil Law of the Family in Marriage and Family Relationship (edited by Dr. Alphonse H. Clemens) (1950) 57 at p. 64. Some of the American states have created impediments which are not in accord with the natural law, such as the

miscegenation statutes prohibiting marriages between whites and negroes, or between whites and Indians or Orientals. But observance of these laws is dictated by prudence grounded on the natural law in the interest of the public peace since they violate the natural law by limiting a person's right to marry, rather than by commanding "a person to do something prohibited by the natural law." See Brown, Brendan F., Foreword xvi, in Del Vecchio, Giorgio, Philosophy of Law (trans. by Rev. Dr. Thomas Owen Martin), 1953.

[60] Vermeersch, op cit. supra note 52 at p. 12.

[61] Canon 1016.

[62] Pope Pius XI, Encyclical Letter, Christian Marriage, op. cit. supra note 46 at p. 32; Sheedy, op. cit supra note 43 at p. 63 citing Canons 1016, 1038, 1960 and 1961.

[63] Sheedy, op. cit. supra note 43 at p. 78.

[64] Pope Pius XI, Encyclical Letter, Christian Marriage, op. cit. supra note 46 at p. 31; Ayrinhac, op. cit. supra note 47 at pp. 352-354, 372.

[65] See Domestic Relations Law of New York, section 7; Civil Practice Act, sections 1132-1133, 1136, 1139, 1141; and Rules of Civil Practice, Section 275 and following; Domestic Relations Law, section 5.

[66] See Gellhorn, assisted by Hyman and Asch, Children and Families in the Courts of New York City, 270-271, 273, (1954).

[67] Voidability implies dissolubility. See Brown, op. cit. supra note 59 at p. 65; Sheedy, op. cit. supra note 43 at p. 77.

[68] 4 Coke 92b, 76 Eng. Rep. 1074 (1602).

[69] L. R. 3 H. L. 330 (1868).

[70] 8 Coke 113b, 77 Eng. Rep. 646 (1610).

[71] 7 Coke 1a, 77 Eng. Rep. 377 (1610).

[72] L. R. 3 H. L. 330 (1868).

E. The Dynamism of Scholastic Natural Law

A. E. Papale, *Judicial Enforcement of Desegregation: Its Problems and Limitations*, 52 *Northwestern University Law Review* p. 301 (1957; reprinted by permission of the author and the Northwestern University Law Review.

Implicit in judicial recognition and enforcement of rights and duties is the rational basis of the principles from which they spring. These principles are constantly appraised and re-appraised to determine whether they are just or unjust, reasonable or unreasonable, sound or unsound, wise or unwise, fair or unfair, right or wrong, good or bad. Those that are just, reasonable, sound, wise, fair, right or good usually endure. Those that are unjust, unreasonable, unsound, unwise, unfair, wrong or bad usually are short-lived or are at least more prone to change. It is of the very nature of the judicial process to evaluate principles in the light of experience and in the light of what is considered the best thinking in regard to them at the particular time.[1] For these reasons it is well to begin with a discussion of the rational basis of the principle from which the right to live in society free from laws requiring segregation on account of race or color is derived.

Brendan F. Brown, A Scholastic Critique of Case Law, 12 Ohio State Law Journal pp 19-22 (1951); reprinted by permission of the Ohio State Law Journal.

It now remains for me briefly to review the materials selected for today's symposium from the point of view of Scholastic Jurisprudence. Significant concepts for this type of Jurisprudence in the cases under discussion are the nature and end of man, law, society, state, constitution, the judicial and legislative processes, and property. Scholastic philosophy postulates that man is a creature, endowed with the distinguishing characteristics of will and reason, with moral freedom of choice between good and evil, under a duty to conform to the dictates of his conscience, informed by reason and experience, perceiving to some extent an externally existent body of ideals, embodied in a higher law.

Man, by nature and by the higher law, ordained by the first Cause of the Universe as a measure of conduct because of the essence of man, ought to form society national and international. This society is at first under the direct discipline of the higher law, which precedes positive law, as a means of social control, and which later ought to receive recognition by the juridical institutions of civil authority, adding physical sanction to an already existing ethical coercion. Scholastic Jurisprudence does not postulate the necessity of any specific type of juridical institution, as long as it achieves higher law justice among men in society. It does not prescribe any precise form of state structure, or administration, or constitution, or system of law for the protection of rights. In the establishment and operation of societal organizations, it does not forbid the interplay of materialistic and utilitarian considerations, as long as they remain within the inhibition of the higher or natural law, which restrains men from evil, but otherwise encourages them to feel free to experiment with their economic, social, political and juridical systems.

The chief excellence of Scholastic Jurisprudence, when compared with other varieties of juristic thinking, is the greater comprehensiveness of its approach in appraising the justice and efficiency of a particular legal order and the decisions made by its agencies in specific situations of fact. It does not mistake the part for the whole. It stresses the elements of reason and experience, the transcendental and the actual, the analytical and the essential, the permanent, idealistic and the transitory, utilitarian. Its ingredients have been selected from universal wisdom, unlimited by historical period, geographic location, or specific civilization, and united by the overall conception that man differs in kind and dignity from all the rest of creation.

But how are these generalities related to the cases which we are considering today? First of all, it may be noted that the judges which decided these cases were divided as to the relative values to be assigned to such interests as freedom of religious belief, property, state-survival, and the acquisition of the use of land by treaty. Each judge passed judgment on each of these interests by weighing it in a scale of his own choice to ascertain its value, for the purpose of deciding whether or not he could clothe the interest with a legal right so as to be protected by the legal order. Each judge accordingly used his own mechanism to measure the relative preciousness of the interests involved, in relation to some fixed standard, whether or not he was conscious of this fact. But in none of the cases was there an effort to justify the standard, or the measuring device. This means that the judicial process, as it functions even in courts of last resort, requires fixed starting points of ethical values, but is not concerned, generally speaking, with the questions of their source, degree of permanence, or reason for their acceptance by the judge.

As a scholastic jurist, I favor the majority opinions in the *Parrish* and *Barnette* cases, and the dissenting opinions in the *Shoshone* and *Oleff* cases. I view each factual situation as a minor premise in a syllogism. My major premise is inductively reached by reason and experience. Reason includes not only my own conscience, but the objective conscience of others, competent in the rational and social sciences. It would be a moral reason, not the reason of the material scientist or mathematician, since I would be dealing with moral phenomena, i.e. right and wrong human conduct. Experience would include a consideration of all relevant historical and social data thus far available. Psychologically, I would be both an introvert and an extrovert. My ultimate aim would be justice. In my effort to reach it, I would not be diverted by such formal devices or techniques, as the mechanical postulation of a presumption for or against the constitutionality of the statute in question. If the legislative process had produced a statute which conformed in a reasonable degree with the ideals of the higher law, according every human being certain inalienable rights, I should declare it constitutional. But otherwise I should declare it unconstitutional, without regard to whether it was a limitation upon property rights or civil liberties, since all rights are human rights, even property rights.

I believe that man is entitled in consequence of the higher law, independent of social contracts, or states, or constitutions, or human wills, to the use and enjoyment of property, sufficient to maintain himself and his family in a manner reasonably appropriate to his person and environmental needs. I would regard the social justice of property relationships, as well as the "mine" and "thine" conception as it affects individuals only.

I subject the rule of *stare decisis* to the test of reason, justice, and experience. As a scholastic jurist, I would not have relied as heavily upon legal precedent as was done in the *Oleff* and *Adkins* cases, for this rule may be used to preserve the value of an interest, which deserves a contemporary devaluation for the sake of justice, i.e. the doing of right, and the avoidance of wrong. I would not attach to a statute or a constitution supreme value, which would be reserved for the higher law. The will of the people, as participants in the democratic process, is a proper source of law, but the resulting imperative law obtains its ultimate vitality from the validity of the pre-existent moral qualities which the legislator has discovered by recourse to the objective natural law, so that in one sense, ultimately the basis of all positive law is discovered; otherwise there could be no inalienable rights, since these presuppose an immutable restraint upon human will, imposed by external, universal will.

As a scholastic jurist, I approve the minority opinion in the *Shoshone* case, because the majority opinion's conception of international law and the rights and duties of nations did not coincide with the notions of the founders of the science of International Law, such as Vitoria, a scholastic, mentioned with approval by Dr. Cohen. Precise land boundaries were mentioned in the Shoshone Treaty. It was obvious that the Indians were using the land in question for the sustenance of life. They had a moral right to the land in virtue of the higher law. In a primitive society, morals are the sole medium of social control. But international society was and remains primitive, for fixed methods of ascertaining legal rights have not yet been created by positive law. Hence under international law, as understood by a scholastic jurist, the Shoshone Indians had title to their land apart from any treaty. This title existed even though there was no recognition of it by the United States in the Shoshone Treaty.

I regret that time will not permit a psychoanalysis of the judges who handed down our cases. The scholastic jurist gives adequate attention to the factor of the mental processes of judges, and of their emotions. Much benefit may be derived from an understanding of the hidden factors of inheritance and environment in the judicial process. But these are subordinate in importance to the judicial factor of the moral freedom of will of the judge in reaching a decision, determined by the choice of ethical values and their relation to the law in action.

Brendan F. Brown, Natural Law: Dynamic Basis of Law and Morals in the Twentieth Century, 31 Tulane Law Review pp. 491-492, 493-494, 495-500, 502 (1957); reprinted by permission of the Tulane Law Review.

I

NATURAL LAW IS THE COMMON BASIS OF LAW AND MORALS

All law originates in the eternal law, that timeless divine plan of government which directs all actions to their appointed ends. This plan is a rule and measure of the whole community of the universe. All other types of law are only limited participations in this plan.[2]

Natural law is a sharing in the eternal law by man.[3]

It is that aspect of the eternal law which directs the behavior of human beings, as distinguished from other forms of creation. The eternal law is the cause of the natural law and exists in man as an imprint on his reason.

The natural law proceeds ultimately from the intellect and will of a Divine Lawgiver, but is made known immediately through reason.[4] It is a source of obligation because it conforms to the essence of rational human nature, and because it has been ordained by the Creator of nature. It is truly law for it is an ordinance for the common good of man and has been promulgated in his intellect by Him Who has the care of all things.

The natural law creates the norm of an objective morality. The *mores* of various peoples in different periods of history do not constitute this norm. But customs will have the force of law if they are an expression of the natural law.[5]

Certain obligations to God, to others, and to subhuman creation result from the natural law. The principal mutual obligations of human beings toward each other are justice and charity.[6] Both moralists and jurists are concerned with the achievement of justice. But the formal object of each is different. The moralist is concerned with the *virtue* of justice, one of the cardinal moral virtues, while the jurist is interested in justice not so much as a virtue or interior disposition, but as a factor of the social order.[7] The jurist focuses his attention upon order and exterior peace, which result from the proper social attitude of the citizen. The jurist looks at the object of the virtue of justice insofar as it commands the attitudes of individuals and even imposes itself upon them by social force and constraint if necessary.[8] But in final analysis, both law and morals are founded on the natural law.[9]

Human law and morals are connected, but distinct, sciences. Their formal objects are different. Morals is the higher of the two norms. Both have the common power to direct and the same subject matter of human conduct. Both seek the same mutual establishment of friendship and orderly relationships among men in society. Both preserve the moral order. They share the same ends.[10]

But law and morals have different sanctions. The sanction of law is primarily exterior; that of ethics, interior.[11] The authority to compel pertains only to law. Law and morals differ, therefore, in the means which they use for the realization of their common ends, and in the respective functions which they perform.[12]

The boundary line between law and morals continually shifts. This is so because enforcement is the distinctive quality of positive law in relation to morals.[13] The lawmaker transforms morals into law whenever public opinion deems this necessary for the well being of the community.

✧ ✧ ✧ ✧ ✧

II

THE NATURAL LAW PROVIDES A DYNAMIC, AS WELL AS A STATIC, BASIS FOR LAW AND MORALS

In the first place, the natural law is immutable in some respects. Its starting point, namely, do good and avoid evil, is an indemonstrable moral fact, falling within the apprehension of the practical aspect of reason, which is principally concerned with ends and means.[14] This starting point corresponds to the proposition that the same thing may not be affirmed and denied at the same time, which comes within the apprehension of the speculative phase of reason.[15] This phase has mainly to do with cause and effect.

The obvious deductions which flow from the self evident, intuitively perceived, starting point are absolute and immutable.[16] Examples of such conclusions are the moral precepts of the Decalogue, social relationships, self preservation, care of offspring, and the

SCHOLASTIC—JURISPRUDENCE

like. These conclusions follow directly from the essential attributes of human nature. Like the properties of a triangle, these conclusions do not change since the essence of human nature does not vary.[17]

The natural law is discoverable by reason alone. It is knowable proximately through the conscience, at least with regard to its more fundamental norms. Its most basic precept, namely, that man must live in accordance with his rational nature so as to do good and avoid evil, is manifest to all.[18] Indeed, it is impossible for its primary principles to remain unknown. But varying gradations and methods of reasoning are required to reach the sub-norms of the natural law. Obvious conclusions can easily be deduced by reason. But the remote conclusions are reached only after considerable study and reasoning.[19]

Man's knowledge of the primary immutable principles may not change, but the natural law may vary both subjectively and objectively with regard to its inferior norms, namely, those detailed proximate conclusions which are drawn from the first category of moral values by deduction, and manifestly from all succeeding categories.[20] In a subjective sense, human knowledge of the remote conclusions of the natural law may increase from time to time. Knowledge within the field of morals grows analogous to that which takes place in regard to other sciences.[21] This knowledge evolves by deductive reasoning. This proceeds from major premises which change as a result of induction based on observation and experience.

New moral judgments with regard to right and wrong may emerge. Thus experience has demonstrated that excessive inbreeding interferes with the primary end of marriage, i.e., the healthy propagation of the human race. This led to a recognition of the evil of marriage within particular degrees of kinship, and resulted in the establishment of the forbidden degrees.[22]

In an objective sense, the remote conclusions of the

natural law may be enlarged and contracted. Thus a change in historical and sociological facts may enlarge the natural law by introducing new secondary or inferior conclusions. These would be for the benefit of human life.[23] Again, changing facts may contract the remote principles of the natural law by subtraction, so that a norm which the natural law prescribes in one period may not be commanded at another.[24]

* * * * *

Thus the natural law provides a dynamic, as well as a static, basis for the moral order by sanctioning evolution within the fixed orbit of the natural tendencies and inclinations of rational human nature. It preserves a delicate and essential balance between the eternal and the temporal good. It distinguishes in kind between the enduring and permanent facts which are beyond the scope of sense, and those which exist in the world of changeable things. It allows for differences of fact-content which exist in various principles. It promotes moral growth toward the morally unchangeable.

In the second place, human law bears an immutable and absolute relationship to the natural law. The juridicity of human law arises from this relationship. Human law has the character of law to the extent that it is derived from the natural law, which is the first rule of reason.[25] The force of a law depends on its justice, which in turn is determined by its reasonableness.[26]

An enactment or a case-decision which is contrary to the natural law may have the appearance of law, but it is not law. Unjust human law does not bind in conscience.[27] But prudence may dictate obedience to certain types of unjust law to avoid public disturbance, as where an unjust law takes away a person's right to a thing forbidden, but does not oblige him to do something intrinsically wrong.[28]

The absolute relationship between natural law and human law requires that human lawmakers reinforce the primary and necessary conclusions of the natural law by means of state-law. If this were not done, some members of the community might not be aware of these conclusions, or else might not be inclined to obey.[29] Besides human reason must devise certain discretionary rules left undetermined by the natural law.[30]

The norms of state-law fall within two spheres, one static and the other dynamic. The fundamental static norms of such law are deduced from an analysis of the nature of man and all his essential relationships. These norms are recognized by all civilized societies to some extent, depending upon their particular level of intelligence.[31] But the dynamic or inferior norms of human positive law express values which are in the nature of temporary generalizations of morals pertaining to the culture of the particular time or place. These dynamic norms are ascertained inductively by way of determinations of the superior principles of the natural law. They are syntheses produced by induction from a variety of facts.[32]

Analysis, synthesis, deduction and induction are rooted in reason. It is reason which deduces the moral norm which forbids theft and confers the right of property from the total expression of the moral law, do good and avoid evil. It is also reason which determines by induction the particular type of property-law which should guarantee the right of property in a particular legal system.[33] This induction will proceed consciously or subconsciously from the consideration of many factors, such as the customs and psychology of the people, their political, economic, and industrial environment, the nature and quantity of the land, and the like.

According to the natural law, human law must be changed whenever it becomes obsolete.[34] Human skill may find more effective methods for implementing the primary principles of the natural law. Lawmakers may discover more successful ways of effectuating the mandate of those principles of positive law which stem from the necessary premises of the natural law.[35]

Again, they may make better determinations, or choices, in the discretionary area of human law. The natural law performs the vital function of providing a critical norm for every positive legal order.[36]

Hence, facts and conclusions therefrom may and do change law and morals except insofar as these latter are founded on the first principles of the natural law. But the inferior norms underlying law and morals do not result entirely from facts which are known by the senses. Moral norms, as such, may not be extracted entirely from sense-facts which belong to a different order than value-judgments.

III

Alternative Solutions of the Problem of Law and Morals Have Failed

Roscoe Pound has written that "next to the nature of law, nineteenth century jurists were troubled about the relation of law and morals."[37] They were disturbed because the Analytical School of Austin which had detached law from morals was proving socially inadequate to solve the contemporary problems of justice. It was becoming increasingly clear that morals, in some sense, must be restored to positive law, if the legal order was to function effectively.[38]

The moral norm of abstract natural rights, based on a state of nature or a social compact, had proven sociologically unsatisfactory. Indeed the Analytical School had gained wide acceptance because it had offset the extreme subjectivism and the excessive tendency toward deduction of the Law of Nature School, which ignored or slighted experience.[39] The Historical School of Maine had reintroduced the factor of experience by its investigations into cultural anthropology and ancient legal systems. But it could not offer the legisator any principle except that of history which would constitute an assured basis of creative law making for the future.[40] In the nineteenth century, legal philosophers had so forgotten the Thomistic doctrine of the natural law as to cause Jhering, one of the founders of the Sociological School of Jurisprudence, to exclaim that he probably would not have written his entire book, if he had been aware of the doctrines of Thomas Aquinas.[41]

The chief problem of Jurisprudence in the twentieth century has been that of how best to restore morals to law in a social context. Various solutions have been proposed by way of juristic doctrine, but none equals that of the Thomistic natural law. No other doctrine offers a greater promise of a legal order which will have the stability of human nature, yet will have sufficient flexibility to meet the ever changing needs of society. No other doctrine can guarantee so well that the legal order will be truly rational with regard to the content of its legal precepts, and its jural postulates. All other doctrines have a blind spot in their failure to locate the source of the authority which communicates stability to law and morals. Stability as well as flexibility is required for a legal order. But the concept of stability has no final significance, if all ideals admit of change, however slow that change may be.

The Sociological School of Jurisprudence attempted a solution with considerable functional success. Jhering had done much in Europe, beginning in the latter part of the nineteenth century, to build law on a morality of interests.[42] These were antecedent to legal rights. Roscoe Pound protested against the abuse of liberty of contract, in the first decade of the twentieth century, and initiated the School of Sociological Jurisprudence in this country.[43] The dominant thought of this School is that the individual, public, and social interests behind the law are to be classified and appraised in terms of the moral ideals of the particular epoch. Legal stability and change are to be reconciled by an analysis from case to case of these interests. Legal rights are merely recognitions of certain interests. Social interests are the most important. They should prevail over the interests of the individual in case of an irreconcilable conflict.[44] Society is regarded as an entity, a faceless mass.

The Sociological School thus far in the twentieth century has made many valuable legislative and judicial contributions to law. Scholastic Jurists, following the Thomistic concept of natural law, have approved these contributions. This is so because the present postulates of American civilization happen to conform, generally speaking, to the morals of the objective natural law.

But the doctrinal weakness of the theory of interests is the absence of any truly permanent norm for determining which interest ought to be legally recognized in the name of social utility.[45] The chief cleavage of thought between the Sociological School and the Scholastic is that the former admits no absolute limit in regard to the satisfaction of social interests. The latter relies on the authority of the restraining first principles of the natural law to guarantee human rights forever.[46]

Secondly, Kelsen has argued that his system of jurisprudence is dynamic and that of natural law is static.[47] Kelsen maintains that the idea of justice is irrational. He excluded it from the field of jurisprudence. His pure theory of law and his hierarchy of juridical norms proceeding from a neo-Kantian logicism is disguised positivism.[48] By conforming law to the ultimate, arbitrary norm of the majority, Kelsen enables law to grow, but not in any particular direction. His pure theory of law can obtain any legal content which force chooses to put into it.[49]

According to natural law, social progress does not consist in mere change. Kelsen's fear "that natural law derives the legal order from certain meaningful notions of justice,"[50] which "hold the legal order within a frame and freeze it into rigidity,"[51] sprang from a misunderstanding of the Thomistic concept. Lon Fuller has correctly refuted Kelsen with regard to this attack upon natural law by stating that it is a "plain fact that ideas are capable of growth."[52]

Both Kelsen and Thomas Acquinas divided law into its static and its dynamic parts. Both agreed that a norm which is directly deduced from a basic norm, without any induction, belongs to a static order.[53] But they fundamentally disagreed in that Kelsen made both types of law mere postulates, while St. Thomas rooted them in reason. Kelsen maintained that the practical reason, which perceives means and ends, as distinguished from the pure reason, which recognizes causes and effects, was actually not reason, but only sentiment. St. Thomas held, however, that each is an essential function of the single faculty of human reason.[54] This is so even though the practical reason deals at times with contingent matters of detail wherein there cannot be absolute rectitude in moral matters.

Thirdly, Holmes, though a man of deep seated moral beliefs, professed a legal philosophy which was static rather than dynamic. It did not provide an ideal toward which the actual might move.[55] General acceptance was his immediate measure of morality, and force the final criterion. His concept of law and morals lacked a vital principle of purposeful growth.[56] Paradoxically, many of his decisions were not consistent with his formal philosophy.

Holmes attacked natural law jurisprudence without distinguishing between the numerous legal philosophies which have adopted that name. Apparently he was not aware of the tremendous dynamism of the Thomistic notion of the natural law.[57] Doctrinally, he would not face up to the compelling fact of the permanence and intrinsic dignity of human personality. In one sense, he unknowingly proved the existence of natural law by absolutely denying that it had universal validity in regard to time and place.[58]

IV

THERE IS POTENTIAL DANGER THAT THE ANGLO-AMERICAN COMMON LAW MAY BE UNDERMINED UNWITTINGLY BY ITS DETACHMENT FROM THE NATURAL LAW

The philosophy of an objective natural law has been accepted for the most part in American constitutional theory. This acceptance is manifested, for example, by the doctrine of judicial supremacy.[59] Historical evidence shows that the Constitution of the United States with its Bill of Rights, like Magna Carta, was an implementation of the natural law. According to the doctrine of judicial supremacy, an act of a legislature which is contrary to the Constitution does not have the force of law, although it may have the appearance of such. Since the Constitution is natural law which has been clothed with positive law, the doctrine of judicial supremacy upholds the legal philosophy of *Bonham's Case*[60] and *Calvin's Case*,[61] decided in the first part of the seventeenth century by Sir Edward Coke. These cases held in effect that legislation which violates the natural law is not law, and hence is not entitled to obedience.

❖ ❖ ❖ ❖ ❖

In conclusion, it is the duty of the legal profession to understand that the separation of morals from the natural law is the first step toward detachment of the Common Law from its ancient moorings. Recognition of this duty is perhaps one of the reasons for the increasing interest in natural law by the American Bar Association as expressed by numerous recent articles on that subject in its Journal. The revival of natural law jurisprudence will succeed to the extent of the knowledge of that particular type of natural law doctrine which this article details.

SCHOLASTIC—JURISPRUDENCE

[1] As stated recently, "Courts have a creative job to do when they find that a rule has lost touch with reality and should be abandoned or reformulated to meet new conditions and new moral values." Traynor, Law and Social Change in a Democratic Society, in Dedicatory Proceeding, University of Illinois 78 (1956). See also Fairman, The Attack on the Segregation Cases, 70 Harv. L. Rev. 83, 91 (1956); Kenealy, Segregation—A Challenge to the Legal Profession, 3 Catholic Lawyer 37, 40 (1957); Chief Justice John E. Hickman of the Supreme Court of Texas, quoted in The Dallas Times Herald, August 29, 1956, §B. p. 1, col. 1-3.

[2] St. Thomas Aquinas, Summa Theologica I-II, 93.3 in corp. (1st American ed., 3 vols., tr. by Fathers of English Dominican Province, 1947), hereinafter cited as "St. Thomas."

[3] St. Thomas I-II, 91.2 in corp.

[4] Id., 94.2 in corp.

[5] Id., 97.3 in corp.

[6] Sheedy, Materials for Legal Ethics 12 (1950).

[7] Id. at 14.

[8] Id. at 15.

[9] Wu, Fountain of Justice: A Study in the Natural Law 253 (1955).

[10] Id. at 249.

[11] Id. at 253.

[12] Ibid.

[13] Rommen, The Nautral Law: A Study in Legal and Social History and Philosophy 212 (1947).

[14] Id., 94.2 in corp.

[15] Ibid.

[16] Id., 94.6 in corp.

[17] Id., 94.4 in corp.

[18] Id., 94.2 in corp.

[19] Id., 94.4 in corp., 94.6 in corp.

[20] Id., 97.1 in corp., Replies Obj. 1, 2 and 3.

[21] 1 Cronin, The Science of Ethics 388 (1939).

[22] Ibid.

[23] St. Thomas I-II, 94.5 in corp.

[24] Ibid.

[25] Id., 95.2 in corp.

[26] Ibid.

[27] Id., 96.4 in corp.

[28] Brown, Foreword XVI, in Del Vecchio, Philosophy of Law (Martin tr. 1953).

[29] St. Thomas I-II, 95.1 in corp.

[30] Id., 95.2.

[31] Rommen, The Natural Law: A Study in Legal and Social History and Philosophy 68, 69 (1947); James, Some Historical Aspects of St. Thomas' Treatment of the Natural Law, 24 Proceedings of the American Catholic Philosophical Ass'n 149-151 (1950).

[32] St. Thomas I-II, 95.2 in corp.

[33] See Pope Pius XI, Reconstructing the Social Order, published in Five Great Encyclicals 136-139 (1947).

[34] St. Thomas I-II, 97.2 in corp.

[35] Ibid.

[36] Id., 95.2 in corp.

[37] Pound, Fifty Years of Jurisprudence, 51 Harv. L. Rev. 777, 811 (1938).

[38] Ibid.

[39] Pound, Outlines of Lectures on Jurisprudence 10-13 (5th ed. 1943).

[40] Id. at 12.

[41] Jhering, Der Zweck im Recht (Law as a Means to an End) 161 note (1886).

[42] Pound, The Scope and Purpose of Sociological Jurisprudence, 25 Harv. L. Rev. 140-147 (1911); see also Pound, op. cit. supra note 39, at 96.

[43] See Pound, Freedom of Contract, 18 Yale L.J. 454-487 (1909).

[44] Pound, op. cit. supra note 39 at 113.

[45] See Julius Stone, A Critique of Pound's Theory of Justice, 20 Iowa L. Rev. 531, 544-550 (1935).

[46] Ibid.

[47] Kelsen, Die Philosophischen Grundlagen der Naturrechtslehre und des Rechtspositivismus 19 (1928), cited by Fuller, The Law in Quest of Itself 113-114 (1940); De Sloovere, Natural Law and Current Sociological Jurisprudence, 17 Proceedings of the American Catholic Philosophical Ass'n 137 (1941).

[48] Wu, op. cit. supra note 9, at 42.

[49] De Sloovere, supra note 47, at 137, 138.

[50] Id., at 137.

[51] Ibid.

[52] Fuller, op. cit. supra note 47, at 113, 114.

[53] See Mulligan, Hans Kelsen and the Problem of Relativisim in the Law, 22 Proceedings of the American Catholic Philosophical Ass'n 185 (1947).

[54] Ibid.

[55] Wu, op. cit. supra note 9, at 165.

[56] Id. at 210.

[57] Id. at 142, 143.
[58] Id., jacket.
[59] Brown, The Natural Law Basis of Juridical Institutions in the Anglo-American Legal System, 4 Catholic U.L. Rev. 91 (1954).
[60] 8 Coke 113b, 77 Eng. Rep. 646 (K.B. 1610).
[61] 7 Coke 1a, 77 Eng. Rep. 377 (K.B. 1610).

PART III. NON-SCHOLASTIC NATURAL LAW JURISPRUDENCE

Non-Scholastic Jurisprudence differs from the Scholastic type in excluding either the factor of a rationally knowable divine Law-Giver, as the Source of the natural law, or else in addition, the element of some immutable, absolute and universally valid ideal, however small. Ilustrative of the former is the neo-Kantian absolutism, transcendental idealism of Giorgio Del Vecchio. As examples of the latter may be cited the ethical rationalism, relative idealism of Morris R. Cohen, and the sociological rationalism, quasi-idealism of Jerome Hall and Lon L. Fuller.

A. *Neo-Kantian-Absolutism, Transcendental Idealism*

Professor Del Vecchio accepts the existence of a divine Law-Giver who has given man a *supernatural* law by revelation, but he does not relate this Law-Giver to the *natural* law. He derives the element of immutability for his juridical idealism from the essence of man rather than from the divine will and reason. This element is not subject to erosion by rational induction or deduction, or by factual sociological variables.

Giorgio Del Vecchio, Philosophy of Law (translated by Thomas Owen Martin) pp. 493-494 (1953); reprinted by permission of the author and The Catholic University of America Press.

Law has, therefore, its principle in the essence or nature of man, just as Morals does, but it differentiates itself therefrom by reason of the *objectivity of the relationship* in which it places and consecrates the absolute character of the person. This character acquires properly a *juridical* meaning and value insofar as it is taken as a criterion and cardinal point of the relationships of common life. In this sense, the maxim is then laid down that *every man can, simply because he is such, demand that he shall not be treated by anyone as if he were only a means or an element of the sensible world.* He can demand that by each one be respected, as he himself is bound to respect it, the imperative. Do not extend your will to the point of imposing it upon others, do not try to subject to yourself one who, of his nature, is subject only to himself.

According to this principle, or idea-limit, of a right which belongs universally to a person, is placed within him, is inalienable and never exhaustible in any fact (the *right to solitude*), must be measured and established all social relationships, so that each of them, whatever may be their particular species, will carry in itself the impress of that Law, will presuppose and imply the recognition of that supreme *virtuality* of the autonomous being, representing an exercise or a function thereof.

It is, indeed, necessary to clarify the point that the person of whom we are speaking is not the empirical individual, but the *universality of the subject,* that universality which becomes concrete in various individual species or figures and represents their common essence and eternal value. To save this value even the sacrifice of the contingent individuality may be necessary. Without this fundamental distinction it is not possible to come to a true theory of Law, as it is impossible to come to a true Morals.

It is useful, further, to consider, in order to avoid errors which are frequent in this matter, that the human person forms itself and develops in virtue of a process which consists in a series of interferences or of relations between subject and subject. Even such relations or interferences must, however, be evaluated *sub specie juris*. To prescind from what, in a subject's mode of existence, represents the effect of the activity of others, annulling the obligations and exigencies which can derive therefrom, would mean to contravene the fundamental principle of justice, which requires precisely the objective evaluation of the person in intersubjective relationships.

Brendan F. Brown, Introduction to Del Vecchio's Philosophy of Law, pp. xiii-xvii (1953) reprinted by permission of The Catholic University of America Press.

But Professor Del Vecchio does not reach the scholasticism of François Gény, born in 1861, perhaps the greatest scholastic jurist of his time, adapting, as he did, the basic principles of Thomas Aquinas to the complex facts of a social order which had changed considerably since the thirteenth century. Professor Del Vecchio has related human reason to religion, by concluding that "the requirements proper to religion," namely, "the supreme aspirations of the soul remain, in truth, absolutely free and complete, without any contradiction with reason,"[1] *i.e.*, hope "in an order beyond this world" and human reason are not in conflict. But it is of the essence of scholasticism, neo-scholasticism, Thomism, or that which the author has called the "Catholic School" of natural law, that such hope may be supported by convictions based on reason apart from revelation. For him, knowledge of a Supreme Being and of His general attributes, as the Creator of Nature, cannot result from human reason alone, but can be achieved only by faith in an immediate divine or supernatural revelation.[2] But the scholastic legal philosopher, as dialectically distinct from the scholastic theologian, believes that theodicy is an integral part of philosophy and clearly distinguishable from theology. The former is a systematic body of knowledge about an eternal and immutable Being, endowed with intellect and will, obtained by human reason alone, while the latter relies on doctrines directly communicated by God to man and accepted on faith.

His distinction between *simple* and *rational* theologism[3] has only a limited relevance for the scholastic. The first locates the authority of law in the will of some transcendental being without any regard whatsoever to reason. The second, regarded as "a noteworthy attempt to connect the requirements of faith with those of speculative thought,"[4] holds that "justice is not what the divinity commands at will, but what it must command because of its content of truth, so that the divine will could not be otherwise."[5] Thus it would relate to the historic dispute among philosopher-theologians, during the middle ages, as to whether the authority of natural law was derived chiefly from the divine will or intellect. But none of these philosopher-theologians ever advocated *simple* theologism, since the unity of God precluded the detachment of His intellect wholly from His will. The dispute was, therefore, one of emphasis since all the disputants believed in *rational* theologism in some degree.

There can be no criterion of truth distinct from and superior to the Divinity[6] which might be created artificially by human reason, because God is the source of all truth and reason. Nothing can be imposed upon the Divinity itself,[7] for His own infinite wisdom forbids Him ever to act unreasonably. All this seems to be admitted by the author, yet his statement that the Divinity is by definition superior to reason is not scholastic. On the contrary, God *is* reason, *i.e.*, in the sense that He is Supreme Intelligence. There can be no conflict between His intelligence and right human reason.

Like scholasticism, the neo-Kantian School, which Professor Del Vecchio espouses, postulates *a priori* the existence of an eternal, immutable and transcendental natural law which imposes certain duties upon all men. But the two Schools disagree as to the nature of this natural law. For the scholastic, this law has its source in the intelligence and will of a conscious First Cause, Who has formulated a master plan for the guidance of the universe. That portion of the plan which applies to mankind is known as natural law. It is perceivable, at least in its more general contours, by human reason, through its own natural ability. This natural law is in accord with the essence of human nature. Conscience dictates obedience to this law.

Professor Del Vecchio has divided "nature" into physical nature and metaphysical nature. In the latter sense, "nature" is "a living principle, which moves the mass of the universe and expresses itself in the infinite and progressive variety of its development. It is that substance which we have already recognized as free from the narrow limits of causality. It is the inner reason which gives a norm to all things and assigns them their proper functions and purposes."[8] The "metaphysical" nature is a division of nature rather than the cause of physical nature, so that the premise would seem to imply a pantheistic notion of God, as contrasted with the theistic concept of scholasticism. Hence, it follows that natural law springs from this metaphysical "nature," as it exists in man, in the form of pure reason. It also explains why man has an absolute value.

This explanation does not satisfy the scholastic jurist, however, who maintains that the authority of the natural law is ultimately derived from the Creator and not from the essence of man, who is only a creature. The nature of man is the proximate norm, however, of natural law. The inestimable value of human nature is not absolute in itself, but only because it has been so created by God. Human reason is not identical with divine reason, but is only its effect or reflection. The value of man must be regarded as infinitely less than that of God. There is no merit in concealing the

NON-SCHOLASTIC—JURISPRUDENCE 177

existence of the final authority, for upholding the intrinsically precious character of the human personality.

Reference has been made above to the God of Theodicy, not the God of Theology. If a legal philosopher is an agnostic, then the integrity of his own conscience will stop him from advocacy of going beyond human reason as his starting point. If he is a pantheist, it will not be necessary to go beyond such reason, for in last analysis it is not distinguishable from the reason of a pantheistic god. But if a legal philosopher accepts the divine positive law, as a consequence of belief in a particular revelation, he will conclude that moral principles, like those embodied in the Mosaic Decalogue, rest upon the authority of reason, in a twofold sense, namely, first, in so far as reason accepts the aptness and necessity of such principles in themselves and as emanating from God, known by reason, and secondly, in the sense that reason accedes to the reasonableness of a divine positive law, and of the obligation to obey it because of the credentials which it presents.

Natural law is not the product, therefore, of human nature, but was made for man by the eternal Lawgiver, because man was created as he was. This objective natural law is not drawn from pure reason, but rather right reason perceives it. The human spirit achieves this perception, producing positive law, but not the natural law itself. The scholastic regards positive law as the implementation of the natural law from which it derives its "juridicity."

If what has the appearance and form of law is contrary to the natural law, according to the scholastic view, it is not law, for it is not just, although one may obey it at times, as a matter of prudence, for the sake of social and political peace, if it contravenes only an *affirmative* precept of the natural law, but not if the positive law commands a person to do something *prohibited* by the natural law, *i.e.*, to violate a *negative* precept of the natural law. Professor Del Vecchio also insists upon justice in law, but it is his opinion that the two may be separated since there is a purely formal concept of law, existing in all systems of positive law, regardless of their degree of "positiveness," whether the law is just or unjust, good or evil. He writes that "the logical form does not tell us at all what is just or what is unjust. It tells us only *what is the meaning of any affirmation of just or unjust*. It is in conclusion, the hallmark of juridicity."[9] Positive law is thus not subordinated to natural law, in one sense, for they are both species of a larger genus, namely, law.

But there are many points of similarity between the legal philosophy of Professor Del Vecchio and scholasticism. Thus, generally speaking, both agree that positive law may be defined as *"the objective coordination of possible actions between several subjects, according to an ethical principle which determines them, excluding the impediments thereto."*[10] They agree that law is *a priori* and relates to a category of values, and that law and morals have their own proper sanctions, *i.e.*, coercibility is a sanction proper to law and remorse to morals. Finally they agree that the most basic elements in the positive legal order are rights and duties, not merely interests, and that some of these rights are inalienable and exist prior to the State, and even to custom.

Similarities between these two Schools predominate when they are applied to the field of the social sciences, for example, to the consideration of society, the State, and the international community. Thus Professor Del Vecchio accepts the Aristotelian notion of the natural fact of human society. He refutes the "contractual" theories of society and the State, as expressed by Hobbes and other writers who believed in a state of Nature. He has described with great insight the value and limitations of the "organic" concept of society, by showing that while several analogies between society and an organism are possible, nevertheless society may not be separated from the individuals who constitute it. He specifically demonstrates that society is not based merely on a biological foundation, although he later shows that the blood bond was the most cohesive force in the period of primitive social organization. He has clearly distinguished society from the State and from the Nation.

According to Kant, the State was only "a combination of men under juridical laws."[11] But Professor Del Vecchio has taken a broader view of the State by defining it as *"the subject of the will which lays down a juridical arrangement."*[12] He agrees with Kant that the State must limit its own action where it would injure the value of human personality. But he does go further than Kant by insisting that the State must promote the good of society by assuming "an ever increasing number of functions."[13] The State must be a "State of law," not merely in the Kantian sense "that it must set the law *as sole purpose* for itself,"[14] but rather "in the sense that the State must operate *on the basis of Law and in the form of Law.*"[15]

---

[1] Philosophy of Law 426.
[2] Ibid.
[3] Philosophy of Law 424-426.
[4] Idem 426.
[5] Idem 425.
[6] Philosophy of Law 426.
[7] Ibid.
[8] Philosophy of Law 434.
[9] Idem 251.
[10] Idem 270.
[11] Bodenheimer, Edgar, Jurisprudence 173, first edition, 1940. See Philosophy of Law 380.
[12] Philosophy of Law 359.
[13] Idem 382.
[14] Idem 383.
[15] Ibid.

B. Ethical Rationalism, Relative Idealism

Some non-Scholastic natural law jurists, like Morris R. Cohen, are relative idealists. Their ideals are logical constants, but there is no immutable element, like the essence of man, in which law has its vital principle. But man is bound to make efforts to formulate a rational ideal which at a given time and place will best "govern the facts of the law."

Morris R. Cohen, Reason and Nature, Preface xiii, pp. 408-409, 412, 419, (1953); reprinted by per- of the Free Press at Glencoe, Illinois.

However, I should also call myself an idealist, not in the perverse modern sense which applies that term to nominalists like Berkeley who reject real ideas, but in the Platonic sense according to which ideas, ideals, or abstract universals are the conditions of real existence, and not mere fictions of the human mind.

* * * * *

The essence of all doctrines of natural law is the appeal from positive law to justice, from the law that is to the law which ought to be;[1] and unless we are ready to assert that the concept of a law that ought to be is for some reason an inadmissible one, the roots of natural law remain untouched. Now, it is true that the issue has seldom been so sharply put, for to do so is to espouse an amount of dualism between the *is* and the *ought* which is shocking to the philosophically respectable. The respectable dread to admit the existence of real conflicts in our intellectual household; they would rather conceal them by ambiguous terms such as *natural* or *normal*. This is most apparent in the most philistine of all philosophic schools, the Stoic, whose tremendous influence in jurisprudence has brought about much intellectual confusion. There have not, of course, been wanting intellectual radicals who, in the interests of a strident monism have clearly and conscientiously attempted to eliminate the chasm between the *ought* and the *is*, either by denying the former, or by trying to reduce it to a species of the latter. Thrasymachus's definition of justice as the interest of the stronger finds its modern form in the definition of right as the will of the sovereign, of the people, or of the dominant group. But few of these radical positivists have had the courage of their convictions; they smuggle in some normative principle, such as harmony with the tendency of evolution, social solidarity, etc., as *the* valid ideal. Marx may have boasted that he never made use of the word *justice* in his writings; but his followers would dwindle into insignificance if they could not appeal against the crying injustices of the present "system." The most courageous of all such positivists, Hobbes and Nietzsche, have not escaped the necessity of admitting, in a more or less thinly disguised form, a moral imperative contrary to the actually established forces. Our analytical school of jurisprudence, pretending to study only the law that is, has been repeatedly shown to be permeated with an anonymous natural law.

The boldest attempt in history to do away with the antithesis between what is and what ought to be is, of course, the Hegelian philosophy, with its violent assertion of the complete identity of the real and the rational. And it is one of the instructive ironies of fate that this most monistic utterance of man should have led to the widest rift that ever separated the adherents of a philosophic school. To the orthodox or conservative right this meant the glorification or deification of the actual Prussian state. To the revolutionary left, of the type of Karl Marx, it meant the denial of the right of existence to the irrational actual state.

* * * * *

We may generalize change as much as we like, saying that even the most general laws of nature that we now know, such as the laws of mechanics, are slowly changing, but this change can be established and have meaning only by means of or in reference to some logical constant. The belief that the world consists of all change and no constancy is no better than the belief that all vessels have insides but no outsides.

Can we abandon the effort to formulate a rational ideal that is to govern the facts of the law? Can the ideal of justice be derived from history or the empirical study of the facts themselves? Obviously not, if history or empirical study is restricted to the realm of existential facts, since our conclusion cannot contain an *ought* if all our premises are restricted to what *is*. But even if we begin with empirical judgments of what ought to be in concrete cases, we need some comprehensive ideal to organize our conflicting judgments into something like a coherent body. It is doubtless true that our ideal grows more definite as our experience expands and we get more opportunity to develop as well as to test our ideal by applying it. Still, any ideal that is to govern facts of conduct must be more simple, uniform and constant than these facts themselves. Otherwise it could not serve as a guide.

Dean Pound has used the postulates of civilization as a justification for the laws that secure the interests of personality, possession and transactions.[2] Certainly without such security our type of civilization is impossible. But these postulates do not undertake to settle questions of justice as to which of two heterogeneous and conflicting interests should prevail.

Morris R. Cohen, Justice Holmes and the Nature of Law, 31 Columbia Law Review pp. 360-362 (1931); reprinted with the permission of the Columbia Law Review.

The decisive role of judicial decisions in modern law leads some behaviorists to substitute the behavior of the judge for that of the people, as the substance of the law. The most direct expression of this is the view of Professor Bingham that the law consists of the actual individual decisions and the rules are no part of the law, but are mere subjective ideas in the minds of those who think about the law.[3]

If we are to have a rational science of law, we must realize the untenability of this position. Such is not the true meaning of Holmes' dictum that "the prophecies of what the courts will do in fact and nothing more pretentious are what I mean by law."

Bingham's position is explicitly based on a dualistic metaphysics which assumes a mind and a world external to it. Judges, cases, and decisions presumably exist in the external world. But

> "Principles and rules cannot exist outside of the mind.... The external expression of them does ... the meaning then exists only in the mind of the speaker or writer as he makes it."

This is an old popular metaphysics going back to medieval times, but it is just old nonsense. If cases existed in the external world and meanings in quite a different world, how could the latter express the former? Rules, we are told, help us to analyze the facts. But how could they do so, if they had nothing in common with the facts and existed in an altogether different realm?

The nominalistic dogma that only particulars exist in nature and that universals exist in the mind only would logically deprive every particular object in nature of all character or meaning. For what can we truly say about anything except in terms of its abstract traits or relations? But there is really no good reason for denying that universals as abstract predicates can denote real traits in the objective world, provided we are careful not to view these abstractions as additional things floating ghost-wise in an ethereal space. They are rather the universal or repeatable abstract qualities, relations, and transformations which characterize objects and events, and constitute their objective meaning. This meaning we may apprehend or not at our peril. Far from its being absurd, as Bingham asserts, to suppose that principles and rules can exist independently of the comprehension of any individual observer, it is exactly what we all assume whenever we undertake to teach any science or systematic truth. And the law is no exception. Certainly when the lawyer argues any case or when a jurist tries to expound any legal doctrine, he tries to make his hearer or reader comprehend that certain rules or general propositions are and have been true. It is desirable that this truth be comprehended. But the comprehension of a proposition does not create its truth. The student does not create the law when he succeeds in understanding it.

If there are any difficulties about conceiving rules or universals in nature, these difficulties are not cured by putting them in the mind. For if the nominalistic logic is good, it should also lead us to deny that there can be any universal ideas in the mind. Indeed, Professor Bingham does exactly this when he argues that there is no real identity between a rule in the mind of A and a rule in the mind of B which in common speech would be called the same rule.[4]

John Dickinson, My Philosophy of Law, pp. 101-102 (1941); reprinted by permission of Julius Rosenthal Foundation of Northwestern University and Boston Law Book Company.

Law in the sense of the rules which are formulated through government for the guidance and control of governmental decisions necessarily derives its content from a source or sources external to itself. This source may be custom,—government may, and in its more primitive stages usually does, simply lend its force to compel compliance with established social usage. On the other hand, it may deliberately formulate a rule to defeat a custom under the influence of some progressive ideal. Men, since they have begun to speculate about law at all, have always been fascinated by the conception of a system of ideal law, to which the actual law applied in decisions ought to, but never quite does, conform. Under the name, 'law of nature', this ideal law, derived from currently active moral aspirations by philosophers, divines, and judges, has supplied not merely a pattern and model, but a powerful stimulus for changes in and additions to the law of a given time and place. Of course, such ideal law can only influence the actual insofar as portions of it are from time to time adopted by judges and legislators. Naturally, the ideal has varied, and not merely from period to period, but from individual thinker to individual thinker; yet, in the large, the pursuit of it has usually represented an effort to discover and give effect to fundamental underlying human values, and the judge who has been influenced by the concept in his decisions has for the most part been doing what he could to build the law according to the better lights of his own age.

Joseph P. Witherspoon, Book Review of the Moral Decision by Edmond Cahn, 1 Natural Law Forum pp. 146, 148, 150-151, 156-157, 158, 163 (1956); reprinted by permission of the author and the Natural Law Forum.

THE MORAL DECISION. By Edmond Cahn. Bloomington: Indiana University Press, 1955. Pp. ix, 342, $5.00.

✻ ✻ ✻ ✻ ✻

If we cannot look to the natural law in our search for moral standards, may we look to the socially established mores, the current social conventions which the positivists urge are the only "standards" of human behavior? Cahn rejects the answer of positivism primarily for pragmatic reasons: "We cannot tell whether 'mores' means (1) what the society desires, or (2) what it popularly articulates, or (3) what it practices, or (4) some combination of these."[5] The positivists would answer, I believe, that Cahn is looking for an inherent will-o'-the-wisp, that there really are no objective moral standards, and that one is free to advocate whatever moral standards he likes—just as Cahn in fact does. After all, they would retort, it is only a matter of opinion; and Cahn does not really address himself to this major facet of their position.

✻ ✻ ✻ ✻ ✻

Thirdly, in *The Sense of Injustice* Cahn criticized

the classical realist thesis of the natural law as being an inadequate base from which to make here-and-now decisions in particular cases. It consisted, he said, of vague maxims incapable of real direction of human conduct and susceptible of supporting either one of contradictory positions one wished them to support. The realist philosophers, however, as Cahn should have known, include in their statement of the principles of the natural law principles substantially similar to the several primary moral principles he now mentions favorably in this book. He now asserts that these and other like principles in conjunction with the "sense of wrong" give an empirical foundation to the moral process.[6] As a matter of fact, if these principles are incapable of providing true moral-direction for human conduct, as Cahn now plainly sees, the whole fabric of his *The Sense of Injustice* and of this book loses its anchor and remits him to the position of moral skepticism which he abhors and denounces. By these principles, therefore, in conjunction with the "sense of wrong," we avoid "relativism and solipsism."[7]

The remaining problem for Cahn is thus one of determining how each person can isolate accurately the primary moral principles and then how, in his particular moral process, he can move objectively from these primary principles to the making of particular moral decisions about concrete moral problems. He thus raises not only the question of how one objectively determines the primary moral principles but also the question of how one likewise determines the moral principles or precepts intermediately placed between the former and the particular moral decisions each person has to make. If each person is his own moral legislator, where shall he go to find the primary and intermediate moral principles and still further to discover how to construe and to apply them properly to concrete moral problems?

Where else shall he go, is Cahn's deceptively simple answer, than to the case law of American courts? Why to the case law, the decisional law of courts? Cahn answers that judges, in performing their official duty to decide concrete cases, are constantly assessing moral interests and resolving problems of right and wrong.

* * * * *

**Why, however, should we look to American as opposed to French, Japanese, or Soviet judges? This question is eventually raised by Cahn himself. He answers: "Because it seems desirable at least, if not strictly necessary, that the decisions grow out of economic conditions and cultural circumstances in a single national society."[8] We can thus expect to find a Soviet morality, a Third Reich morality, and an American morality, each good in its own sphere but only accidentally good elsewhere. We can also expect that the amount of required critical evaluation of intermediate moral precepts proffered by the judges will vary heavily from country to country. This is truly the notion of a "gentilitial" morality. As the Soviet cloak spreads to more countries, we can even anticipate the problem of conflicts not of law, but of morality.

We must also ask how it is that Cahn expects to find all the categories of moral good dealt with in the rules announced or developed by judges in resolving controversies between people. It would seem very clear from Cahn's statement of purpose, from the title, as well as from his discussion of the good for man, that his book is at least concerned with the moral good in all its scope, and not merely with the narrower problem of justice in the relations between men. In his discussion of the good for man he classifies the philosophical contributions on this subject, either as viewing the good for man as "happiness" or "righteousness."[9] He rejects these contributions as being too narrow in view and supports the notion of a "mixed government" of the good which combines both notions of the good for man: "happiness" and "righteousness." Whatever Cahn means by "happiness" and by "righteousness"—and he does not define or describe what he means—his joining them together into an amalgam notion of the good for man is indicative that he is concerned with an expansive notion of the moral good and the moral decision concerning which he seeks to illuminate the thinking of others.

Yet can Cahn seriously contend that his reader may expect to find in the decisions of judges, even American judges, moral knowledge bearing upon the primary and intermediate principles concerning love, friendship, charity, humility, temperance, courage, veracity, sobriety, modesty, magnanimity, patience, perseverance, and constancy? We are indeed fortunate if we can obtain just judges who know something about justice and who seek justice in their decisions. We can hope they will in fact be charitable, temperate, courageous, and humble, but we will hardly look to their decisions for guidance in these matters. After all, Cahn has himself stated in his earlier work that the end of the positive law is justice. What we in fact expect to find in the development and application of positive law by judges is an approximation of justice. The principles they develop and apply are intended to be of legal justice. The problem to which positive law is directed is the problem of justice: how the conduct of one man which bears upon another is to be judged. It is not directed to the problem of courage, of moderation, and the other myriad moral problems where the problem relates to how the conduct of one man is to be judged apart from its bearing on another person. Thus, despite Cahn's exposition of the good in general for man, the statement of the purpose of the book, and his title, we must say that he is concerned with the primary and intermediate principles of justice. For this reason, he might better have entitled his book *The Just Decision*.

❖ ❖ ❖ ❖ ❖

When we examine the "prismatic" cases in which the court holds certain conduct to be wrong, we can expect to discover more about "prismatic" method, for it is this type of case for which the book plainly indicates the method is primarily designed, since there is a derivative criterion for determining what is good human conduct.

The first case to which Cahn applies "prismatic" analysis is one in which a sailor was charged and convicted of manslaughter for having thrown a ship's passenger out of a liftboat into which some of the crew and passengers of a sinking ship had gotten after the ship had struck an iceberg.[10] When the act was done it was highly probable that the boat would have sunk and all would have perished in the sea. In all, fourteen passengers were thrown to a watery death and possibly two additional women passengers, although the latter may have leaped into the water to be with their dying brothers. In his charge to the jury, the judge stated that only those sailors who were indispensable for operating the boat were entitled to remain in it and that if there were surplus passengers upon this basis, those to be thrown over the side must be chosen by lot. Cahn disagrees with the decision. He takes the position that "if none sacrifice themselves of free will to spare the others—they must all wait and die together." [11]

The point here is not so much whether one agrees or disagrees with Cahn's position concerning what is the morally good conduct here. It is rather, for the limited purposes of this reviewer, to determine the nature of the "prismatic" analysis by which he arrives at such a position. How does he determine that the court is wrong in the rule it announced and how does he determine that his position gives the right rule for the moral problem here involved? As a matter of fact his position is one of four positions that have been taken by judges and legal scholars as to what the legal rule should be. The first thing to be noted, then, is that "prismatic" method as applied here involves a situation in which the operative result of the "sense of wrong" varies depending on who is judging the moral problem.

The second thing to be noted is, as Cahn says, that "[t]his question could never be resolved if our appraisal of human life were a strictly *subjective* process." [12] We must, therefore, make an *"objective* examination of the value of being alive." [13] Without defining what an objective examination is, the author then states that such an examination may be found reported in the Babylonian Talmud which had been made by two competing famous schools of rabbis.[14] As the content of the examination to which he refers is not explained in his book, we cannot know the basis upon which it was or could be termed an objective examination. The next hint as to what an "objective examination" is comes when the author states that "[t]he *objective view* does not hold that under every conceivable human set of circumstances each human life has an indestructible value."[15] He then refers to the fact that everyone knows the law recognizes justifiable homicides, excusable homicides, drafts men into armed forces to face death in wartime, and executes certain convicted criminals. While this is not a definition of what is "objective," it obviously by implication gives some tentative shape to his use of the term. We can now surmise he refers either to the law or to "what everyone knows" as a standard of what is objective. We must, for obvious reasons, reject the idea that law can be a standard for objectives in determining what are correct primary and intermediate moral principles and accept the other alternative. That we are not far from the author's actual position is quickly discovered for he refers to a statement by Justice Holmes from another case and says his "appraisal was objective" concerning the value of being alive.[16] The statement of Justice Holmes so approved was the following: *"By common understanding* imprisonment for life is a less penalty than death." [17] We can now conclude that an appraisal or an examination of the value of being alive, for the purposes of resolving a moral problem in a court case, is "objective" when it is framed to reflect what the "common understanding" is of that value with regard to that moral problem.

To be "objective," then, we must look to what the common understanding is of the value of being alive in the situation presented by the sailor-passenger-sinking-lifeboat case. As we have already said, four different views have been taken as to what the value of being alive (more properly, the value of being allowed to live) is in this situation. This naturally leads us to conclude that this is a case presenting a moral problem in which no objective examination of the moral value involved is possible, for the simple reason that there is no "common understanding" with respect to it. The fact that it is commonly understood that human life does not have "an indestructible value ... under every conceivable human set of circumstances" does not help us. For this "objective appraisal" does not tell us how to determine what to do under *these* circumstances. The first aspect, then, of Cahn's "prismatic" method of case analysis can not get off the ground in a case where there is no "common understanding" for the courts to expound.

"Prismatic" method, however, does not stop with an analysis of common understanding, for Cahn proceeds to examine the principal case and rejects the court's solution as well as any which has been proffered other than his own. If we consider that his "prismatic" method is still "objective," clearly that notion must take on new contours of meaning. In support of his position, he observes that "of course" the life of any person in the lifeboat is worth as much as the life of anyone else in the boat.[18] Is this self-evident, and if not, why is this proposition true? Cahn does not answer this question directly. His "of course" may in fact mean that he takes it to be self-evident that the proposition is true; but this would be inconsistent with his over-all presentation, for he expresses extreme doubt about what is morally good conduct in this situation.

The "moral constitution" is just another term for what Cahn has called a "sense of wrong." The latter has not been explained in this book insofar as it commands one result rather than another in a particular case. Cahn has said his last word on the matter. Either what he has said is self-evident or it is not. Cahn has denied by his own analysis that it is self-evident; therefore, from his point of view, there must be a reason or basis for his position. He makes statements for his position but he does not show why they are reasons.

* * * * *

This book is in fact a venture into the field of practical philosophy insofar as it raises philosophical questions. It is a venture also into the field of normative knowledge below the level of practical philosophy insofar as it aims at a knowledge which will serve as the proximate basis for the prudential judgment. One must indeed sympathize with Cahn in his denunciation of the positivism which pervades so much of our thinking today. Yet he does not show that the positive position is a false one. More basic, however, is the conclusion which this review justifies: that he takes a position which does not substantially differ from and may be reduced to the basic positivist position. This is true because he neither shows the legal cases to be productive of moral knowledge nor does he identify in any discernible manner the extrinsic standard of "morality" by which he purports to test the validity of the norms he meets in those cases. The position of one who refers to but does not or cannot identify an objective standard for moral judgment is hardly to be preferred or distinguished from one who asserts, as does the positivist, that there is no objective standard for moral judgment. Finally, by failing to examine carefully the classical realist thesis of natural law and disfiguring some of the essential facts about it, he violates the time-tested procedure for bringing about genuine progress in the two areas of knowledge referred to at the outset of this paragraph.

[1] For this reason I must reject Professor Fite's attempt, in his *Individualism*, to reduce natural rights to a question of intellect-power, or intelligent self-assertion. It seems to me a subtle way of reducing questions of right to a species of might. Basing his theory on an analysis of consciousness, Professor Fite consistently arrives at the position that the unintelligent have no rights. If that were so, we would have to say that infants, before the age of self-consciousness, and the senile or demented have no rights whatsoever, and any one who takes advantage of his superior intelligence in dealing with them is exercising his rights. In one case, at least, Professor Fite does not hesitate to follow his theory to such a conclusion. A nation, he tells us, which allows valuable public lands to pass into private hands through lack of interest and intelligence should not complain of being robbed. If Professor Fite were consistent, he would have to say, not only that the public has no right to complain of being robbed because of its ignorance, but that the robber is perfectly justified, so long as the public does not know a way of recovering it. This, indeed, would be reducing questions of right to questions of might, but it would really make the predicate *right* devoid of all meaning.

[2] See his Introduction to the Philosophy of Law (1922).

[3] Bingham, What is the Law? (1912) 11 Mich. L. Rev. 109 et seq.; Bingham, Legal Philosophy and the Law (1914) 9 Ill. L. Rev. 96.

[4] 9 Ill. L. Rev., at 114. But why stop here? If the same rule cannot exist in two different minds, can it exist in the mind at different times? Indeed, how can any existing mind or any objective whatsoever remain identically the same if there is no identity in nature? But if identity and diversity, unity and plurality do exist in nature, there are universal principles which form the substance of the meaning of things.

[5] The Moral Decision 26.

[6] Id. 27-38, 25-26, 30, 63.

[7] The Sense of Injustice 13, 24.

[8] The Moral Decision 52.

[9] Id. 12-14.

[10] Id. 61-71.

[11] Id. 71.

[12] Id. 63.

[13] Ibid.

[14] Id. 63-4.

[15] Id. 64.

[16] Id. 65.

[17] Ibid.

[18] Id. 68-9.

C. Sociological Rationalism, Quasi-Idealism

Some natural law jurists, like Jerome Hall and Lon L. Fuller, may be described as quasi-idealists because of the great relativity of their ideals. They believe that there are correct ideals for the evaluation of the conduct of man, a rational and social creature. They further believe that those ideals exist outside of the mind in a metaphysical order. But according to these jurists, all of these ideals are the variable products of thought working on ever changing sociological phenomena.

1. In General

Thomas A. Cowan, A Report on the Status of Philosophy of Law in the United States, 50 Columbia Law Review pp. 1095-1097 (1950); reprinted by permission of the author and the Columbia Law Review.

The influence of idealism in American juristic writings represents a very definite break with, or at least clear opposition to, sociological jurisprudence. This break, however, is only a contemporary reemergence of an influence always existing at least in an inarticulate condition in American legal thought for, although classical natural law doctrines faced growing hostility in this country from the adoption of the federal Constitution, it cannot be said that natural law influence ever suffered extinction. As a source of inspiration for "higher law" theories, for exaltation of received traditions, for principles of unity and coherence over the body of the law, and for emphasis upon the necessity of converting moral obligations into legal ones, the "ideal" element in the law has been the constant concern of able jurists since the beginning of the American legal system. Pound has never ceased to teach the importance of this tradition and in recent years seems to be stressing it.

Three American jurists in particular are at present working out an approach to a recognizably idealistic position in legal philosophy. They are Lon L. Fuller[1] of Harvard, Jerome Hall[2] of Indiana and Edmond N. Cahn[3] of New York University. While stressing at all times the social nature of all legal phenomena, these men have nevertheless opposed the pragmatic philosophical position in two main respects. They attack its pluralism as leading to cultural determinism and scepticism and they attack its alleged amoralism. For them, the ideal element in law needs conscious elaboration in order (1) that competing ideals may be examined and evaluated and the fundamental purposes of law be given unified direction; (2) that value judgments themselves may be put on a rational basis so that the gap between morality and law be closed; and (3) that the effects of legal scepticism may be overcome by a reaffirmance of faith in American legal and political ideals, that is, ideals of justice and democracy. All this is directed to the end that the law may be placed upon a firm support in ethics and value theory.

Fuller's book, *The Law in Quest of Itself*,[4] most nearly approaches the temper of idealism. The claims of idealism are opposed to positivism, and while that movement rather than pragmatism is most severely scored, it is apparent that the author is more concerned with pragmatism than with the generally discredited positivism. Fuller shows in this book quite clearly the links of modern legal idealism with natural law. In fact, he just barely misses calling for a revival of natural law. It is too bad for the idealists that the tempting phrase "natural law" is still a little too hot to touch. Its free use would at least put the present-day idealists in a rich historical tradition, a tradition which they feel unable to accept but for which a nostalgic longing pervades their writings.

Jerome Hall's recent book on *Living Law in a Democratic Society*[5] is less clearly in the idealistic tradition. His concern like Fuller's is with the harmful effects of "positivistic" separation of law and morals, with ideals of jural purpose, such as democracy and justice, and with the preservation of ancient wisdom in the classical philosophical and legal texts.

Philosophy for the idealists traditionally has been more concerned with wisdom than with science. Wisdom is conservative, subtle, classical, moral and self-conscious. Wisdom protects itself from excess and asks youth to bring its aims to the level of self-consciousness and at the same time suggests what these self-conscious aims ought to be. The idealistic philosophy especially prizes consistency or coherence. Among our legal idealists these demands apparently call for a leap backward beyond Hegel whose dialectical system actually rendered infinitely more difficult the idealists' task of making nature coherent and consistent. My own personal distress with idealistic legal philosophers stems from their tendency to sound a retreat to Plato. Their failure to face up to Hegelian idealism deprives them of an opportunity to make their idealism modern.

It is common knowledge that Hegel really made it impossible for idealists to escape the dilemma of absolutism. After him all idealistic systems must either arrest progress and stagnate in some species of absolutism; or, forswearing the absolute, come to grips with the relativism of modern science. For better or for worse, knowledge has become dialectical and the ancient dilemmas—is and ought, freedom and necessity, idealism and realism—are dissolving away. Not alone Marx and Freud, but Kierkegaard, Husserl, the phenomenologists and existentialists owe their existence to Hegel, as do the modern pragmatists. It will be recalled that the greatest of them, John Dewey, began as a Hegelian, and that all pragmatists are or ought to be grateful to Hegel for relativizing "fact," and for the notion of interpenetration of "fact" and "law." [6]

Edmond Cahn in his recent book, *The Sense of Injustice*,[7] seems to have escaped the dangers of regression to Ancient Greece. He does not regard the old positivistic-idealistic contradictions as fruitful sources of inquiry. In his work recognition of the influence of Hegel appears through the German romantics, and the secular ethics of humanism rather than an appeal to a revived natural law is looked upon as the source of the "ideal" element of law. *The Sense of Injustice* is an attempt to lay a foundation for the scientific study of man as an emotional animal whose feelings find expression over the range of an enormous number of law situations.

2. In Particular

Lon L. Fuller, The Law in Quest of Itself pp. 5-6, 99-104, 135-137 (1940); reprinted by permission of the author and the Foundation Press.

By legal positivism I mean that direction of legal thought which insists on drawing a sharp distinction between the law *that is* and the law *that ought to be*. Where this distinction is taken it is, of course, for the sake of the law *that is*, and is intended to purify it by purging it of what Kelsen calls "wish-law." Generally —though not invariably—the positivistic attitude is associated with a degree of ethical skepticism. Its unavowed basis will usually be found to rest in a conviction that while one may significantly describe the law *that is*, nothing that transcends personal predilection can be said about the law *that ought to be*.

Natural law, on the other hand, is the view which denies the possibility of a rigid separation of the *is* and the *ought*, and which tolerates a confusion of them in legal discussion. There are, of course, many "systems" of natural law. Men have drawn their criteria of justice and of right law from many sources: from the nature of things, from the nature of man, from the nature of God. But what unites the various schools of natural law, and justifies bringing them under a common rubric, is the fact that in all of them a certain coalescence of the *is* and the *ought* will be found. Though the natural law philosopher may admit the authority of the state even to the extent of conceding the validity of enacted law which is obviously "bad" according to his principles, it will be found in the end that he draws no hard and fast line between law and ethics, and that he considers that the "goodness" of his natural law confers on it a kind of reality which may be temporarily eclipsed, but can never be wholly nullified, by the more immediately effective reality of enacted law. So far as the question of ultimate motives is concerned, it is fairly obvious that if the positivist insists on separating the *is* and the *ought* for the sake of the *is*, the natural-law philosopher is attempting to serve the *ought* when he refuses to draw a sharp distinction between it and the *is*.

* * * * *

So far we have been almost exclusively concerned with the difficulties encountered in the search for some criterion which will separate the law that is from the law that ought to be. Our attention has been concentrated on the obstacles which beset the law's quest of itself. I have attempted to reveal the essentially sterile nature of any form of legal positivism which purports to divorce itself from a definite ethical or practical goal; I have tried to demonstrate the bankruptcy of those formalized varieties of positivism which purport to deal analytically and descriptively with an assumed "pure fact of law." Does this rejection of the claims of "scientific" positivism imply a recommendation that we should go the whole way in the opposite direction of legal thought? Am I to be understood as asserting, in effect, that almost any system of natural law is to be preferred to legal positivism? If not, then what attitude is here implied toward the various theories of natural law that have come down to us from the speculations of the past?

In answering these questions, I should like to have it understood at the outset that any compliments which may here be cast in the direction of natural law are not addressed to the doctrine of natural and inalienable rights. This warning would probably be unnecessary if it were not for the fact that we have got into the habit of identifying these two notions and of assuming that some conception of the natural rights of man must lie at the heart of every system of natural law. As a matter of fact, if we take into account the whole course of legal philosophy from its beginnings with the Greeks, the notion of natural rights appears not as an integral part of the theory of natural law but as a passing episode in the history of ethical and legal speculation. Even in its heyday the view was neither received unanimously, nor entertained by its philosophic adherents in the unqualified form it assumed in political documents. But there is no need here either to beat dead horses or to review their pedigrees. I am not advocating the doctrine of natural rights, and I may add that in my opinion the notion of "imputed rights," or rights in the positivistic sense, is open to many of the objections which have been advanced against natural rights.

Not only am I not proposing to re-fight the philosophic battles of the American and French Revolutions, but I am not attempting to set myself up as sponsor for any of the various systems of natural law which have been advocated in the past. In particular, I should dislike being called upon to undertake a defense of all the things which have been said in the name of that excellent philosopher, Saint Thomas Aquinas. On the other hand, I believe that there is much of great value for the present day in the writings of those thinkers who are classified, and generally dismissed, as belonging to the school of natural law, and I regard it as one of the most unfortunate effects of the positivistic trend still current that it has contributed to bring about the neglect of this important and fruitful body of literature. Ironically enough, one of the things which has rendered this literature unacceptable to the modern legal mind is a quality which ought really to have had precisely the opposite effect. It is one of the tenets of modern legal science that law is an integral part of the whole civilization of a society, and that fruitful work in the law presupposes a familiarity with the other social sciences such as psychology, economics and sociology. Yet this is only the rediscovery of a point of view which has always been taken for granted in natural law speculation. Unfortunately for the natural law philosopher, however, this interest in subjects outside his immediate field has as its price the possibility that his work may soon become dated. By relating his legal philosophy to the other social sciences, he runs the risk that the progress of those sciences may leave his work behind. So today, when we read in Ahrens' *Cour de Droit Naturel* that the theory of evolution is disproved by the fact that monkeys cannot be taught to talk,[8] we put the book back on the shelf in disgust and we forget, or fail to learn, that it contains an excellent discussion of the function of contract law, a discussion which is perhaps even more valuable today than when it was written. We fail also to realize that it was after all more significant that Ahrens' conception of law should have been broad enough to make the truths of biology legally relevant, than that he should have rejected a particular biological theory which was still a great novelty in his day. Of course the work of the positivists is essentially timeless; by abstracting law entirely from its environment and defining it not in terms of its content, but of its form and sanction, they run no risk either of being outdated or of ever contributing anything to the development of the law except restraints and inhibitions. Austin's theory, which suffered no contamination from the backward state of the social sciences of his day, remains today just as true, and just as lacking in significance for human affairs, as in 1832.

The chief value of the older books on natural law for us of the present day does not lie so much in the systems they expound, as in the kind of legal thinking they exemplify. The broader and freer legal method of these books is in a double sense "natural law." In the first place, it is the method men naturally follow when they are not consciously or unconsciously inhibited by a positivistic philosophy. When there is no warning stop sign, reason naturally pushes as far ahead as it can. In the second place, when reason is unhampered by positivistic restraints, it tends inevitably to find anchorage in the natural laws which are assumed to underlie the relations of men and to determine the growth and decay of civilizations.

* * * * *

It has been the service of a vigorous Swedish school of legal thought to bring home to us a realization of the extent to which the law, particularly judge-made law, shapes common morality.[9] They have shown us how false is the common picture according to which there exists outside the law, and wholly independent of it, a body of moral precepts which exerts a kind of one-way gravitational pull on the law, against which the law opposes a constant inertia, so that it lags always behind morality and only meets those minimum ethical demands which relate to the most pressing social needs. This whole "extra-legal" body of moral precepts is to a large extent a creature compounded of paper and ink and philosophic imagination. Actually, if we look to those rules of morality which have enough teeth in them to act as serious deterrents to men's pursuit of their selfish interests, we will find that far from being "extra-legal" they are intimately and organically connected with the functionings of the legal order. I may think that I drive carefully because it is my moral duty to do so as a good citizen, and I may suppose that the law merely takes over my standard of driving—which is, of course, that of the prudent man—as a test to apply to drivers less virtuous than myself. I forget to what extent my conceptions of my duty as a driver have been shaped by the daily activities of the traffic police. I forget that behind my standard of driving there may lie a vague fear of the ignominy involved in having to appear in traffic court, and that this fear may have had a great deal to do with shaping my conceptions of traffic morality.

It should be noted that the view I am expounding

here does not assert that men are, in the ordinary affairs of life, consciously deterred by legal penalties. It concedes that the effective deterrents which shape the average man's conduct derive from morality, from a sense of right and wrong. What it asserts is that these conceptions of right and wrong are themselves significantly shaped by the daily functionings of the legal order, and that they would be profoundly altered if this legal order were to disappear. As business men we may perform our contracts not because we are afraid of a law suit, but because we feel that it is our duty to do so. But would this same conception of duty exist if the law enforced no contracts at all? In the moral environment out of which this conception of duty arises, is not the law itself one of the most important elements?

Lon L. Fuller, American Legal Philosophy at Mid-Century, 6 Journal of Legal Education pp. 467-469, 470-472, 479 (1954); reprinted by permission of the Journal of Legal Education, published by the Association of American Law Schools. Copyright, 1954, by the Association of American Law Schools.

NATURAL LAW
Some False Issues

Current disputes about "natural law" in this country generally revolve about certain issues that seem to me to be futile in the sense that a discussion of them leads to no clarification of the essential problems of law and justice. One of these is the notion that adherents of natural law are committed to "absolutes," while those who reject it are "relativists." This is a distinction commonly accepted on both sides.

I have to confess I have no clear idea what an "absolute" is. In philosophic discussions an "absolute" is something that is not related to anything else, but since I cannot think without employing relations I cannot conceive what this unrelated thing would be like. If an "absolute" is taken to mean a moral imperative that yields a clear principle of decision under all circumstances then, again, I know of no "absolute." Human life is in this sense as close to an absolute as anything we have, yet it furnishes little guidance to the hospital that has only enough of a scarce drug to cure one patient when three are dying for lack of it.

So far as I can see, the expressions "absolute" and "relative" as they are employed in current discussions about natural law are simply unanalyzed terms of censure and praise. The believer in absolutes is either an unpleasant dogmatist or a man of firm principles. His opposite number, the relativist, is either a fellow who shows a commendable flexibility in the face of a changing reality, or a spineless creature drifting with the tides of circumstance. Neither term seems to me to present anything like a justiciable issue.

Another diversionary controversy that prevents profitable discussion is aroused by the notion that natural law sets itself above positive law and counsels a disregard of any enactment that violates its precepts. When it is suggested that this attitude toward positive law be adopted, not only by the citizen, but by the judge and state official as well, there is certainly ground for real concern.

But the issue of fidelity to positive law is certainly severable from that of natural law generally. If the matter is examined candidly it will be found that there is no one who cannot imagine himself, even as a judge, being faced by a law so infamous that he would feel bound to disobey it. For most of us such a situation could only arise in the event of some great dislocation in the ordinary processes of government, such as might be occasioned by a dictatorship or an occupation by enemy forces. Perhaps a certain distaste for the notion of natural law is engendered precisely because it reminds us of such unpleasant and unlikely possibilities.

Most philosophers of natural law have regarded the duty of obeying the positive law as founded on natural law itself and as being subject to exception only in extreme cases. Certainly it is clear that the obligation of fidelity to positive law cannot itself be derived from positive law. Even so great an enemy of natural law as Gray had to desert the positivist position when he came to explain why in modern states judges must consider themselves bound by statutes. "This," he wrote, "may be said to be a necessary consequence from the very conception of an organized community of men." [10]

If in our society a man accepts a judicial post with a commitment to disregard laws duly enacted by the same democratic and constitutional procedures that created the office he assumes, a serious issue is presented. That issue will not be clarified, but obfuscated, if it is converted into a general philosophic discussion of the natural law position.

The great merit of Patterson's discussion of natural law[11] is that it discriminates. He recognizes that in the course of history the term has had different meanings and that these meanings must be appraised separately. In so far as Patterson may be said to have an attitude toward the general direction of thought represented by natural law, it is approximately that of Maine: although intellectually indefensible, the notion has in practice probably done more good than harm.

For my own part, I have two major criticisms of Patterson's treatment of the natural law philosophy, which I shall try to express in what follows.

THE DIRECTION-GIVING QUALITY OF PURPOSIVE FACTS

When the question is discussed today, How can ethical judgments be justified?, two propositions are generally accepted as truisms: (1) there is a difference in kind between statements about what ought to be and statements about what actually exists; (2) it is impossible to derive from a statement about what exists any conclusion about what ought to be. Neither of these assertions would have appeared as a truism to Plato or Aristotle, and those philosophers would probably have had difficulty extracting a clear meaning from them. It is only in more recent times, and chiefly through the influence of Kant, that these propositions have reached the status of axioms among philosophers and laymen generally.

In principle, at least, Patterson accepts "the dichotomy of fact and value" and the impossibility of deriving "value judgments" from "facts." [12] In this I differ from him, for I believe that this time-worn dichotomy requires serious modification when applied to purposive human behavior as a simple illustration will show.

* * * * *

As for the application of the dichotomy of *is* and *ought* to the law, it is fairly clear that with legal precepts, as with the instructions for assembling a machine, what a direction *is* can be understood only by seeing toward what end result it is aimed. The essential meaning of a legal rule lies in a purpose, or more commonly, in a congeries of purposes. Within the framework of this purpose, or set of related purposes, the sharp dichotomy between fact and evaluation cannot be maintained; the "fact" involved is not a static datum but something that reaches toward an objective and that can be understood only in terms of that reaching.

In criticism of the view just expressed, it has been asserted that it destroys the possibility of defining what the law actually is and prevents the taking of any distinction between what is in fact law and what ought to be law.[13] This criticism would be justified only if the view I am advocating permitted the interpreter of a statute or precedent to read into it any purpose he saw fit. No such abandonment of ordinary principles of interpretation is here proposed or implied. All that is asserted here is (1) that a law must be interpreted in the light of some purpose; (2) that this purpose should not be subjected to a false "logic" derived from experience in dealing with **non-purposive facts.**

It may be said that this is all very well, but that it has little or nothing to do with natural law. Indeed, commenting somewhat obscurely on an obscure passage from a book of mine, Patterson seems to say just this.[14] I believe, on the contrary, that the question whether the dichotomy of *is* and *ought* can be applied to purposes goes to the heart of the philosophic issue of natural law *v*. positivism.[15] (I stress the fact that I am speaking of the philosophic issue, because many defenses of the natural law view made in the name of religion seem to me to lack anything resembling philosophic analysis.)

An insistence on attempting to apply the dichotomy of *is* and *ought* to purposes seems to me to permeate the thinking of all those who have explicitly rejected the natural law philosophy. Kelsen's whole system is an elaborate effort to deal with purposive arrangements as if they had not purpose.[16] His attitude comes plainly to the fore in his discussion of "dynamic" and "static" norms. A norm or rule can for Kelsen be "dynamic" only if it is devoid of material content, only if it is simply a procedural rule defining the sources of law. A rule that says something on its own account, as it were, is necessarily "static."[17] On a common sense level, this means that if A has attempted to articulate in words a purpose he has in mind, B could not possibly help him to improve the statement of his purpose. For Kelsen there can be no meaning in Mansfield's famous phrase to the effect that the common law, proceeding from case to case, gradually "works itself pure." For Kelsen, a substantive rule is "pure" to start with and there is no such thing as a collaborative articulation of shared purposes.

It is no mere accident of the history of ideas that those who can see nothing but fraud or self-delusion in the notion of natural law should be those who are also unable to see the essential inapplicability of the dichotomy of *is* and *ought* to purposes. For one who has seen clearly that this dichotomy loses its validity in the face of a single purpose will be led, I believe, to see that it loses its force before the problem of the justification of ethical judgments generally.

A purpose is, as it were, a segment of a man. The whole man, taken in the round, is an enormously complicated set of interrelated and interacting purposes. This system of purposes constitutes his nature, and it is to this nature that natural law looks in seeking a standard for passing ethical judgments. That is good which advances man's nature; that is bad which keeps him from realizing it. Just as the dichotomy of *is* and *ought* does not apply to the act of reaching toward the realization of a single purpose, so it is equally inapplicable to a whole purposive system. From the reaching that is imbedded within that system, we can learn in what directions it should reach.

When the natural law view is defined in this way the question is not *how much* we can learn from studying man's nature, but whether this is the proper place to look for guidance in deciding what is right and what is wrong. Viewing the matter in this light, a professed skeptic might accept natural law, saying, "I agree that the only possible source of ethical judgments lies in man's nature, viewing that nature as a striving and not as a fixed datum. But I don't think you will derive much of substance even from that source."

❋   ❋   ❋   ❋   ❋

The great mistake of the natural law school was, however, not to keep the problem of ends in a sufficiently intimate contact with the problem of means. Instead of holding means and ends open for a reciprocal adjustment with respect to each problem, the writer on natural law was apt to reach abstract resolutions on ends and then to trace out the implications of those resolutions for the various branches of the law.

This mistake of the older natural law school is being repeated, I believe, by Professors McDougal and Lasswell.[18] Their philosophy is "value-oriented," which means preference-oriented, since a "value" is defined as being a "preferred event." With the aid of a table of eight fundamental "values" (which include, incidentally, neither freedom nor scurity) the philosopher or legal reformer is supposed to determine what values are to be effectuated—in other words, what he wants. The rest is a mere matter of technical implementation with which Professors McDougal and Lasswell have no direct concern and for which they assume no responsibility.

Joseph P. Witherspoon, The Relation of Philosophy to Jurisprudence, 3 Natural Law Forum pp. 124, 126-129 (1958); reprinted by permission of the author and the Natural Law Forum. This note is a comment on the first two stages of the discussion between Professor Fuller and Professor Ernest Nagel, which appears in this issue of the Natural Law Forum at pp. 68-104.

The problem can be more simply stated as follows: "Is it possible to attain to philosophical science concerning the right ends and means of human action?" The first objection to its affirmative answer is the assertion that man is unable to determine his terminal end by analysis and observation. The second objection is the assertion of the datum of interaction between means and ends at the prudential level of decision.

      ✻   ✻   ✻   ✻   ✻

It remains that if Professor Fuller wants a full-dress discussion of his problem, among those to whom he must certainly turn are those who earlier have carried on and those who today still carry on the tradition of the *philosophia perennis*. They have been obtaining a constantly increasing audience in the twentieth century throughout the world of intellectual discussion. The difficulty arises as to just how a discussion between them and Professor Fuller should begin in order to maximize on the mutual exchange. Professor Fuller has not only raised a philosophical question but he has given two reasons for giving it a negative answer that ousts philosophy from one of its traditional tasks. On the other hand, the classical realists in philosophy have not only asked this same question but also have given an affirmative answer and have supported it by a foundation of explication that has continued to grow in depth and explicitness in this century. Since the collective method of Aristotle appears to be the only adequate approach in philosophy (even for non-Aristotelians), I should affirm that Professor Fuller, having raised a philosophical question **and provided the basis for his tentative answer to it, is** entitled to have his objections seriously considered and that he, in turn, should now state why, if it is the case, he is not prepared to accept the reasons of the classical realists for their affirmative answer to the same question. This latter, it seems to me, is a fundamental obligation of those who enter philosophic discussions.

  ***I would like to examine the first basis utilized by Professor Fuller for concluding tentatively that philosophical knowledge of proper human ends is not possible. Let me quote his precise statement of it: "The other line of thought leads, with equal persuasiveness, to the conclusion that this activity [of choosing 'an apt means for the realization of a given end'] must have a terminal point and that the end ultimately pursued cannot be determined by analysis or observation, but must in some manner or other be projected upon events." [19] Professor Maritain, in a criticism of Bergson, shows his full agreement with Professor Fuller in one sense of this statement. He has stated: "Aussi bien nul philosophe ne peut-il nous dire quelle est en réalité l'ultime fin de notre existence. C'est Dieu qui nous l'appris, lui qui nous a faits pour qu'en définitive nous le voyions comme il nous voit." [20] This was in answer to Bergson's contention that man is made solely for his action (*homo faber*), i.e., particularly for transitive as opposed to immanent action. We do not and cannot know in this life "en réalité l'ultime fin de notre existence," which is God. The terminal end in question here, of course, is our supernatural one. There is an end short of our supernatural end to which one may refer as in some sense terminal. Some have called it our natural or temporal terminal end.[21] It is the latter which the context indicates Professor Fuller has in mind.

What then are we to say about his objection that the natural end of human living cannot be determined "by analysis or observation"? Since there is no philosophical or other analysis in his paper devoted to the support of this objection, and the matter is not self-evident, the reason he has for reaching his conclusion cannot be examined. Some of his discussion could be taken to indicate that he would support this conclusion upon the basis of the psychological datum that men at the level of prudential decision do not have a very firm notion of the ends they wish to pursue. If this were to be offered (and I do not assert that it has been) as the basis for concluding that knowledge concerning the natural terminal end of man is not possible, it must be replied that this mode of proceeding begs the very issue for discussion. Men are always uncertain before they attain certainty, without knowledge before they attain knowledge. The very issue is whether they can attain knowledge of a certain sort. To assert that because they are uncertain or do not have knowledge of something, they cannot attain certainty or knowledge about that thing is to foreclose discussion of the issue raised. Consequently, I do not believe that Professor Fuller would rely upon this argument. Yet I do not know what his argument is as to why man cannot achieve scientific knowledge concerning what his terminal end is in this world and concerning universal means for attaining it. It seems to me that to support his position he must inevitably show why the position of classical realists who assert that knowledge about man's true ends in this world is attainable and has been attained in increasing measure is wrong. I have particularly in mind, as a basis for possible future discussion, such material as the Treatises on The

Last End, Human Acts, Justice, and Law of St. Thomas Aquinas.[22] These should be examined for errors and inadequacies as well as for the substantial truths they may contain upon the question which Professor Fuller raises. This comment applies especially to the Treatise on Law. As Adler has observed of this treatise in an article that will richly repay reading for all in philosophy of law and jurisprudence:

> St. Thomas does not pretend to write the philosophy of law in a manner that is adequate to its principles and problems. Here, as elsewhere in the *Summa*, he uses philosophical knowledge and analysis in the service of theology, as an instrument to achieve some understanding of revealed truth. This does not mean that philosophical truth is not present in the *Summa;* it is neither lacking, nor obscured. But it is subordinated, and many points are treated too briefly and too simply which, if the aim were exclusively philosophical, would demand much more extensive discussion and much more complicated analysis than is needed or justified in a theological work. We have no right to complain, we can only regret, that St. Thomas did not write about human and natural law with the fullness proper to philosophical discussion in itself and apart from theology. Nor need we rest there, for within the scope of a few compact questions St. Thomas has given us enough to enable us to do a job which, under the exigencies of his life and times, he was not called to do. We not only can, but should, write about law in a purely philosophical manner.... That sort of work is our historical vocation, as St. Thomas had his.[23]

I should like to add to Dr. Adler's statement the comment that the Treatise on Law is most likely to be misunderstood by moderns unless read *after* or at least in conjunction with the other Treatises I have mentioned, especially the Treatise on Justice.

The second base from which Professor Fuller concludes tentatively that philosophical science of human means and ends is not possible is the datum of interaction. It should be noted that neither in this paper nor in his previous writings does Professor Fuller define the datum of interaction. He does give an example in his first paper of how a person may shift from one purpose to another in a given sequence of action and of the difficulty with which either that person or an observer of him has in determining what his real purpose is or when he has in fact shifted from one purpose to another. Somewhat later he states that forms of language "are an awkward instrument for dealing with interaction."[24] In the immediate context he refers to the choice of ends and means as seeming to be described aptly as a reasoning process. He also states that at the level of prudential decision ends and means no longer arrange themselves "in tandem fashion."[25] All these statements are suggestive of several senses in which he may be using the notion of interaction. It becomes important to determine what the sense is or the senses are in which the notions is used, since it is claimed that datum of interaction in some way prevents the possibility of philosophical science of proper human ends and means. Yet a claimed result cannot be properly assigned to a given cause unless that cause is known. Moreover, it is important to know the argument made by Professor Fuller as to why or how it is claimed that the datum of interaction is operative to prevent a philosophical science of proper human ends and means. This is true because although it may be true that interaction between ends and means, in some sense, does occur, it may nevertheless not be true that this prevents philosophical science of proper human ends and means.

Since Professor Fuller neither specifies the sense or senses in which he uses the datum of interaction nor develops the reasons why the datum is operative to prevent philosophical science of proper human ends and means, it would be entirely appropriate to bring my discussion to a close by the observation that he does not show that the problem as reformulated should be answered one way rather than another.

Jerome Frank, Fate and Freedom, p. 296 (1945); reprinted by permission of Simon and Schuster.

Fuller concedes that virtually all that he means by "natural law" is that ideals of justice should be an acknowledged vital component in the thinking of judges when deciding cases. As today most American judges frankly and consciously think in that fashion —endeavoring, within the limits allowed by statutes and well-settled precedents, to make their decisions conform to their ideals of justice—Fuller's program perhaps requires no great amount of advertising. But, if it does, it would be far wiser to publicize his program in an outright manner—to speak directly of justice—than to obscure it by a phrase which must be translated in order to be generally understood.[26] If you want a waiter to bring you a glass of water, you do not think of saying, "Please fetch me a transparent brittle container nearly full of aqueous fluid." Fuller asserts that natural law connotes that there are "conditions of successful group living" which "determine the rules" judges ought to apply; but he confesses that "natural law says at the most only one clear thing about society, namely, that it is impossible without some kind of order"—a discovery made by every sane lawyer or layman, whether or not he speaks of Natural Law.

Jerome Hall, The Progress of American Jurisprudence in The Administration of Justice in Retrospect pp. 36-37, (1952); reprinted by permission of the author and the Southern Methodist University Press.

When it is suggested that the present period is marked chiefly by the rise of a natural law jurisprudence, what is intended is the following:

1. The thesis that there are objectively better or worse solutions to legal problems; that, in brief, valuation makes sense, that there is truth in the realm of ethics and law.

2. That man is a rational creature; i.e., in addition to his powerful instinctual drives and deeply rooted

emotions, there is a very significant functioning of intelligence. That is the central thrust of the psychology of human nature which the current development shares with older natural law philosophies. (A corollary of the above theses is that through persistent use of their rational functions, human beings can discover objectively better solutions—e.g., morally valid laws and decisions.)

3. That although the effect on law of fortuitous, economic, and dictatorial forces must be recognized, and while the perspective of lawyers' law initially often ignores valuation and concentrates upon the formal aspects of law, nonetheless, as regards large portions of case law and so-called customary law as well as with reference to other types of spontaneously made law, value is an essential element. These norms are characterized by the efforts of the problem-solvers —legislators, judges, officials, and private persons—to seek morally valid solutions within the limits of their authority; that fact is reflected in the interpretation of lawyers' law. In sum, as Frederick Pollock states, "The Law of Nature . . . is a living embodiment of the collective reason of civilized mankind, and as such is adopted by the Common Law in substance though not always by name."[27]

If the above theses are valid foundations of a defensible natural law philosophy, it is apparent that there have always been many natural law philosophers in this country and that most legal scholars and lawyers here are, in fact, practicing natural law philosophers.

Jerome Hall, Living Law of Democratic Society pp. 56-58, 94-100 (1949); reprinted by permission of the author and the Bobbs-Merrill Co., Inc.

Even the theory that law represents merely the impact of the dominant forces in the society concedes that there is reason in the process. For unless the rulers are insane, their edicts represent deliberate end-seeking and the use of generalizations to attain their goals.

That sort of rationality, however, is hardly a sufficient foundation for a defensible philosophy of law. More significant in that regard is Aristotle's observation that certain laws are found in all societies whereas others are not. The former, he declared universal and natural, the latter, particular and conventional. As was pointed out above, the Stoics took the decisive step in the development of this theory by insisting that justice ("virtue," "Natural Law") is an essential attribute of positive law.[28] Though it was subjected to continuous attack and was modified and restated in various ways, the Stoic theory of law prevailed for over a millenium and a half.

This perennial perspective rests ultimately on the position that human beings are rational and social. What do these words mean, and how can that position be defended in view of man's evident passion and aggressiveness? "Reason" is a term pregnant with endless ambiguity. It has been restricted to the recognition of logical implication, correct reasoning. It has, on the other hand, been taken to mean no less than the apprehension of universals, "the one in the many." It may designate only scientific thought or it may mean practical judgment exhibited in the efficient attainment of desired ends. It means merely the recognition of self-interest and it means wisdom, including knowledge of moral as well as factual truth. "Reason" has been defined to include all of these and, no doubt, other meanings. The common thread running through most of these meanings is that human beings manifest certain, probably distinctive functionings in generalizing and in the invention and use of symbols to communicate their ideas and ideals.

The other ultimate component of human nature, sociability, stems from the Greek view that man is a "political animal" and it has been stressed in secular Natural Law theory beginning, in modern times, with Grotius. Reason, alone, being regarded as insufficient for the discovery of what is right or good, the "social nature of man" became an essenital complement. This sort of sociability must be distinguished from the gregarious instinct. For example, no one has ever recorded any Thoreau-like behavior among bees or ants.[29] On the other hand, there is ample evidence to support the insight that man's intelligence permeates his gregariousness and that human co-operation therefore reflects a unique sociability.

Behaviorist psychology, Kohler's studies of apes, Pavlov's experiments, as well as the recent resurgence of primitive savagery in Europe have cast doubt on the traditional psychology of human nature, especially on any claim to superior distinctiveness; indeed, it is recognized that no mere beast is capable of the inordinate cruelty of *homo sapiens*. These challenges require drastic modification of optimistic psychologies just as they compel us to read the traditional Natural Law postulates as emphases on certain differentials rather than as assertions that men are wholly rational and social.

But they do not invalidate the traditional insights. We have only to point to the theoretical structure of science, to philosophy, to advanced legal systems, and to the progress in political ideals as evidence of human rationality. It is significant that this is the position of a distinguished biologist, Julian Huxley, who writes, "The first and most obviously unique characteristic of man is his capacity for conceptual thought . . . ;" "cumulative tradition . . . capable of indefinite improvement in quality and increase in quantity" is another distinctively human attribute. He notes that " . . . man is the only organism normally and inevitably subject to psychological conflict." He stresses man's "conscious reason," his "conscious purpose and his set of values." "There may be other beings in this vast universe," concludes Mr. Huxley, "endowed with reason, purpose and aspiration; but we know nothing of them. So far as our knowledge goes, human mind and personality are unique and constitute the highest product yet achieved by the cosmos." "Biology thus reinstates man in a position analogous to that conferred on him as Lord of Creation by theology."[30]

This instrumentalist viewpoint toward law, though helpful in describing intermediate aspects of problem-solving, misses the all-important consideration that legal experience is moral experience and that moral experience is intrinsically valuable. Thus, especially the legal system of a democracy is a repository of social values, an abundant concretization of value by reference to more or less specific situations. The ultimate value can be generalized, with some degree of success, as the basic norm of the legal order (*e.g.*, anyone who harms a legally defined value must be coercively subjected to prescribed sanctions). Thence, the values, very widely implicit in extensive constitutional provisions and in the broad principles of case law, find their general incidence in statutes. The values are more specifically represented in individual cases; and they are very narrowly embodied in the execution of particular judgments. This entire hierarchy of value represents legal experience, a distinctively human experience which does not operate in a separate compartment that merely parallels the moral experience of the race. It is part of that moral experience.

The law of democratic societies is distinguishable from that of other polities in that it represents the maximization of values. It facilitates more and higher value-experience than does that of any other form of polity because, in the first place, the conditions for sound valuation are present in greater degree— democratic process, especially the activities which actualize the Bill of Rights, means, in this connection, sound methods for discovering the right answers to social problems. Morality implies voluntary conduct, wherein obligations are recognized. Thus, secondly, regardless of how wise and good a dominating élite might be, the rules they laid down could not begin to approximate the values experienced by a population legislating for itself, itself discovering the right answers and voluntarily laying down the rules to govern inter-personal relations, which are recognized as morally binding. Creativity in the realm of moral experience, no less than in the exact sciences, is stimulated by the quality of democratic law, which is the decisive relevant institution though not, of course, the only important influence in this regard.

That law is valuation also implies that law is an on-going process, that the process is meaningful in relation to the solution of social problems, and that legislation and adjudication are ways of discovering and using the ethically valid answers, which it is feasible to implement by force.

We must therefore question the common assertion that any legal order embodies only a minimum of morality. Sometimes, to be sure, it does even less than that. For example, even a minimum of morality would oblige an expert swimmer to save a drowning child if he could do so without endangering himself. But, though he need only reach out his arm to rescue the child, our law requires no such action by him. So, too, a minimum of morality would require individuals not to indulge in the vicious libel of minorities. But that and many other grossly immoral acts and omissions are legally privileged.

On the other hand, our law sometimes imposes a great deal more than a minimum of morality. For example, a railroad has been held to owe a duty of care to the heroic rescuer of a stranger. A right to privacy is becoming increasingly recognized. And, as regards trustees and guardians, our law has long imposed a standard of morality that is rigorous enough to satisfy the most sensitive conscience. Thus, it is not so much a minimum that is significant in legal valuation as are certain other criteria, namely, the feasibility of enforcement by coercive measures; the clash with other, superior values, *e.g.*, whether it is possible to bar certain anti-social acts such as the libel of minorities, without at the same time repressing freedom of speech; and there is also the doctrine *de minimis,* which postulates the opposite of the traditional notion, namely, that the pettiest wrongs are too insignificant to receive legal recognition.

But if the theory that law enforces a minimum of morality is oversimple, it also contains an important truth. Its valid implication is the distinction which the Puritans drew between law and grace, *i.e.,* beyond the moral duty of the law, though not uninfluenced by that, is the boundless area of individual sacrifice and devotion.

The values incorporated in democratic law represent the more stable policy decisions which it is wise and feasible to implement by compulsion. But such value experience understood *vis a vis* problem-solving usually involves varying degrees of uncertaintly not only up to the point where the goals are definable with sufficient precision to render group action possible but even after "the" correct answers have been discovered. The problematic aspect of law-as-valuation, especially the tensions between any given implemented valuation and competing values is a permanent phase of the democratic process.

This is perhaps most evident in the clash between the values of freedom and those of equality. The following dilemma is presented: The expansion of law limits freedom but may increase equality; on the other hand, if people are left free, inequality increases. It is possible to indicate what goes on incessantly in the democratic process by noting that the resolution of this dilemma involves evaluation in *specific* factual situations and with reference to relatively narrow issues; that any given determinations are held tentatively and subject to improvement; and that specific interpretations of the meaning of "liberty" |and| "equality" are derived, which are often formulated in precise laws.

It is in this context of specific problem-solving that one must interpret the ideal of legal equality implied in the uniformity of law. The generality (impersonality) of the substantive law as well as the objectivity of legal method are the corresponding, implementing constructs. But the generality and uniformity of law only guarantee that, if it is discriminatory, it discriminates against an entire class. "Equality before the law" therefore stipulates that the generalized rules must be ethically valid. But this criterion, related to actual social problems, also implies that certain kinds of inequality, *e.g.*, those indicative of superior merit, are desirable. Moreover, the grant of equal opportunities not only carries no assurance that inequalities will not arise; it can be confidently predicted that inequalities will arise. The social objective is to confine them to rational ones.

That equality does not mean that all persons must be treated alike in all situations and relationships may be seen in the legal cognizance taken of social and economic facts, differences in sex, age, income, and so on. Laws limiting the employment of children, the working hours of women, the labor contract, insurance, the operation of factories, railroads and banks, etc., single out certain classes of persons upon whom special limitations are imposed. This means differential legal treatment. But it is not discriminatory in an objectionable sense. There is often a conflict between the ideal and a specific obligation to care for certain persons. If one has only enough food to sustain his family, and a neighbor is hungry, the law of family relations imposes unequal distribution. Equal incomes would provide more wealth for many persons but it would also doom the efficient operation of the economy. So, too, income tax laws impose differential burdens. Finally, there are deeply rooted attitudes and loyalties which obstruct direct or early application of legal provisions for equality in some spheres of social life. Only a harsh egalitarianism would ignore these sensibilities. Only a smug complacency would ignore the problems.

Just as the ideal of political equality must not be confused with actual power to influence policy-determination, so, too, the ideal of legal equality must not be confused with the actual functioning of the legal system. The conditions of men vary in power, wealth, intelligence, and resourcefulness; these undoubtedly affect the operation of the law. There is certainly point in the criticism that it takes money to retain counsel, to appeal an adverse decision, and to employ lobbyists. The legal ideal falls short of complete realization because the facts often render that impossible; moreover, opposing values inhibit efforts to solve the problems by changing the facts. Solution takes the path of amelioration in specific areas, e.g., legal aid societies, volunteer committees of Bar associations, public defenders, laws waiving court costs, and the organization of labor unions and other associations whose resources are sufficient to place their members on a parity with any litigant.

Thus, "freedom" and "equality" are not only essential democratic, though vague, ideals; they also raise many difficult problems. Democratic society holds fast to the central insight of the equal claims of personality, as such; hence, it seeks to determine what is arbitrary and to oppose unfair claims to special privilege. It provides the conditions wherein sound decisions can be reached regarding competing values. Its legal order represents a relatively refined instrument, stipulating and determining what values to advance, how far, and at what cost of other values. It represents a series of the more definite value judgments applied in limited areas, where not only equality but also many desirable inequalities are sanctioned. Actual capacity, need, merit, predictions regarding the consequences of certain policies, and many other factors are reflected in the legal system. The net result is a series of considered judgments representing differential specific applications of the principles of freedom and equality.

The problematic character of law in a democratic society is further revealed when we consider that, whereas morality presupposes freedom, law involves coercion. Yet, in law, morality is forcibly sanctioned, presenting a union of antinomies. We rationalize the situation by asserting that the law exists for bad people and that its purpose is to achieve a uniformity of conduct by compelling them to do what most persons do of their own volition. In addition, by restraining evil men, law enables good men to carry on worthy activities.

In a deeper sense, the legal order helps all of us to discover the correct solution of moral problems and to do the right thing. It aids solution of difficult moral problems by making readily and precisely available much of the accumulated ethical knowledge of the past. It stimulates us to do the right thing so much because we are deterred by fear of sanctions as by rendering it easier for us, more or less unconsciously, to repress our anti-social instincts and to remain emotionally satisfied despite our inhibitions.[31] That law checks the rush of destructive instinct is obvious. That, in doing so, it frees energy for devotion to worth-while endeavor is only slightly less apparent. In thus conditioning conduct, law functions as a major determinant of human nature. In this process men receive much of their moral education.

We may state the principal conclusions reached thus far: positive law consists of propositions stated in the form of hypothetical-imperative judgments; the formal source and the enforcer of these bilateral rules is the maximum power center in the society; the rules of law stand highest in the hierarchy of norms in the sense that, in case of conflict with other norms, law prevails; the sanction of legal rules is enforced, ultimately, by physical power which operates unconditionally; the rules of law, by and large, implement interests inclusive of the entire society; the rules of law are coalescences of the ideas, signified by the rules, with value; and this attribute is divisible into (a) conformity to ethical principles and (b) self-rule —the distinctive quality of the law of democratic society.

NON-SCHOLASTIC—JURISPRUDENCE 223

[1] See Fuller, Problems of Jurisprudence (1949); Fuller, The Law in Quest of Itself (1940); Fuller, Place and Uses of Jurisprudence in the Law School Curriculum, 1 J. Legal Educ. 495 (1949); Fuller, Reason and Fiat in Case Law, 59 Harv. L. Rev. 376 (1946).

[2] See Hall, Living Law of Democratic Society (1949); Hall, General Principles of the Criminal Law (1947); Hall, Integrative Jurisprudence in Interpretations of Modern Legal Philosophies (1947); Hall, Place and Uses of Jurisprudence, 1 J. Legal Educ. 475 (1949).

[3] See Cahn, The Sense of Injustice (1949); Cahn, Jurisprudence in Annual Survey of American Law (1944-49); Cahn, Goethe's View of the Law, 49 Columbia L. Rev. 904 (1949).

[4] Fuller, op. cit. supra note 1.

[5] Hall, op. cit. supra note 2.

[6] Positivism, on the other hand, is a throwback beyond Hegel to seventeenth century empiricism. And it is melancholy, though perhaps inevitable, that eighteenth century intuitional idealism should be resurrected today to lay the still more ancient ghost of seventeenth century positivistic empiricism.

[7] Cahn, op. cit. supra note 3.

[8] Vol. 1 (8th ed. 1892) p. 254. The discussion of contract law is found in Vol. 1, p. 143, and Vol. 2, p. 223.

[9] See Olivecrona, Law as Fact (1939); Lundstedt, Superstition or Rationality in Action for Peace? (1925); Lundtstedt, Die Unwissenschaftlichkeit der Rechtswissenschaft (1932). The leader of this school is Alex Hägerström, whose principal works are unfortunately available only in Swedish.

In connection with the point made in the text, it is interesting to compare the observations of Timasheff in An Introduction to the Sociology of Law (1939) 132, n. 17, concerning the effect of Soviet legal reforms on Russian conceptions of morality.

[10] John Chipman Gray, The Nature and Sources of the Law § 273 (1909).

[11] Chiefly in Chapter 13, pp. 332-375.

[12] "One of the great contributions of the German philosopher, Immanuel Kant, was his separation of 'reality,' the realm of science, from value, the realm of ethics ... to the great benefit of both intellectual disciplines." P. 42. Cf., "In so far as the author has a coherent theory, it is 'axiological realism,' that legal evaluations should always be determined on the basis of facts." P. vii. (Does this simply mean that you ought to get the facts straight before you decide what ought to be done? If so, "axiological realism" seems a rather pretentious description for so simple an idea.) Cf. also, "Professor Dewey's most im-

portant contribution to ethical theory is his controversial view that valuation can be an empirical process..." p. 495.

[13] Cohen, Should Legal Thought Abandon Clear Distinctions? 36 Ill. L. Rev. 239 (1941) (being a review of Fuller, The Law in Quest of Itself (1940)).

[14] "Professor Fuller ... defines natural law as 'the view which denies the possibility of a rigid separation of the *is* and the *ought* and which tolerates a confusion of them in legal discussion.' However, the teleological or purposive interpretation of statutes or of case law is not dependent upon the acceptance of such a confusion, nor is it an exclusive property of natural law." P. 369. Patterson wants a purposive interpretation, but no "confusion" of *is* and *ought*. Does he mean to assert that he can take any given rule of law and tell just where the rule as it leaves off and where the rule as people think it ought to be begins? If he cannot effect this separation, then, though he may not like my paradoxical form of expression, he too is compelled to tolerate a "confusion" of *is* and *ought*.

[15] Since I have been arguing for this position for a good many years I am encouraged to find that in two recently published works the authors have arrived independently at a substantially similar point of view. John Wild, Plato's Modern Enemies and the Theory of Natural Law (1953); Leo Strauss, Natural Right and History (1953). (Neither of these books is written from a Roman Catholic point of view.)

[16] A perceptive Soviet legal philosopher (now repudiated) once observed that in Kelsen's system the model of the legal rule must be "thou shalt..." and not "thou shalt...in order that...." Kelsen's system is incapable of absorbing the second kind of imperative. Pashukanis, The General Theory of Law and Marxism, in Soviet Legal Philosophy 111, 114 (Babb's transl. 1951).

[17] General Theory of Law and State 112-113 (1945).

[18] McDougal, The Comparative Study of Law for Policy Purposes: Value Clarification as an Instrument of Democratic World Order, 61 Yale L. J. 915 (1952). A generous bibliography of previous writings by Professors McDougal and Lasswell will be found in the notes to this article.

[19] 3 Natural Law Forum 71 (1958).

[20] Maritain, La Philosophie Bergsonienne 323 (2nd ed., 1930). ["Likewise no philosopher can tell us what, in reality, is the ultimate end of our existence. It is God who has taught us this, He who has made us in such a way that finally we may see Him as He sees us."] Of course, there are truths about God

which human reason can investigate, and there is a science whose subject matter is God.

21 Adler and Farrell, The Theory of Democracy: Part II, 3 The Thomist 598-607 (1942).

22 Summa Theologica, I-II, QQ. 1-21 (The Last End); I-II QQ. 22-48 (Human Acts); I-II, QQ. 57-122 (Justice); I-II, QQ. 90-108 (Law).

23 A Question about Law, Essays in Thomism 207 at 208-9 (1942).

24 Op. cit. supra, note 19 at 72.

25 Id. at 72.

26 I hasten to add that, although I have long been an ardent semanticist, I cannot agree with those who would do away with a word like "justice," merely because it is vague. Its vagueness has the advantage of allowing for expansion; see Frank, If Men Were Angels, p. 313. "Justice" does not have the disadvantages which attach to the term "natural law."

27 Pollock, The Law of Reason, 2 Mich. L. Rev. 173 (1903); Cf. Lord Wright in [1955] Cambridge L. J. 163.

28 See notes 40, 41, 42 supra, namely:[40] "Law is the ruler over all the acts both of gods and men. Law must be the director and governor and guide with respect to what is honorable and base, and therefore the standard of the just and unjust; for all beings that are social by nature, it directs what must be done and forbids what must not be done." Chrysippus, On Law, quoted by Sabine and Smith, Introduction to Cicero, On the Commonwealth 22 (1929).

Cf. "And the things which are in the power of a fool are not law." The Discourses of Epictetus 350 (Long ed. 1877). The editor comments as follows: "The will of a fool does not make law, he says. Unfortunately it does, if we use the world law in the strict sense.... The strict use of the word 'law' is independent of the quality of the command, which may be wise or foolish, good or bad. But Epictetus does not use the word 'law' in the strict sense." Id. at 350 n. 11. Cf. Infra note [8]. See Fuller, Reason and Fiat in Case Law, 59 Harv. L. Rev. 376 (1946). [41] Cicero, De Legibus I, vi, at 319 (Loeb Lib. ed., Keyes trans. 1928). [42] Id. at II, v, p. 385.

29 Cassirer, An Essay on Man 223-224 (1944).

30 Huxley, The Uniqueness of Man, 28 Yale Review, 475, 491, 500, 476 (1939).

31 West, Conscience and Society (1945).

Index to Natural Law Reader

A

Adler, Mortimer, 1 et seq, 27, 211-212
"Alssein," 38
America, 28
American Bar Association, 168
Aquinas, St. Thomas, 2, 22, 23, 61, 66 et seq, 167
Aristotle, 22, 23, 49 et seq
Austin, John, 9-10, 23, 149

B

Babbitt, Irving, 8
Behaviorism, 10, 216
Bentham, Jeremy, 9, 23
Bergson, Henri, 5
Betancour, Cayetano, 31
Blackstone, 99, 104 et seq
Bouscaren, Timothy L., S.J., 27
Brito, Francis, 31
Brown, Brendan F., 14 et seq, 27, 82 et seq, 101 et seq, 109 et seq, 128 et seq, 154 et seq, 174 et seq

C

Cahn, Edmond, 185 et seq. 195
Capitalism, 4
Capograssi, Giuseppe, 42
Cardozo, Benjamin, 11, 121
Case system, 11
Catholicism, 3, 24
Catholic Historical Review, 29
Catholic Philosophical Association, 24, 27
Catholic University, 26
Cicero, 54 et seq

Clarke, William F., 29
Cohen, Morris R., 21, 180 et seq
Coing, Helmut, 32, 35
Common law, 15
Comte, August, 6
Communism, 125
Connor, James T., 28
Constitutional law, 141
Corwin, Edward S., 110 et seq
Cowan, Thomas A., 194 et seq
Curran, John W., 27

D

Dabin, Jean, 32
Darwinism, 6
Davitt, Thomas E., S.J., 101 et seq
de Amoras Lima, Alceu, 31
Dewey, John, 11
Dickinson, John, 184
Dillon, William T., 25, 26, 27
del Vecchio, Giorgio, 40, 172 et seq

E

Economic determinism, 10
Ellis, Adam C., 27
Esposito, Carlo, 42
Existentialism, 38, 39

F

Farrell, Walter, O.P., 28
Fasso, Guido, 39 et seq
Fechner, Erich, 38
Field, 13
Figuereida, Jackson de, 31
Fitzgerald, John C., 27
Ford, John C., S.J., 29

Fordham University, 24
Fragueiro, Alfredo, 31
Frank, Jerome, 213
Friedmann, W., 20 et seq
Friedrich, Carl Joachim, 101 et seq
Freudianism, 10
→ Fuller, Lon J., 195-196, 197 et seq, 209

G

Geny, François, 174
Georgetown University, 24
Goethe, 89
Gray, John C., 204
Grotius, 100, 216

H

Hall, Jerome, 172, 195, 213 et seq
Hart, Charles A., 27
Hartmann, Nicolai, 35
Hernandez, Rafael Preciado, 31
Hobbes, Thomas, 9, 177
→ Holmes, Oliver W., 10, 11, 118-119, 121, 167, 182, 190
Hooker, Richard, 23
Huxley, Julian, 216

I

Iustitia, 40

J

Jhering, 165
Jus, 40
"Jus naturale," 16, 17, 18, 82
Justinian, 87, 105, 140

K

Kant, Immanuel, 9, 88 et seq, 179
Kearney, James J., 27
Keenan, Joseph B., 109 et seq
Kelsen, Hans, 88-89, 166, 206-207

Kenealy, William J., S.J., 117 et seq
Kennedy, Walter B., 27
Kilmuir, Viscount, 113 et seq
Kocourek, 136
Kuchenhoff, Gunther, 34
Kunz, Joseph L., 30 et seq

L

Laissez-faire, 9
Lasswell, 207
Law Merchant, 143-144
Legaz y Lacambra, Luis, 32
Legislative law, 12
"Lex naturalis," 83
Lilly, Linus, S.J., 27
Lucey, Francis, S.J., 29, 145 et seq

M

Magna Carta, 123
Maihofer, Werner, 38
Manion, Clarence, 29
Marquette University, 24
Marriage, 132 et seq
Mc Dougal, 207
Mc Kenna, Daniel J., 29
Messner, Johannes, 33
Mill, John Stuart, 9
Monogamy, 128 et seq
Mott, O. H., 30
Moyles, William P., 28

N

Nationalism, 3-4
Naturalists, 1
Natural Law Forum, 24
Natural Law Institute, 24
Neo-Hegelianism, 34
Neo-Kantian, 33, 35, 88, 172 et seq
Neo-Scholastic Philosophy of Law, 25
Neo-Thomism, 21, 30, 32, 33, 39
Nicolini, Ugo, 42
Nietsche, Friedrich, 5
Noonan, Father, S.J., 27
Notre Dame University, 24

NON-SCHOLASTIC—JURISPRUDENCE 229

P

Palmer, Ben W., 3 et seq
Papale, A. E., 153 et seq
Passarelli, Santoro, 42
Philosophy, Committee on the of Law and Government, Repot of, 25 et seq
Pius XI, 40
Pius XII, 40
Plato, 47 et seq
Pollock, Frederick, 23, 119, 214
Positivists, 1, 10, 19
Pound, Roscoe, 12, 21, et seq, 32-33, 165
Pragmatism, 11
Prismatic method, 189 et seq
Property law, 138
Pseudo-natural law, 13
Puritans, 219,

Q

Quiles, Ismael, S.J., 31

R

Radbruch, Gustav, 36
Relativism, 5
Renan, 8
Reuschlein, Harold G., 112 et seq
Rhyne, Charles S., 123 et seq
Ricardo, 9
Rio, Manuel, 31
Robles, Oswaldo, 31
Romanticism, 5-6
Rommen, Heinrich A., 61 et seq
Rooney, Miriam Theresa, 25, 28
Rousseau, Jean-Jacques, 5, 8, 11
Russell, Franklin F., 28
Ryland v. Fletcher, 138

S

St. Augustine, 63
St. Germain, Christopher, 90 et seq

St. John Chrysostom, 61
St. Johns University, 24
St. Thomas More Institute of Legal Research, 24
Scheler, Max, 35
School, Men, The, 61 et seq
Schopenhauer, 5
Science, 6-8
"Selbstsein," 38
Slade's case, 134 et seq
Smith, Adam, 9
Sociological School of Jurisprudence, 164-165
Southern Methodist University, 24
Spencer, Herbert, 6, 9
Stammler, Rudolf, 88-89
Stoic-Thomistic Doctrine, 3, 16, 47 et seq, 94
Suarez, Francisco, 94 et seq
Summa Theologica, 69 et seq
Summi, Pontificatus, 41

T

Ten Commandments, 103
Torts, 136

U

Union of Catholic Jurists, 41
Utilitarianism, 9

V

von der Heydte, Freiherr, 33 et seq
von Hippel, Ernst, 34
von Kempski, Jurgen, 34
von Laun, Rudolf, 35, 39
von Verdross, Alfred, 34

W

Welzel, Hans, 37
White, Robert, 29
Wigmore, Dean, 136
Wilson, James, 23
Witherspoon, Joseph P., 22 et seq, 185 et seq, 208 et seq
Wolf, Erik, 34, 37

THE DOCKET SERIES

Julius J. Marke, *General Editor*

Selected readings in law, politics, and government, edited by recognized authorities in their respective fields

$3.50 cloth $1.35 paper

1. **THE HOLMES READER**
   Julius J. Marke

2. **THE FREEDOM READER**
   Edwin S. Newman

3. **THE MARSHALL READER**
   Erwin C. Surrency

4. **THE WILSON READER**
   Frances Farmer

5. **THE DANIEL WEBSTER READER**
   Bertha Rothe

6. **THE MEDICO-LEGAL READER**
   Samuel Polsky

7. **THE BRANDEIS READER**
   Ervin Pollack

8. **THE AMERICAN JURISPRUDENCE READER**
   Thomas A. Cowan

9. **THE ALEXANDER HAMILTON READER**
   Margaret E. Hall

10. **THE FREDERICK WILLIAM MAITLAND READER**
    Vincent T. H. Delaney

11. **DEANS' LIST OF RECOMMENDED READING**
    Julius J. Marke

12. **THE AMERICAN CONSTITUTIONAL LAW READER**
    Robert B. McKay

13. **THE NATURAL LAW READER**
    Brendan F. Brown

14. **READINGS FOR REPUBLICANS**
    Franklin Burdette

15. **READINGS FOR DEMOCRATS**
    Edward Reed